California Street Gang & Prison Slang

ERIC "SUPERMAN" STURGESS

Rose Of Sharon
PUBLISHING

California Street Gang & Prison Slang

ERIC "SUPERMAN" STURGESS

Printed Worldwide First Printing 2026

First Edition 2026

10 9 8 7 6 5 4 3 2 1

Rose of Sharon Publishing books may be ordered through booksellers or by contacting:

Rose Of Sharon Publishing roseofsharonpublishing.com

P.O. Box 186

Floresville, Texas 78114

ISBN: 978-1-970335-18-7 Paperback

DEDICATION

I dedicate this book to all the people who did not have a positive, strong, and moral male role model while growing up. Most men in prison came from fatherless homes, or if the dad was around, he was a horrible role model. Absentee fathers are causing society to pay a high price for their low living and lack of leadership.

By the Grace of God, I have given my children everything I never had as a child. God bless the men who take their responsibility as fathers seriously and are positively involved in their children's lives. More than ever, we need strong and moral men to lead their families boldly and set an example of how to live.

"When my mother and father forsake me, then the Lord will take care of me,"
Psalm 27:10.

FORWARD

Every culture has distinct regulations, principles, customs, and dialects, and the prison environment is no exception. As a former correctional officer, Eric has acquired firsthand knowledge of the California prison system's jargon. He has amassed an extensive collection of slang words commonly used in California prisons. Eric's unwavering dedication to this subject is evident in the countless hours we have spent discussing these words and their meanings. His profound expertise on the subject has left me thoroughly impressed.

Boxer, 20 years in the CDCR.

PREFACE

I am in contact with numerous convicts who are currently incarcerated in the California Department of Corrections and Rehabilitation. They have helped me with some words I had never heard, and with specific details in a few other definitions. They have over 250 years combined in the California prison system, and they are in different prisons around the state. I strive for accuracy in this book, and I require at least two reputable sources to confirm a slang term with which I was unfamiliar. This process has been painstaking. I started this immense task over 15 years ago as a hobby, and it took on a life of its own.

At the end of the day, my name is on this book, and I will stand on whatever I say. I humbly submit to you, my magnum opus. I hope and pray you enjoy this compendium of gang and prison slang words that pertain to the California prison and street gang culture.

I want to extend a special thanks to all the talented individuals who contributed to this book; you know who you are. The editors and people behind the scenes spent hundreds of hours making this book something we could proudly stand behind. Without the help of God and you, this book would have never been possible.

God bless you all.

Contents

INTRODUCTION

This exceptional and one-of-a-kind book is a prison slang dictionary with over 4,000 individual entries. This book contains words, sayings, phrases, and historical events related to California gangs and prisons. Most of the terms contained herein are what you would hear if you walked into a prison today. I have also included words spoken decades ago in prisons, such as "Screw," which refers to a correctional officer.

This street gang and prison slang dictionary also incorporates prison administration technical terms and other words about various programs available to inmates in state prisons. I chose these words to give the reader a broader understanding of the prison system.

There will be capitalized words in quotation marks, which means you can look up the definition in this book if you need to become more familiar with that particular word. I hope you enjoy this unique journey into the belly of the beast.

Remember, there is only one thing in the streets and prison you can trust behind your back: a concrete wall. Your homies, with whom you break bread, will put a "Banger" in your neck if the "Big Homies" give the order. There is nobody you can fully trust in the cold game of gang banging.

A

A Fair One: To treat an adversary respectfully and give them a fair fight. For example, "I will give you a fair one, homie. What you wanna do?"

A Group Doesn't Make A Man He Makes Himself: This saying means being part of a "Faction" doesn't make you tough. A man only gets respect in prison because of how he carries himself. Respect is earned in prison daily by your actions.

A Lame With A Paint Job: This means a person has numerous tattoos but is a "Punk." For example, "Scars is a punk; he is just a 'Lame' with a paint job. His comrades don't even respect him."

A Needle Hanging Out Of His Arm: An inmate always doing heroin in prison. For example, "Dopey is just an old 'Tecato' who did his time with a needle hanging out of his arm."

AB: Another name for the "Aryan Brotherhood" prison gang, a White prison gang formed in San Quentin Prison in 1967. The Aryan Brotherhood started as the "Blue Bird Gang" in the 1950s, and as a result of a vicious war with the "Black Guerrilla Family," they joined forces with other smaller White gangs to form the Aryan Brotherhood.

About It: A convict known for "Putting In Work" and putting anyone in check who comes at him "Sideways." For example, "Rook is about it; don't play with him."

About The Business: A convict known for "Putting In Work" and putting anyone in check who comes at him "Sideways." For example, "Capone is about the business. He's a real one."

Above The Program: When people believe the rules and regulations that govern their "Faction" don't apply to them. For example, "Some of the 'Fellas' think they are above the program."

AC: This acronym stands for "Adjustment Center." These were the "Isolation Wings" of San Quentin, Soledad, Chino, Tracy, and Folsom Prisons. These are the areas of a prison where inmates were placed for disciplinary, medical observation, or safety and security issues. These isolation wings are generally referred to as the "Hole."

Academy: The California Department of Corrections and Rehabilitation training academy is in Galt, California. The academy has a 13-week duration; housing and food are provided.

Ace Deuce: A homie who has remained steadfast through thick and thin, whether on the streets or in prison. For example, "That's my ace deuce, so look out for him."

Act Of Redemption: When a convict messes up, he is given an opportunity for an act of redemption to make his name good again within his "Faction." An act of redemption means he will do a "Cleanup" and "Blast" someone who has fallen out of favor with his comrades.

Act Of Treason: When a gang member fails to defend his "Household," shows cowardice, snitches, or fails in other responsibilities. A gang member guilty of treason will be "Removed" from the yard. For example, "Diablo committed an act of treason. He has to go."

Active vs Inactive: Active inmates are pushing a "Hardline" on "Prison Politics," and inactive inmates are just trying to do their time peacefully, such as inmates on Level I and II yards. An active inmate cannot go to an inactive yard and "Program" and still retain his active status from his comrades. Active inmates consider themselves "Mainline," and they regard inactive inmates as "SNY."

Ad-Seg: Ad-Seg stands for "Administration Segregation," where inmates are sent for breaking the rules in prison. Basically, Ad-Seg is a jail within a prison. The inmates are in their cells for 23 hours a day. They have limited personal items due to security reasons. The inmates are allowed a shower once every three days. They can exercise on a small yard behind the "Housing Unit" with "Gun Coverage."

Adjustment Center: These were the "Isolation Wings" of San Quentin, Soledad, Chino, Tracy, and Folsom Prisons. These are the areas of a prison where inmates were placed for disciplinary, medical observation, or safety and security issues. These isolation wings are generally referred to as the "Hole."

Administration Segregation: This is where inmates are sent for breaking the rules in prison. Basically, Administration Segregation is a jail within a prison. The inmates are in their cells for 23 hours a day. They have limited personal items due to security reasons. The inmates are allowed a shower once every three days. They can exercise on a small yard behind the "Housing Unit" with "Gun Coverage."

Administration Segregation Unit: This is where inmates are sent for breaking the rules in prison. Basically, the Administration Segregation Unit is a jail within a prison. The inmates are in their cells for 23 hours a day. They have limited personal items due to security reasons. The inmates are allowed a shower once every three days. They can exercise on a small yard behind the "Housing Unit" with "Gun Coverage."

Adverse Action: When the prison administration takes formal action against officers who break the rules. These sanctions may include an official reprimand, salary reduction, suspension without pay, demotion, and dismissal.

Africanos: A word that translates to Africans, and some "Factions" use it to refer to the Black inmates in prison.

After Hours: At night, convicts turn their radios and televisions down so they won't disturb others in their area. If a convict is loud after hours, he will be disciplined by his "Faction."

Against The Grain: To go against the "Program" in prison. To be a "Lone Wolf" and put your life in danger. For example, "Redwood, you are 'Heading For A Wreck.' Stop going against the grain."

AIC: This stands for "Authority In Charge." He is the "Norteño" who oversees an entire prison or jail.

AIMS: This acronym stands for Allegation Inquiry Management Section, and it is a staff investigation unit that handles complaints from inmates pertaining to misconduct by officers. When inmates make formal complaints alleging officer abuse or misconduct, AIMS personnel will investigate so that resolutions will be made outside of the prison setting to ensure impartiality.

Ain't Built Like That: When a person acts like they are down for the "Cause," but they are a "Buster." For example, "Porky ain't built like that. You should have known better than to trust him to 'Hold His Mud.'"

Ain't Nobody Bigger Than The Program: If you go "Against The Grain" in prison, you will end up in a "Wreck." At the end of the day, you will mind someone, and you will "Mind Your Manners."

Ain't Running Nothing: When an inmate acts like he is calling shots, but in reality, they aren't running anything but their mouth. For example, "He said that? Lips ain't running nothing but his mouth."

Air Freshener: When inmates want to make their cell or area smell better, they have a couple of ways to do that. One method is to soak a paper towel in body wash or oils and leave it sitting out. Another way is to throw baby powder in the air for the same effect.

Airlifted: When an inmate gets assaulted so severely, they are flown on a helicopter to an emergency room at a local hospital. For example, "Chopper got airlifted after they 'Poked' him."

Air Out Your Laundry: When a person confronts someone about their bad behavior in front of others.

Airing It Out: To speak on something publicly. For example, "You aren't even from this 'Car,' why are you speaking on our business? Why are you airing it out?"

Alice Baker: Another name for the "Aryan Brotherhood" prison gang, a White prison gang formed in San Quentin Prison in 1967. The Aryan Brotherhood started as the "Blue Bird Gang" in the 1950s, and as a result of a vicious war with the "Black Guerrilla Family," they joined forces with other smaller White gangs to form the Aryan Brotherhood.

All Bad: When things go terribly wrong for an inmate. For example, "Bozo came at me 'Sideways,' and it was all bad for him."

All Day: A life sentence in prison.

All Day & A Night: A life sentence without the possibility of parole.

All Money Ain't Good Money: This means some "Come Ups" aren't worth the risk of prison time or the consequences from another "Faction" taking retaliation if you "Burn" them.

All Sides Of The Rag: This refers to the gangsters and gangs on opposing sides in a gang conflict. For example, "I'm a Crip, and I had many friends who were Bloods in prison. After being in prison long enough, you start to see past that and realize there are good individuals on all sides of the rag."

Alone Time: When an inmate needs time alone in his cell to masturbate. If they are on "Lockdown," he will sign his "Cellie" up for a doctor's appointment to get some alone time. During normal "Program," alone time will be when his cellie is at work, school, yard, or "Dayroom."

Americans: Old-school term used by some "Factions" to describe the White convicts who pushed a "Hardline" of "Prison Politics."

Animal Control: The nickname for the "Adjustment Center" at San Quentin State Prison.

Anniversary: The date that an inmate started doing their time in prison. For example, "Today is my four-year anniversary since I got 'Cracked.'"

Appliances: The electronic items and cooking devices an inmate is allowed to keep in their cell or locker. For example, "In the 'Hole,' we didn't get to have our appliances. These days, they get a radio and television."

Area Spread: A unique community meal for homies from your area that everyone contributes to. Then, when it's done cooking, everyone eats together like a barbecue at a park.

Armor: Extra clothes, jackets, books, and magazines are worn by inmates to protect them in a melee from being "Blasted." The books and magazines are placed inside clothing so they are not seen.

Aryan Brotherhood: In 1967, this White prison gang was formed at San Quentin Prison. The Aryan Brotherhood started as the "Blue Bird Gang" in the 1950s, and as a result of a vicious war with the "Black Guerrilla Family," they joined forces with other smaller White gangs to form the Aryan Brotherhood.

Asante: This word means thank you in Swahili, and some Black inmates use Swahili words in prison to get back to their cultural heritage.

Asian Car: The Asian "Car" is under the umbrella of the "Other" car in prison.

Ask For A Seat: When a high-ranking "Camarada" would "Land" on a prison yard and ask to be placed on the "Mesa." For example, "Lazy just 'Drove Up,' and he asked for a seat. But there are no seats open."

ASP: Avenal State Prison.

Ass Backwards: When an inmate "Rolls It Up" and goes "PC" due to fear and intimidation from other convicts. For example, "I heard Dumps went out ass backwards."

Assed Out: When an inmate disrespects an officer, and the officer refuses to give him things. For example, a "Problem Child" asks an officer for a favor, and the officer replies, "You're assed out. You got 'Nothing Coming.'"

Associate: A person who hangs around gangs and even does things of a criminal nature with them, but they aren't a bonafide member.

ASU: This stands for "Administration Segregation Unit," where inmates are sent for breaking the rules in prison. Basically, the Administration Segregation Unit is a jail within a prison. The inmates are in their cells for 23 hours a day. They have limited personal items due to security reasons. The inmates are allowed a shower once every three days. They can exercise on a small yard behind the "Housing Unit" with "Gun Coverage."

At Peace With Their Program: When a convict just wants to do his time and make his "Date" to get to the streets and be with his family. A convict at peace with his "Program" will stay out of the drama others are involved in on the prison yard. For example, "A lot of the homies just want to be at peace with their program."

At The End Of The Day: It's pretty common for inmates to use this phrase while talking to you. Basically, it's used at the end of a dialogue to summarize what they were talking about.

Authority In Charge: This is the "Norteño" who oversees an entire prison or jail.

AW: This acronym stands for the Associate Warden of the prison.

Awake, Aware, Alert: This is a mindset that most "Factions" instill into their members. They demand their members are up early, working out hard, on point, and representing themselves well in prison based on their conduct.

Aztecs: A more advanced variation of a "Burpee."

B

Back: The "SHU," or the "Hole," where the "Heavy Hitters" are "Locked Down." Basically, it is a prison within the prison. It's where convicts are placed when their presence on the "Mainline" is deemed problematic to the administration. For example, "The 'Big Homie' Venom is in the back."

Back At It Like A Crack Addict: To get back to doing something and going all out with it. For example, "I am 'Hitting' again, so I'm back at it like a crack addict."

Back Door Parole: When an inmate dies in prison. For example, "Graybeard got that back door parole."

Back Door Politics: When a gangster is betrayed by his homies. When a gangster fails to understand "Prison Politics" and falls victim to a savvy comrade looking to move up the ladder in the organization. For example, "Bad Luck got 'Crossed Up' by back door politics."

Back Doored: When a gangster is betrayed by his homies. When a gangster fails to understand "Prison Politics" and falls victim to a savvy comrade looking to move up the ladder in the organization. For example, "Pretty Boy got back doored by Pirate."

Back To Front Charlie Row: Charlie Row is a section in the L.A. County Jail. The inmates on either end of Charlie Row are tasked with being "On Point" for their "People." When the inmates in the back hear the officers' keys coming towards them, they yell, "Back to front, Charlie Row." This verbal warning would notify the homies to stash any "Contraband" and stop illegal activities.

Back Up Off My Program: This means you better leave a convict alone and stop pressuring them. For example, "Back up off my program, 'Lame!' You aren't running nothing around here."

Back Wall: An area in prison where inmates are concealed from the view of correctional officers. The back wall is where inmates go to settle disputes among themselves. For example, "Stop talking out the side of your neck. Take it to the back wall!"

Backpiece: Tattoos that cover the back of an inmate. For example, "Did you see Big Herm's backpiece? It's off the chain, homie."

Backwards: When an inmate "Rolls It Up" and goes "PC." For example, "Shaggy went out backwards like a 'Lame.'"

Bad Call: When a "Shot Caller" gives the "Green Light" to have someone "Removed," and it turns out the victim didn't do anything wrong. Usually, when this happens, the shot caller will face severe repercussions for making the bad call. That's why shot callers must be sure and have "Paperwork" before they have one of their people "Whacked."

Bad Case: When an inmate is convicted of rape, snitching, molestation, abusing women or the elderly, etc. Most prison gangs will violently attack these inmates and remove them from the yard. These inmates are "No Good."

Bad Charges: When an inmate has any of the following on their "Paperwork;" rape, snitching, molestation, abusing women or the elderly, etc. Most prison gangs will violently attack inmates with these things on their "Black & Whites" and "Remove" them from the yard.

Bad Jacket: This is when an adversary spreads lies about another person in prison to "Smut Up" their name. This is done by someone who is "Politicking" against them. For example,

"Iceman is trying to give me a bad jacket by saying I never paid the homie what he had coming."

Bad For Business: A saying in prison that refers to violence between different "Factions." If things "Kick Off" between two different factions, there will be a "Lockdown" afterward. Once both groups are on lockdown, they will lose significant amounts of money because it will disrupt their drug trade and many other money-making ventures.

Bad Graces: An inmate put on the "Shine" by his gang. His gang won't talk or associate with him until he redeems himself by doing a "Cleanup."

Bad Look: When a person does something that makes them look bad. For example, "Wino, you are drinking too much 'Pruno' and not taking care of yourself. It's a bad look, homie."

Bad News List: Every prison gang has a ledger of "No Good" former members who are targeted for attack whenever the opportunity becomes available. Every prison will have a copy of this list, usually kept in the "Hole." These lists are very extensive and can have hundreds of names on them. The bad news list is usually "Hooped" for safekeeping.

Bad Paperwork: When an inmate has any of the following on their "Paperwork;" rape, snitching, molestation, abusing women or the elderly, etc. Most prison gangs will violently attack inmates with these things on their "Black & Whites" and "Remove" them from the yard.

Bad Politics: This is when a gang member goes against the established policies and procedures in a particular prison setting. For example, if an inmate in a prison gang "Pokes" someone without clearing it first with those in charge, that is bad politics. Inmates in most gangs in prison need permission from the "Shot Callers" to do certain things, or they will face serious repercussions.

Bad Standing: When a prison gang member is under investigation by his comrades for wrongdoing. He will be kept to the side, and no gang business or "Politics" will be shared with him until he is cleared of any violations.

Badge Heavy: A correctional officer who unnecessarily throws their weight around to compensate for their many shortcomings. For example, "Who is that 'Robocop' trying to impress? There is no need to be badge heavy with these convicts; they are 'Programmers.'"

Bag Work: Bag work is when a convict does various exercises with a "Water Bag." Weights were taken away in 1997 by the California Department of Corrections and Rehabilitation. Convicts use water bags for weights. For example, "I'm going to go and do some bag work in my cell."

Bakers: Some "Factions" in prison from Bakersfield will refer to their city as Bakers. For example, "Icepick from Bakers pushes a 'Hardline.'"

Bakersfield: Most people regard gangs in Bakersfield and below as Southern California; any gangs in cities above Bakersfield are considered Northern California.

Balas: This word translates to "Bullet." In prison, it means to do one year behind bars. For example, "I have been down 20 balas, homie."

Baller: A person in prison who has their shelves stocked with "Groceries" and "Hygiene," and rarely goes to the "Chow Hall."

They only go to the chow hall to give their food tray away to their homie. For example, "Bird is a baller; he never goes to the chow hall."

Banger: A banger is an inmate-manufactured weapon. For example, "Bandit had a banger on him, and he 'Booked' that 'Chomo' when he caught him slipping."

Banging At Them: When an inmate purposely exposes his penis to a female officer or "Free Staff." For example, "Lowdown is a 'Gunslinger,' he is always banging at them female officers."

Bar: A lock on the wall that prevents the cell doors on that "Section" of a "Tier" from being opened when it's engaged. The bar lock is activated after the last count of the night and deactivated during the morning count.

Bar Lock: A metal box on the wall that prevents the cell doors on that tier from being opened when engaged. The bar lock is activated after the last count of the night and deactivated during the morning count.

Barrio: A word some gangsters use for their neighborhood.

Barrio Hard Candy: This is a "Green Light" put on an entire "Barrio" versus a Green Light put on a specific person. For example, "Whittier Varrio Locos have a barrio hard candy on them."

Bastille: An old-school term used for San Quentin State Prison.

Bastille By The Bay: An old-school term used for San Quentin State Prison.

Basura: A word that means garbage or trash. When an inmate has any of the following on their "Paperwork;" rape, snitching, molestation, abusing women or the elderly, etc. Most prison gangs will violently attack inmates with these things on their "Black & Whites" and "Remove" them from the yard.

Batch: A bag of "Pruno" just cooked and ready to drink. For example, "I just cooked a batch. Do you want a cup, homeboy?"

Baton: The metal, plastic, or wood striking device officers carry on their "Duty Belts."

Battery Pack: Rechargeable batteries in a makeshift cardboard carrying case that inmates use to charge their devices. Inmates can rig a battery pack to charge their "Contraband" cell phones.

Battery Packed: When convicts put batteries or bars of soap in a sock and then swing it as a weapon. These weapons inflict significant damage and are a great choice when a "Banger" isn't available to use. For example, "Gunner was 'Talking Out The Side Of His Neck,' so I battery packed him."

Bay Area Brothers: A nickname for the "Kumi 415," a well-organized "Faction" consisting of Black convicts.

Bay City: A nickname for San Quentin State Prison.

BCOA: The Basic Correctional Officer Academy is 13 weeks long. It is located in Galt, California.

Be On Your Toes: To be aware of what's happening around you and not fall victim to an "Okey Doke."

Bean Chute: The small opening in the cell door or wall whereby food is given to the inmates. Inmates are also cuffed through this opening while still inside their cells.

Bean Slot: The small opening in the cell door or wall whereby food is given to the inmates. Inmates are also cuffed through this opening while still inside their cells.

Beat The Brakes Off Him: To win a fight against someone decisively. For example, "The next time I see Popcorn, I'm going to beat the brakes off him."

Beat The Brakes Off You: To win a fight against someone decisively. For example, "Don't ever talk to me like that again, or I will beat the brakes off you."

Beat Up From The Feet Up: When a person, thing, or situation looks terrible. For example, "That new officer thinks he is all that, but he is beat up from the feet up."

Beating The Brakes Off Him: To win a fight against someone decisively. For example, "I was beating the brakes off him until the homies broke it up."

Beauties: The term used for something of a good quality. For example, "Check out these beauties; I can't wait to 'Poke' someone with them."

Bed Card: A card with the convict's picture and gang affiliation kept in the "Control Booth." When transferred between buildings on the same yard, they take this with them and give it to the officers in their new "Housing Units." Each bed card has a color that correlates to the inmate's race.

Bed Move: When an inmate is moved from one bunk or cell to another within a prison.

Bed Roll: Item given to a "Fish" inmate, which consists of a towel, two sheets, a blanket, and one pillowcase.

Beef: To have an active conflict with another person or organization. For example, "I don't have a beef with you."

Beefed Out: This means to catch a case and get transferred out of a prison facility. For example, "I beefed out of Folsom and ended up at High Desert."

Beefing: To have an active conflict with another person or organization. For example, "We were beefing hard with those 'Nazis' at Folsom."

Behind The Gate: This describes things that happen in prison. For example, "I put in a lot of work behind the gate."

Behind The Iron Gate: This describes things that happen in prison. For example, "I did twelve years behind the iron gate, comrade."

Behind The Wall: The "Vocational Training" area of a prison where inmates learn a trade like welding, woodworking, silk screening, working on cars, etc.

Being Loud In The Vent: Convicts in prison cells can communicate with their neighbors by talking in the vent for the air conditioning. Sometimes, when inmates get drunk or too rowdy, they yell in the vent and disrespect their neighbors. This activity is highly frowned upon because it can cause "Tension" between different "Cars." For example, "Stutter, you need to stop being loud in the vent. You were 'Out Of Pocket.'"

Belly Chain: This restraining device is used when inmates travel outside the prison for various reasons. The handcuffs are secured to the belly chain on each inmate's side.

Belly Up: When an inmate can't take the pressure on a prison yard and tells the officers they need "Protective Custody." For example, "Beetle went belly up after being Mister Tough Guy."

Berdoo: Some "Factions" in prison from San Bernardino will refer to their city as Berdoo. For example, "Maniac from Berdoo was 'Running The Program' back at 'County.'"

BGF: Acronym for the "Black Guerrilla Family" prison gang. The BGF was formed in the 1960s at San Quentin Prison consisting of Black "Convicts." In the early 80s, they had a notable war with the "Crips" that lasted several years.

Bible: The rules and regulations of a prison gang that all members must follow. The Bible is also referred to as "Household Policies," "Household Rules," "Constitution," or "Code Of Conduct."

Bic: The preferred haircut in prison by some inmates is a shaved head. One reason is that a barber isn't always available while locked in their cells, so it's easier for them to shave it themselves. For example, "Hey homeboy, do you have a razor so I can bic my head?"

Bid: A prison sentence of various lengths. For example, "I just got done doing a ten-year bid."

Big Bertha: The nickname for thc 40mm launcher that the officers use to stop fights and riots.

Big B*h:** This is a name given for a life sentence. For example, "Playboy just caught a big b***h!"

Big Five: These were the five main prison gangs in the California Department of Corrections and Rehabilitation at one time. These gangs are: "Aryan Brotherhood," "Mexican Mafia," "Nuestra Familia," "Black Guerrilla Family," and "Nazi Low Riders."

Big Four: These were the four main prison gangs in the California Department of Corrections and Rehabilitation. These gangs are: "Aryan Brotherhood," "Mexican Mafia," "Nuestra Familia," and "Black Guerrilla Family."

Big Homie: A term used by "Southerners" for a member of "La

Eme" or "Mexican Mafia."

Big House: Another word for prison. For example, "From the big house to your house."

Big House Prison Museum: This museum is located near the entrance of Folsom State Prison and is filled with many artifacts about its legendary history.

Big M: Another name for the "Mexican Mafia."

Big Q: Term used by convicts for San Quentin State Prison.

Bigger Than The Program: When people believe the rules and regulations that govern their "Faction" don't apply to them. For example, "Some of the 'Brass' think they are bigger than the program."

Biker: This term is used in prison to describe a dirty person who keeps a dirty cell. For example, "Big Nasty is greasy. The homie is living like a biker."

Biker Status: This term is used in prison to describe a dirty person who keeps a dirty cell. For example, "Caveman is on biker status. He is funky."

Billy Club: The old-school term used for the correctional officer's "Baton."

Bindle: A small measurement of tobacco or weed that's used to barter with. For example, "I will give you four bindles for those 'Kicks.'"

Binky: A prison-made device used to inject intravenous drugs. The Binky is made of an eye dropper, a sharpened guitar string, and a shaft of a plastic ink pen that has been cut down to size.

Bird Bath: When convicts use the water from their sink to clean themselves with soap and water.

Birdcage: The telephone booth-shaped cage that convicts are placed in for short periods. The birdcage looks like a telephone booth with mesh wire for walls.

Birds On The Line: Warning that someone is listening to a conversation.

Birthday Spread: A special community meal for birthday celebrations in prison that everyone in the "Car" contributes to. When it's finished cooking, they eat together like a barbecue at a park.

B*h Up:** When an inmate has succumbed to pressure or intimidation and no longer feels safe on the "General Population" and "Checks In" to "Protective Custody."

BKS: This is short for the city of Bakersfield, and some gang members from there will tattoo BKS on them.

Black: Prison slang used for heroin. For example, "Do you have any black left, homie?"

Back Fade: This refers to when a comrade "Drives Up" to a "Compound" and runs a "Fade" with a person who a member of his "Car" just ran a fade with. For example, "My homie Looney just ran a fade with Bam Bam, I am about to run that back fade."

Black & Whites: This is the "Paperwork" that shows what crime a convict was incarcerated for and all relevant court documents. Every convict in a "Car" has their black and whites checked by other members to verify they don't have any "Bad Charges."

Black & Whites Don't Lie: This saying means that the "Paperwork" concerning a convict's crimes can be relied upon to determine if they have "Bad Charges." For example, "You know what they say, homie, the black and whites don't lie."

Black August: In California prisons, many Black convicts come together in August and pay homage to the Black men who came before them and fought the "System." Men like George Jackson of the "Soledad Brothers" are prime examples. During Black August, these convicts also fast during the day, workout together, and refuse to go to "Canteen."

Black Box: The black device that connects the waist and leg chains on inmates transported on the "Grey Goose." When restrained in this manner on the prison bus, it is very uncomfortable for the inmates, and they hate it.

Black Boxes Walking: This is yelled by the officers in "L.A. County Jail" when inmates going to court in full restraints with a "Black Box" are walking around other convicts. When this is yelled, the other inmates must turn around and not look at them so they can't pass messages.

Black Guerilla Family: A prison gang formed in the 1960s at San Quentin Prison consisting of Black "Convicts." In the early 80s, they had a notable war with the "Crips" that lasted several years.

Black Glove Gang: An alleged group of officers at "New Folsom Prison" who would put on black gloves before they gave inmates a "Tune Up." For example, "The black glove gang has 'Priors' for doing our 'People' dirty."

Black Patches: These officers are members of the "Goon Squad." They have black patches on their jumpsuits, hence the name. Black patches stand out from regular correctional officers because their patches are a different color. Black patches are officially named the "Investigative Services Unit."

Blade: An inmate-manufactured weapon used for slashing and cutting. For example, "Homie, you better have your blade on you today. Things might 'Jump Off' with the 'Others.'"

Blammer: An inmate-manufactured weapon made out of metal, melted plastic, or any other hard material that can be sharpened to a point.

Blanket Party: When several inmates get a blanket and throw it over their victim's head. They will beat and kick him while they hold the blanket tightly over him.

Blast: To get "Poked" with an inmate-manufactured weapon. For example, "That fool keeps 'Bumping His Gums.' I'm going to blast him during 'Dayroom.'"

Blast Grenade: Numerous grenades utilized by the California Department of Corrections and Rehabilitation contain various chemical agents. These types of devices are employed to break up fights.

Blast Him Out His Boots: To viciously "Poke" another inmate. For example, "Psycho keeps 'Mean Mugging' me. I'm going to blast him out his boots."

Blasted: To get "Poked" with an inmate-manufactured weapon. For example, "That White boy blasted that 'Chomo' in the neck."

Blasted: When a convict is covered in tattoos or the actual process of getting a tattoo in prison. For example, "Have you seen Toon? That fool is blasted." Or "Dreamer blasted these 'Patterns' on me back at Calipatria Prison."

Blasted Out Of The Movement: When gang members remove a member from their "Car" by stabbing him. For example, "All of the 'Big Homies' in the 'Hoyo' agreed that Silent should be blasted out of the movement."

Blaxican: A term some "Factions" use for Black inmates who run with the "Southerners."

Blend Him: To attack someone violently. For example, "Stand back bro, me and the homies are about to blend him."

Blessed Me: When a homie gives you something that helps you out. For example, "When I 'Landed' at Folsom, Jet blessed me with a 'Care Package.'"

Blessing: When a convict gets permission from the "Big Homies" to run a prison yard. For example, "Beast has the blessing from Popeye. You better fall in line, comrade."

Blind: An area in prison where you are concealed from the view of correctional officers. Many inmates are lured to a blind, and then they are "Blasted" or "Smashed" by other "Convicts."

Blitzed: When an inmate gets violently attacked by a person or group of people. For example, "Soldier Boy got blitzed by the homies."

Block: A concrete and steel structure with 100 cells that hold two convicts each at Centinela Prison. Each block has four phones, twelve benches, eighteen metal tables, one clothes iron, two sinks, two water fountains, two televisions, and eight showers. Two "Floor Officers" supervise all 200 convicts in the block, and they ensure that all inmates receive their "State Issue," i.e., showers, phone calls, yard, "Dayroom," mail, medical appointments, visits, and meals.

Block Channel: The "Norteño" who is responsible for all messages and reports in his "Block" that need to be relayed to other "Channels" in his chain of command.

Block Name: A convict's nickname that all gang members call him by. For example, Bugsy, Casper, Sniper, Creeper, Danger, Jackal, Wicked, Nutty, Maniac, Sinner, Shadow, Trouble, Green Eyes, Gunner, Sharky, Oso, Payaso, etc.

Block Sergeant: In old school prisons, it's the sergeant in charge of a "Block." For example, "Ramos is the block sergeant, so get at him."

Blood: A street gang formed in Los Angeles, California. The color red identifies Bloods, and they have a rivalry with the "Crips."

Bloodism: A Blood's belief on how a true "Blood" should conduct themselves. For example, "Bandit is a brotha whose Bloodism is on point."

Blood Alley: A notorious area at San Quentin State Prison where numerous inmates have been viciously attacked over the decades.

Blood & Honor: A tattoo that some "Peckerwoods" get that means they will be honorable and loyal to their "Cause."

Blood In, Blood Out: This is the process by which someone is accepted into some gangs. This means they have to kill to get in, and their death is the only way to get out.

Blood Line: Blood Line is an old-school organization formed in California prisons consisting of "Blood" gangsters.

Bloquero: A "Sureño" in charge of a "Housing Unit" in prison. The bloquero is on the "Mesa" and works directly under the "Yardero" who runs that yard.

Blow Up The Spot: When an inmate draws attention to himself or an area, and the officers come around because of it. Now that the officers are there, any illegal activity will be discovered. For example, "Sleepy, every time you are late for lockup, you blow up the spot because that dumb cop comes over here."

Blower: An inmate-manufactured weapon made out of metal, melted plastic, or any other hard material that can be sharpened to a point.

Blowing Holes In Them: The act of viciously stabbing someone in prison with a "Banger." For example, "Icepick was blowing holes in them fools!"

Blowing Up The Spot: When an inmate draws attention to himself or an area, and the officers come around because of it. For example, "Reckless, you keep blowing up the spot. 'Slow Your Roll' homeboy."

Blown Out: When a convict gets filled with pride and starts acting out of character and taking advantage of his people. For example, "Cordless 'Had The Keys' on Charlie Yard, and he was so blown out that he started taking advantage of our comrades."

Blue Bird Gang: During the 1950s and 1960s in the California Department of Corrections, this was the biggest White prison gang. The Blue Birds were at war with the "Black Guerrilla Family," so they allied with the smaller White prison gangs, which was the start of the "Aryan Brotherhood."

Blue Flagging: When gang members who claim blue wear it proudly and don't hide their gang affiliation even if they are outnumbered.

Blue Magic: Blue Magic is an old-school organization consisting of "Crip" gangsters that were formed in California prisons.

Blue Note: Blue Note is an old-school organization consisting of "Crip" gangsters that were formed in California prisons. Their mission, when created, was to bring the Crips back to their greatness when they first started. They also wanted unity among Crip gang members.

Blues: When something terrible happens to a convict, like an extended prison sentence, or he gets "Blasted." For example, "You got to watch yourself little homie. You don't want to catch the blues."

Board: When an inmate goes to the parole board to get released early.

Board Hearing: When an inmate goes to the parole board to get released early.

Board Of Parole Hearings: The Board of Parole Hearings performs parole suitability hearings and nonviolent offender parole reviews for the California Department of Corrections and Rehabilitation.

Boarding Up: When an inmate blocks his cell window with cardboard or other materials so the officers can't see in. The inmates usually do this when they have a grievance. Officers need to see inmates during the count, so the issue must be resolved when they board up. If the inmate refuses to clear his window, a "Cell Extraction" will be done.

Bob Barker's: This term refers to items such as "Jap Flaps," combs, toothbrushes, and white T-shirts that the company Bob Barker produced.

Body By Ramen: An out-of-shape inmate whose body looks like he has been eating "Soups" and "Spreads" all day. For example, "Gordo has a body by ramen, and he is always in his rack."

Bogus Mission: When a convict is supposed to get his wind taken, but he barely gets injured in the attack. For example, "The 'Brass' wants Diamond killed. They don't want a bogus mission where he gets hit and rolls it up."

Bomb: A rolled-up piece of toilet paper shaped like a doughnut and set on fire. The inmates use it to cook food or heat water in their cells. Inmates are allowed "Hot Pots" for this very purpose, but "Indigent" inmates can't afford one, so they use this primitive method to heat their food or water. They also use a bomb to make a "Banger" from melted plastic.

Bombed On: When a person gets attacked violently. For example, "Grumpy was asleep during 'Gallo.' That's why he got bombed on by the homies."

Bomber: This is an inmate-manufactured weapon. For example, "Boogie had a bomber on him, and he 'Booked' that 'Diaper Sniper.'"

Bombers: These are the convicts involved in a "Removal." Their job is to physically attack their victim and cause a distraction after the "Hitter" "Pokes" the target so the hitter can get away and dispose of the weapon.

Bombs: In old-school prisons with bars on the prison cell doors, throwing homemade bombs into enemies' cells was not uncommon. This happened at prisons like San Quentin in the 50s-80s.

Bompton: "Bloods" don't use the letter C, so this is how they say and spell the city of Compton.

Bonaroo: This means to iron and crease up clothes to make them look really nice and clean. For example, "I have a big visit this weekend, so you know everything is going to be bonaroo."

Bonecrusher: A large inmate-manufactured weapon that causes devastating injuries.

Bone Out: To leave an area or group of people. For example, "Homie,

I'm about to bone out; see you later."

Bone Yard: The area where the wife of an inmate stays the night with him on prison grounds during a "Conjugal Visit." A secure fence surrounds the building. It has a small kitchen, bedroom, and seating area. The visitors can bring food to cook in the kitchen during their short stay.

Boo Bop: When a person gets beaten badly in a fight. For example, "That 'Punk' came at me sideways, so I gave him the old boo bop!"

Book: This means to "Poke" someone with an inmate-manufactured weapon. For example, "I'm going to book that fool the next time I see him."

Booked: When an officer does a "Write Up" on an inmate for breaking the rules. For example, an officer might say, "I booked Wino because I found a bag of 'Pruno' in his cell."

Booked: This means to "Poke" someone with an inmate-manufactured weapon. For example, "Creeper got booked because he didn't pay his debts."

Books: This is where an inmate keeps his money to buy things in prison or from approved vendors. Family members can deposit money into an inmate's account, and any money earned from his prison job goes there. This account is also called the "Inmate Trust Account."

Books: This refers to books of stamps, and in prison, books are a form of currency. For example, "Lips wants 20 books for those 'Kicks' you like."

Books Are Closed: When a prison gang stops recruiting new members into their organization.

Books Of Higher Learning: Prison gangs require their members and prospects to read several books that deal with war and political strategy. The most popular books are The Art Of War by Sun Tzu, The Prince by Machiavelli, The Book Of Five Rings by Miyamoto Musashi, and The 48 Laws Of Power by Robert Greene.

Boot Hill: These are the names of the two cemeteries at Folsom and San Quentin Prisons. There are over 650 inmates buried at San Quentin's Boot Hill and over 600 at Folsom.

Boot Up & Suit Up: When a convict expects smoke, he will be ready for battle. They will stay ready, so they don't have to get ready. For example, "When in prison, you are expected to boot up and suit up and handle your business."

Booty Bandit: An inmate notorious for using other inmates as a "Punk."

Boss: An old-school term for a correctional officer.

Bottom Bunk Chrono: This "Chrono" requires that inmates with it be assigned a bottom bunk. This Chrono is usually given to inmates with medical conditions that limit their ability to climb into a top bunk.

Bottom Bunk Seniority: Whoever has been in the cell the longest gets the bottom bunk, even if it is not assigned to him. The bottom bunk is more desirable because you don't have to climb to get into it like the top bunk. Sometimes, the inmate with seniority will give the bottom bunk to an older "Cellie" since it's harder for him to climb to the top bunk.

Bounty: "Bloods" don't use the letter C, so this is how they say and spell County when referring to County Jail.

Bow & Arrow: This weapon is used to shoot from inside a cell through the "Tray Slot" opening at someone outside the cell. The arrow and bow are made from tightly rolled paper, each layer strengthened with soap. The bowstring is made from elastic from a pair of boxers. This weapon is powerful enough to go several inches into the flesh. Some convicts will add "Poison" to the arrow tip to promote an infection.

Bow Down: When you confront a person aggressively, and they immediately back down because they are scared. For example, "I told Stomper if he ever got at me like that again, I would put hands on him. I knew he would bow down."

Box: Another term for a prison cell. For example, "If you go 'Against The Grain' in here, you might end up in another box with nothing but you and a mattress."

Box: This is another term used for the "Security Housing Unit." The Security Housing Unit is where the most violent and influential convicts are placed due to their threat to institutional security at other prisons. These convicts are in their cells 23 hours a day and are allowed very little personal property due to security reasons. These convicts are given a shower once every three days and exercise on a small yard for an hour every day.

Brand: Another name for the "Aryan Brotherhood" prison gang, a White prison gang formed in San Quentin Prison in 1967. The Aryan Brotherhood started as the "Blue Bird Gang" in the 1950s, and as a result of a vicious war with the "Black Guerrilla Family," they joined forces with other smaller White gangs to form the Aryan Brotherhood.

Branded: When a person gets chosen to be a member of the "Brand." For example, "The 'Aryan Brotherhood' was looking at a few

'PENI' members who were well respected to be branded."

Brass: The leaders of a prison gang or "Car" who wield significant influence over their "Faction." For example, "I need you to pass this 'Filter' to the homies. It's coming from Corcoran, it's coming from the brass."

Break Bread: This refers to paying "Taxes" from illegal profits to the "Brass." Taxes are usually one-third of profits gained. For example, "If you don't break bread this month, the 'Big Homies' will start asking questions."

Break Down To State: Inmates are allowed certain possessions according to the "Title 15." This term simply means to take all "Contraband" and excess items from an inmate and dispose of them. For example, "Sleepy was late for lockup again. I'm going to break him down to state."

Break Him Down: To attack another inmate and demolish him. For example, "On the 'Mainline,' the great equalizer is your knife; it doesn't matter how big a guy is; if you know how to use your knife, you will break him down real quick."

Break It Down: When an inmate has succumbed to pressure or intimidation and no longer feels safe on the "General Population" and checks into "Protective Custody."

Break Them Off: When something is given to another person or group of people. For example, "If those dudes don't pay what we have coming, we are going to break them off."

Breaking It Down: To back down from physical confrontation. For example, "I got in his face, and he started breaking it down and apologizing."

Breaking Razors: Refers to taking a razor apart and separating the blade from the plastic to make a "Tomahawk." For example, "Powder is in the cell breaking razors."

Brew: An alcoholic beverage made from the following ingredients: apples, oranges, fruit cocktails, ketchup, and sugar. It is cooked for three days in a plastic trash bag until it ferments and produces an alcoholic beverage. Pruno has a putrid taste and smell; depending on what fruit is used, its color can vary from red to orange. The going rate for a cup of pruno in prison is $8.00, and for a cup of the more potent "White Lightening," $20.

Brims: Brims are part of the "Bloods" family. Brims are Bloods, but not all Bloods are Brims.

Bring In Heat: When a convict regularly gets drugs from a visitor, "Free Staff," package, mail, or corrections officer. For example, "If you are bringing in heat, you need to pay 1/3 to the 'Big Homies' in the 'Back.'"

Bring It To The Yard: When a convict brings an issue to his "Car" so they can decide what to do as a group. For example, "Trouble was having a serious issue with Psycho, so I told him to bring it to the yard so it could get handled."

Broadway: An area of the prison inmates use as a main thoroughfare.

Brocha: A word that translates to brush, but in prison, it means a thick mustache. For example, "That vato Crow is old school homie; check out his brocha."

Broke It Down: When an inmate backs down from a physical confrontation. For example, "That punk broke it down once I caught him alone."

Broke My TV Down: To break something down and use material from it to make an inmate-manufactured weapon. For example, "I broke my TV down and made a knife. Then I 'Poked' my cellie."

Broke Off: When something is given to a person. For example, "The homie just got broke off for a 'Hot One.'"

Bros Before Hoes: This was a reasonably common tattoo I observed

on inmates. This concept means never letting a woman come between you and your homies.

Brought Back In The Fold: When a gangster is allowed back in "Good Standing" after walking away from his comrades. The price to get back in good standing is either a large sum of money or doing a "Cleanup." For example, "Wolfie was brought back in the fold. He had to pay the 'Big Homie' $5,000."

Brown Cards: The security passes issued to staff volunteers at the prison.

Brown Eagle: A more advanced variation of a "Burpee."

Brownies: The dark gloves a gangster or "Convict" will put on right before they "Put In Work."

Bubble: In most county jails in California, this is the control room where the deputies are.

Buck: To fight back in a situation. For example, "If he decides to buck, he will get what he was looking for, and it won't be nice."

Buck 50: The scar on an inmate's face caused by a severe slash from a "Tomahawk." A Buck 50 is also called a "Puto Mark," which usually starts by the ear or corner of the lips and spans the length of the face. The Buck 50 is only for snitches, drop-outs, or other "No Good" inmates. The large and very noticeable scar forever brands them.

Buck Roger's Date: This term describes any lengthy prison sentence. For example, "Spanky has a Buck Roger's Date."

Buglers: This refers to cigarettes. For example, "I rolled him up a few Buglers and I sent them in his 'Care Package' when 'Drove Up.'"

Buggy Whips: A man with skinny arms and no muscle definition. For example, "Tweek has some buggy whips; he needs to hit the 'Weight Pile' and eat more food."

Build Them Don't Break Them: This means to build your fellow gang members up and don't break them down. It's a mindset of not victimizing your people but making them better so your "Car" becomes more potent due to their growth.

Building: A concrete and steel structure with 100 cells that hold two convicts each at Centinela Prison. Each building has four phones, twelve benches, eighteen metal tables, one clothes iron, two sinks, two water fountains, two televisions, and eight showers. Two "Floor Officers" supervise all 200 convicts in the building, and they ensure that all inmates receive their "State Issue," i.e., showers, phone calls, yard, "Dayroom," mail, medical appointments, visits, and meals.

Building Rep: The leader of a prison gang or "Car" in a "Housing Unit" who wields great influence over his comrades. If an officer has a persistent problem with a convict, they usually talk to the building rep to resolve the issue. Building reps in prison help keep things in order, and I have asked them numerous times to put their homies in check before they head into a "Wreck."

Bull: An old-school term for a corrections officer.

Bulldog: To bully other inmates and throw your weight around. For example, "Check this out, Scarface, you aren't going to come here and bulldog your way around this yard."

Bulldogs: The Fresno Bulldogs are a prison gang from Fresno, and unlike most gangs, they do not have "Shot Callers." Due to the fact the Fresno Bulldogs don't have shot callers, they are harder to manage in a prison setting because they do whatever they want without a leader keeping them in check.

Bullet: Doing one year behind bars.

Bump Around The Cell: When two inmates in a cell fight each other, and during the fight, they slam each other against the walls, tables, lockers, and bunk. For example, "Check this out, homie; if you ever do that again, we will bump around the cell."

Bump Your Head: When a person acts out of character. For example, "Why are you acting stupid, homie? Did you bump your head?"

Bumping Heads: When two people or groups constantly have problems with each other. These types of situations eventually lead to a physical altercation. For example, "Toro and his cellie keep bumping heads."

Bumping His Gums: When someone is being disrespectful and running their mouth. For example, "Lips was bumping his gums, so I 'Took Off' on him."

Bundle: Back in the early 80s, in "Receiving And Release" at Soledad Prison, they would give a bundle to new inmates. The bundle consisted of a rolled-up towel with some tobacco inside, two books of matches, and two blue bandannas. During this same time at Tracy prison, the inmates would get two red bandannas in their bundle.

Bundle: "Contraband" such as drugs, knives, or sensitive documents wrapped in cellophane and usually "Hooped" in the rectum by a convict.

Bunk Status: When convicts in a "Dorm" setting are confined to their bunks and are not allowed to move without permission. This is the dormitory version of a "Lockdown." Gang members also discipline some of their members in the same way. For example, "Check this out, Bronco, you are going to be on bunk status for two days as punishment for losing that 'Kite.'"

Bunked Up With: This is the person you share a cell with or a bunk bed in a "Dorm" setting. For example, "I was bunked up with Sleepy on A Yard."

Bunky: In a "Dorm" setting, it's the person you share a bunk bed with.

Burn: To agree to pay for something (usually drugs) without the intention of actually paying for it. Then, when you are "Fronted" the drugs, you don't pay the person who gave them to you. For example, "Those fools would never burn me because the drugs I was selling belonged to the 'Big Homie.'"

Burn Artist: An inmate who is known for ripping people off. Usually, these types of inmates are dope fiends. For example, "Watch out for Dopey; he is a burn artist."

Burner: An inmate-manufactured weapon. For example, "Sniper, you got your burner on you, homie? It looks like these fools are about to move on us."

Burner: The "Contraband" cell phones that convicts get smuggled into prison.

Burning Ink: When inmates burn things such as Pomade,

racquetballs, chess pieces, and numerous other plastics under their stainless steel toilets covered with a wet sheet that funnel the smoke into the vent. After burning the materials, they will scrape the soot from the toilet and mix it with shampoo or baby oil to make their tattoo ink. They will use a sharpened guitar string for a needle in their tattoo "Rig."

Burnt: When something or someone is "No Good." For example, "Mule Creek is a 'No Landing Zone' homie. It's burnt."

Burp The Baby: When making "Pruno" in prison, you must release the gasses from the plastic trash bag, or the bag will burst. This process is called burping the baby. For example, "Hey, homie, you need to burp the baby because your bag is about to burst."

Burpee Line: The "Burpee" line is for people who violate "Household Policies," and they have to do burpees as punishment.

Burpee Monster: A convict who can do more "Burpees" than most other people. Usually, the standard for a burpee monster is 1,000 burpees in an hour. For example, "Hulk is a burpee monster. Nobody can keep up with him."

Burpees: The most common exercise in California prisons, in its simplest form, is doing a push-up and then standing up. Most inmates perform burpees several hundred times a day. The primary purpose of this exercise is to build up an inmate's endurance so that their stamina is at near maximum level when they fight.

Burping The Baby: When making "Pruno" in prison, you must release the gasses from the plastic trash bag, or the bag will burst. This process is called burping the baby.

Bus Therapy: A cruel, painful tactic of keeping convicts on the "Grey Goose" for prolonged periods as punishment. For example, a troublesome inmate will be constantly transferred from various prisons to keep them on the Grey Goose for weeks or even months. Convicts despise being transported because the seats and "Transport Jewelry" used on the bus are very uncomfortable on extended trips.

Business Card: The prison gang's official tattoo is their business card.

Bust A Grape: To become violent and attack somebody verbally or physically. For example, "That dude is a 'Lame,' he isn't going to bust a grape."

Bust A Hole In You: This means to "Poke" someone in prison with a "Banger." For example, "If you don't have my money in 48 hours, I will bust a hole in you."

Bust A Mission: The process of carrying out a "Mission." For example, "Check this out, homie, we need you to bust a mission on Stranger."

Bust A Move: When a person or "Faction" attacks another person or faction. For example, "Felony rushed Solo on the yard today. I'm surprised it took that long for him to bust a move after the way he did him dirty."

Bust A Spread: When an inmate makes a "Spread" because he is hungry.

For example, "I need a summer sausage to bust a spread."

Bust Down: When an inmate does his workout routine. For example, "Homie, after I wake up, I'm going to bust down and do 1,000 'Burpees.'"

Bust Down Routine: The workout routine that a convict does in prison.

Bust You Out Your Cell: When an officer opens a cell door to let an inmate out. For example, "Homie, I'm going to have the cop bust you out of your cell so we can handle that issue."

Bust Your Spokes: When a convict places items of "Contraband" in his rectum to avoid discovery by officers. Some convicts become very proficient at this and can do it in seconds. When a "Banger" is placed inside the "Prison Safe," it will have a protective layer of cellophane to prevent his insides from being perforated.

Busted: When a person gets arrested and sent to prison.

Buster: Refers to a lazy, sloppy, and good-for-nothing person nobody respects in prison.

Buster: This is the shortened version of the term "Sodbuster." Sodbuster is a derogatory term "Southerners" used for "Northerners."

Busting Laps: When convicts walk around the "Dayroom" or "Track." For example, "The homies were busting laps in the dayroom."

Busting My Ear: This means someone is irritating you by what they say. For example, "My old lady was busting my ear about the same old drama."

Butt Hurt: When you tell someone the truth about their bad behavior, and they get offended. For example, "Why are you getting butt hurt? I'm just keeping it real with you, homie."

Butte County Gangsters: A "Peckerwood" "Car" in prison from Butte County.

Butterfly Tattoo: Some old-school "Mexican Mafia" members used a butterfly tattoo many years ago. It is commonly called the "Mariposa," which translates to butterfly.

Buyback Policy: A policy whereby "Southerners" who were deemed "No Good" could pay $10,000 to get back in "Good Standing."

Buzz Him In: When a "Control Booth Officer" presses a button to open a cell door. For example, "I had the police buzz him in so he could get some 'Hygiene' to give to the 'New Booty.'"

C

C-File: This is the main file for each convict, where all information is maintained regarding their history and behavior while in prison.

C-Nation: The "Crip" collective as a whole. For example, "Homie, all I care about is the C-Nation unification; we need to stop this 'Set Tripping' and come together."

C-Status: A "Privilege Group" of inmates where most of their "Program" is restricted. For example, "I was on C-Status for getting caught with a cell phone."

Cadillac: Term used for the actual weight used for "Fishing" in prison. Fishing is the process of sliding a long string with a Cadillac attached to the end under the cell door and into another cell to pass "Kites," "Bangers," and other "Contraband." For example, "Shoot your cadillac, homie."

Cadillac Cell: When an inmate customizes a prison cell and is very clean and nice looking. Inmates can get various materials inside the prison, making their cells unique.

Cadillac Coffee: This is coffee with cream and sugar. Some inmates add cocoa to make Cadillac Coffee. For example, "Me and the homie were killing time telling 'War Stories' while having a Cadillac Coffee."

Cadillac Draw: This is what the maximum "Canteen" "Draw" is referred to. The canteen is the inmate store on prison grounds, and they can buy food and hygiene items once a month. The Cadillac draw these days is $240 a month.

Cadillac Job: This is a highly sought-after job in prison by inmates. For example, the "Visiting Room Porter" is a Cadillac Job.

Cadillac Rack: A rack in a "Dorm" that doesn't have a bed stacked on top of it, unlike the other ones, which are bunk beds. This term also refers to the bottom bunk.

Cage: Some inmates call their prison "Cell" a cage. For example, "You are looking for Muggsy? He is in his cage."

Cal: Calipatria State Prison.

Calendar: A term used in prison to describe one year served behind bars.

For example, "I did ten calendars behind bars, homie."

Calentada: This is when an inmate has violated the "Reglas" of his gang, and for punishment, his homies will assault him for 13 seconds. For example, "Sniper has a calentada coming."

California AB: The "Aryan Brotherhood" that runs the California prison system for White inmates. They are allies with the "Federal AB," which has a different "Commission" and runs the Federal prison system in America for White inmates.

California Car: In the federal prison system around 1993, the Black convicts from California united to strengthen themselves as a people because the cats from D.C. were pushing a "Hardline" on them.

California Model: The California Model represents a comprehensive transformation initiative within the California Department of Corrections and Rehabilitation and California Correctional Health Care Services. This model incorporates best practices from both national and international contexts to foster a cultural shift within the prison system, enhancing the correctional environment. It achieves this through the provision of staff training, as well as the development of tools and resources aimed at promoting the health and well-being of both employees and inmates.

California Youth Authority: This is where juvenile offenders, ages 1225, went when they got convicted of crimes in California. The California Youth Authority is notorious for being very violent, with the state's wards fighting each other daily.

Calipat: The nickname for Calipatria State Prison.

Calipatria Program Office Attack: On June 5, 1995, five "Crips" rushed into the "Program Office" while the door was unlocked at 0930 hours and attacked the officers inside with inmate-manufactured weapons. Eight officers got stabbed and were taken to outside hospitals for treatment. A female sergeant suffered severe stab wounds during the violent attack. The motive for this attack is unknown, but two months prior, an officer shot and killed an inmate during a fight. This attack changed the California Department of Corrections and Rehabilitation's policy on Level IV yards because, after this, they installed fences separating the Program Office from the rest of the prison yard. They also sectioned the yard off with two buildings in one section and three in the other.

Called It Quits: When a prison gang member stops gang banging and lays down his flag. For example, "Did you hear about Monster? He called it quits like a punk. He 'Went Out Backwards.'"

Called Me In The Vent: When your neighbor in prison calls you through the vent that connects both cells to talk. For example, "Wino called me in the vent and asked me if I had any 'Pruno' left."

Calling Out Doors: When inmates in their cells yell out the cell number of another inmate to tell them something. For example,

"Cell 206, you are a punk! When I catch you on the yard, it's on and cracking!"

CALPIA: Acronym for the California Prison Industry Authority, which the State of California runs. It employs inmates for a meager wage to make merchandise for sale at a significant profit. The inmates make anywhere between .30 to .95 cents an hour before deductions.

Calpulli: A "Nahuatl" word some "Southerners" use when referring to "Pelican Bay" or the "SHU." For example, "This order is coming from the Calpulli."

Camarada: A high-ranking gangster with a lot of "Status."

Came Up Missing: When a person or something of value disappears either from getting murdered or by getting stolen. For example, "Cartoon, I heard that cat who killed your homie came up missing. He had that issue coming, homie."

Camp: The California Department of Corrections and Rehabilitation minimum security facilities for firefighting and conservation work. They are commonly referred to as "Fire Camp."

Camp Snoopy: A low-level prison yard where people are trying to get home and not pushing a "Hardline" or any "Prison Politics."

Campaigning: To use your "Status" in your "Car" to try and get another member "Removed," "Disciplined," or just to "Smut Up" his name because you don't like him. Campaigning means pushing a "Hardline" against any group or person in prison.

Campaigning For Votes: This is when the "Big Homies" are talking to other "Mexican Mafia" members, trying to get the necessary votes to get one of their homies to become a "Carnal." For example, "I was at the Tehachapi SHU when the 'Fellas' were campaigning for votes."

Campers: The inmates who are assigned to "Fire Camps." For example, "It is hard work for those campers fighting fires."

Can I Holla At You: When some convicts want to talk to you privately, they will say this to you.

Can We Get Some Volume On That: This is how some convicts in their cells ask their "Neighbors" to turn their radio or television down if it's too loud. For example, "Hey, cell 212, can we get some volume on that."

Can't Play Varrios In The County: This is a "Mexican Mafia" rule that "Southerners" who are at war with each other on the streets have to get along while in County Jail.

Canteen: Store on prison grounds where inmates buy food and other supplies. Inmates can purchase a maximum of $240 a month from the canteen. Canteen is also used to describe items from the canteen. For example, "I got a bunch of canteen in my cell, homie."

Cap: A cap refers to a small amount of tobacco or marijuana. The term cap is used because inmates use a Chap-Stick cap to measure cannabis or tobacco. A cap of weed in prison varies in price depending on where you are, $20-100. A cap of tobacco goes for $10.

Cap: A cover for a knife that prevents it from poking you when you are "Hooping."

Car: Term used for the actual weight used for "Fishing" in prison. Fishing is the process of sliding a long string with a car attached to the end under the cell door and into another cell to pass "Kites," "Bangers," and other "Contraband." For example,

"Shoot your car, homie."

Car: The people one associates with or the gang members from one's county.

Care Package: When a new arrival "Lands" at a prison or yard, his homies will give him food and hygiene items to help him until he gets on his feet.

Career: This is the reputation a gangster has and the "Status" they achieve among their peers. Gangsters advance their careers by "Putting In Work" on the streets and in prison.

Carga: A term that refers to heroin. For example, "Where can I get some carga on this yard?"

Carnal: A member of the "Mexican Mafia."

Carnales: This word means brothers.

Carnalismo: To have love for your brothers.

Carnival Talk: Coded words that inmates use when discussing illegal activities so law enforcement who may be eavesdropping on their conversation won't know what they're talking about. For example, an inmate on a "Contraband" cell phone with his homie says, "Venom is going to drive Cherilo to the car show." This coded sentence means Venom is going to kill Cherilo.

Carry A Flag: To belong to a movement and push their beliefs and agenda. For example, "I don't carry a flag for anything now. I carry my own flag. I stand by my values, not anybody else's."

Carry Your Weight: When an inmate puts in work for his gang. Every prison gang member will carry their weight by doing things that must be done for their comrades. For example, "Check this out, youngster, you need to carry your weight around here."

Cased Up: When an inmate goes into "Protective Custody" out of fear for their safety. Protective Custody prison yards are the majority in CDCR now. These yards are considered "No Good" by the "General Population" convicts. Most inmates in Protective Custody are there for drug or gambling debts. Protective Custody yards tend to be more chaotic and violent than the "Mainline" because the gang structure is less rigid than the general population gangs. For example, "I was in 7 'Block' at 'Susanville' when Nails cased up."

Cat: A term used to describe a person. For example, "Rocky is a cool cat."

Catch A Bus: When inmates are transferred between prisons, they are chained together and put on the "Grey Goose" prison bus. The seats are very hard, and being chained the way they are makes these trips uncomfortable for the inmates. For example, "I'm waiting to catch a bus to Soledad."

Catch A Chain: When inmates are transferred between prisons, they are chained together and put on the "Grey Goose" prison bus. The seats are very hard, and being chained the way they are makes these trips uncomfortable for the inmates. For example, "I'm waiting to catch a chain to Folsom."

Catch A Fade: A challenge to a one-on-one fight between two adversaries. For example, "I am tired of you 'Selling Wolf Tickets,' let's catch a fade."

Catch A Mainline: When inmates are at one of the California Department of Corrections and Rehabilitation's "Reception Centers," they get assigned a prison. For example, "I was at Wasco Reception and waited a long time to catch a mainline."

Catch A Ride: To ask a friend with drugs if you can get high with them. For example, "Hey man, can I catch a ride?" It can also mean hanging out with your friends, "Hey, can I catch a ride with you?"

Catch A Square: To challenge another inmate to a fight. For example, "You talk too much, punk! It's time to catch a square!"

Catch The Blues: When something terrible happens to a convict, like an extended prison sentence or he gets "Booked." For example, "You got to watch yourself on this yard, youngster. You don't want to catch the blues."

Catting Off: This means acting crazy and clowning around like a "J-Cat." People who know you would think you went crazy. For example, "The homie got a hold of that 'Pruno,' and now he is catting off."

Catwalk: A high walkway above inmates in various buildings and areas in prison where officers observe inmate activities.

Caucasian: A "Non-Affiliated" White inmate. A term used by "Peckerwoods" to describe a White inmate who does not get involved in "Prison Politics."

Caught A Body: This means to murder someone. For example, "I caught a body at Folsom Prison."

Caught Down Bad: When someone is confronted, and they don't have their "Banger" on them.

Caught My Number: When a convict goes to state prison and is assigned their "CDCR Number." A CDCR number is the inmate's identification for their tenure in prison. It's a social security number for their new birth in the prison system. For example, "I caught my number in 2020."

Caught Out Of Pocket: When someone is confronted, and they don't have their "Banger" on them.

Caught Slipping: When someone is confronted, and they don't have their "Banger" on them.

Caught That L: When someone gets a life sentence in prison.

Caught Up: Getting so involved in a situation that you become oblivious to reality.

Cause: A gang's mission and all members must be down for them to remain in the "Car." For example, "I'm down with the cause, homie."

CC: Every inmate is assigned a correctional counselor, and their jobs are to interview the inmates, evaluate their progress in programs, summarize reports from the inmate's files, and assist them with parole suitability.

CC Riders: Many years ago, the Compton "Crips" had a "Car" in prison, and this was their name.

CCO: Consolidated Crip Organization is an old-time organization consisting of "Crip" gangsters who were pushing a "Hardline."

CDC 115: A disciplinary report issued to inmates. There are two types of reports: administrative and serious.

CDC Number: The five-digit number assigned to all California Department of Corrections convicts. For example, C-57861, D-60986, F-71252, H-91241, J-24978, and T-65243.

CDCR: The California Department of Corrections and Rehabilitation.

CDCR 115: A disciplinary report issued to inmates. There are two types of reports: administrative and serious.

Cell: The California Department of Corrections and Rehabilitation prison cells are only on Level III and IV yards. A cell is an enclosed room roughly 6 x 12 feet with a double bunk made of steel and a small steel table with a steel stool attached to the floor. There are two small steel shelves, one for each inmate, and a steel toilet with a small sink attached to the top. There is one electrical outlet and lights that convicts control. A narrow window in the back of the cell is roughly six inches wide and three feet tall. A highly polished piece of rectangular steel is also attached to the wall that is used as a mirror. There is one air conditioner vent that many convicts will cover the opening with wet toilet paper until it dries into a thick paste because they claim it is too cold. Inmates immaculately clean their prison cells. Their homies will discipline them if they keep a dirty cell. They will sit to pee so they don't splash drops of urine on the floor. Inmates might get "Smashed" by their "Cellie" for a thing as little as a pee drop on the floor.

Cell Etiquette: Convicts are usually extremely meticulous about keeping themselves and their cells clean. Some of them will scrub their entire cell down with a cleaner daily. Some standard rules convicts have to maintain this level of cleanliness are sitting to pee. They sit to pee to avoid urine droplets on the walls and floor. They will spit in the toilet when brushing their teeth because doing that in the sink is prohibited. They employ the "Drop One Flush One" technique when going poop so their cellie doesn't have to smell their feces. If they have to fart, they will sit on the toilet and flush it while farting, so it sucks the smell out. No dirty clothes are allowed in the cell, and everything must be hand-washed after being worn to avoid stinking up the cell. Most convicts are deadly serious about a clean cell, and if a cellie disrespects their nose by being smelly or dirty, they will be attacked after a few warnings.

Cell Exercise: Many years ago, this was a punishment in the "Adjustment Center" at San Quentin, Soledad, and Folsom Prisons. This punishment meant an inmate would not be allowed out of his cell to exercise for several days. Basically, this meant an inmate would be in his cell 24 hours a day. For example, "The pigs gave me ten days of cell exercise for 'Fat Mouthing' them."

Cell Extraction: When a convict refuses to exit his cell and all other options have been exhausted, they will be forcibly removed. Several officers wear protective clothing, helmets, a large Plexiglas shield, and other equipment, and then they enter the cell and place "Mechanical Restraints" on the occupants of the cell. Convicts would commonly spill shampoo or lotion on the concrete floor of their cell to make the officers slip when they all rushed in.

Cell Extraction Football: An old-school game that some convicts play in prison. They use a roll of toilet paper as a football and try to exit their cell with it during a "Cell Extraction." A cell extraction is when several officers in riot gear rush into a cell to handcuff and remove the inmates who have refused to come out peacefully. It is worth three points if the inmate playing football can get the toilet paper roll past the door threshold as the officers rush in. If the inmate can exit his cell and cross the "Out Of Bounds" line painted on the concrete three feet in front of the cell during the cell extraction, that is a touchdown worth seven points.

Cell Feeding: When inmates are locked in their "Cells," you give them a tray of food through the "Food Port."

Cell Rep: In a County Jail or prison, this is the person in charge of a particular "Car" for that cell or "Pod."

Cell Soldier: When an inmate talks tough inside his cell behind the locked door, but when his door opens, he shuts up because he is scared.

Cell Status: This is when a convict is confined to a cell and not allowed to leave.

Cell Time: When an inmate needs time alone in his cell to masturbate. If they are on "Lockdown," he will sign his "Cellie" up for a doctor's appointment to get some cell time. During normal "Program," cell time will be when his cellie is at work, school, yard, or "Dayroom."

Cell Warrior: When an inmate talks tough inside his cell behind the locked door, but when his door opens, he shuts up because he is scared.

Cellie: The person who shares a cell with an inmate.

Central Control: It refers to the nerve center of Centinela Prison, where the inmate "Count" is maintained and access to other key areas via locking gates and doors. Central Control is inside the prison facility at the entrance of the two yards. "Yard Officers" "Chit Out" their equipment from Central Control with circular brass tokens with their initials on them. Central Control also controls the access to the two gates that open to the prison yards. A sergeant and two officers work that position.

Central File: This is the main file for each convict, where all information is maintained regarding their history and behavior while in prison. The Central File is commonly referred to as the "C-File."

Certified Riders: This is another name for the "Northern Riders."

The Northern Riders originally were "Norteños" who rebelled against their gang's politics that they disagreed with. They eventually became a well-respected and violent group on the "SNY" yards.

Chad: This is the nickname for the N. A. Chaderjian School in Stockton, California. This "California Youth Authority" facility was notorious for being very violent.

Chain: When convicts are transported on the "Grey Goose" to a prison, they are chained together to prevent escape. This term also refers to handcuffed inmates escorted anywhere on prison grounds. For example, "Cisco is on the chain to the 'Infirmary.'"

Chale: A word that translates to no way or hell no!

Channel: A gang member who relays messages and reports between gang members on different prisons, yards, "Buildings," or the streets.

Channel Jumping: A highly frowned upon activity when a "Norteño" usurps his chain of command and talks to another "Channel" because he feels his direct channel isn't addressing his grievances. Any Norteño who engages in this activity gets disciplined.

Chapel: The chapel on prison yards has religious services for inmates. The chapel services are for various religious groups at different times of the week. The chapel in prison is notorious for being a place where inmates go to fight to settle disputes.

Charlie 5: This was the nickname of my "Housing Unit" Charlie 5 on the Level IV yard at Centinela State Prison. It was called this because it was "Rocking," and bloodshed was very common inside its walls. On my day off, my partner was stabbed in the neck by a "Crip." On another occasion during this same time, two

Crips violently beat an officer, and they tried to pull him into cell 217 and close the door so they could kill him. That officer barely escaped with his life, and I visited him at his home a few days later. He looked terrible because of the injuries on his face. Even the "Booty Bandit" in Charlie 5 would threaten officers with beatings if he didn't get his way. I was assigned to this building as a "Fish" because the "Regular" officers either quit or were off because of stress or injuries.

Chase: Between each "Cell," a small locked enclosure called a chase houses the shut-off valves for the water in each "House."

Chasing The Dragon: This mainly refers to heroin addicts seeking the drug-induced stupor that they crave so much. This term can also refer to a person seeking a high from any drug they are addicted to.

Chavalo: This term describes a person who is used as a "Punk" in prison.

Check: When an inmate breaks "Household Policies," his homies will discipline him. This punishment can range from cell or "Bunk Status" to a violent beating.

Check-In: An inmate who has succumbed to pressure or intimidation and checks-in to "Protective Custody" for his safety.

Check-In: There were some prison gangs like the "Nazi Low Riders" who required their members to report to the "Hole" and check-in with the "Big Homies" when they returned to prison. To do this, they would have to physically attack someone so they would get sent to the hole.

Check-In: To report in with a higher authority in your "Car" to ask permission for something or to request advice. For example,

"Before I give the okay for that, I need to check-in with the 'Big Homie' at Pelican Bay."

Check Move: When an inmate breaks "Household Policies," his homies will discipline him. This punishment can range from cell or "Bunk Status" to a violent beating.

Check This Out: This is what is said to another person when you want them to pay close attention to you. For example, "Check this out homie, you need to 'Slow Your Roll' because you are 'Heading For A Wreck.'"

Checked: When an inmate breaks "Household Policies," his homies will discipline him. This punishment can range from cell or "Bunk Status" to a violent beating.

Checked In With The Squad: This is when a convict is working as an informant with the "Goon Squad." For example, "Big Country checked in with the squad at Corcoran and crossed up several of our comrades."

Checked Out: When an inmate "Rolls It Up" and goes "SNY" or "PC." For example, "I heard that Ghost checked out."

Checker: A convict who is sent on a "Mission" to "Remove" or "Discipline" other people.

Checking: When an inmate breaks "Household Policies," his homies will discipline him. This punishment can range from cell or "Bunk Status" to a violent beating.

Cheeking: When an inmate hides drugs or a "Banger" between his butt cheeks. It differs from "Hooping" because there is no anal penetration while hiding the "Contraband."

Chequeada: This is when a "Southerner" has violated the "Reglas" of his gang, and for punishment, his homies will assault him for 13 seconds. All blows will be from the neck down, with no face shots. For example, "When Spider gets to the 'Back,' the homies are going to give him a chequeada."

Chest Plate: When an inmate's chest is completely covered in tattoos. For example, "That's a nice chest plate you have, homeboy. Who slung that ink on you?"

Chester: This term refers to a child molester. They are commonly referred to as "Chomo."

Chicken Fights: Between 1989 and 1994, it is alleged that officers at Corcoran State Prison orchestrated confrontations between rival gang members in the Security Housing Unit (SHU). During this period, seven inmates were fatally shot, and 43 others sustained severe injuries due to officers discharging their firearms.

Chicken On The Bone: This is the name inmates use for one of their favorite meals served in prison. For example, "We are having chicken on the bone. That's a good meal. I love that tray."

Chicken Wing: When a law enforcement officer pushes up on a person's arm while it's behind their back, and it causes severe pain.

Chill: When a comrade is in "Violation," but a "Big Homie" raises his hand for him and orders a "Red Light" so they won't be attacked. Usually, this is done for selfish reasons, such as the comrade in violation is putting money in the pocket of the big homie. This is a prime example of "Homeboy Favoritism."

Chilling: When a comrade is in "Violation," but a "Big Homie" raises his hand for him and orders a "Red Light" so they won't be attacked. Usually, this is done for selfish reasons, such as a comrade in violation putting money in the pocket of the big homie. This is a prime example of "Homeboy Favoritism."

Chill Game: What you say to a homie when they are telling stories that you know aren't true. For example, "Chill game, Sleepy. I know what happened, stop 'Fronting.'"

Chin Check: To punch somebody in their mouth.

China White: Prison nickname for the drug heroin.

Chirp: A term used for a "Contraband" cell phone in prison.

Chirped Up: When a convict has a "Contraband" cell phone. For example, "I was always chirped up when I was behind those walls."

Chirujo: To be used as a "Punk" by another inmate.

Chisme: A word that translates to gossip. For example, "The 'Big Homie' is straight up. He doesn't get involved in chisme or any type of snake stuff."

Chit: A brass token with an officer's name or initials that they use to "Chit Out" equipment needed to perform their duties.

Chit Out: This is the process whereby an officer uses their "Chit" to exchange for the equipment they will use during their shift.

Chiva: This term refers to heroin. For example, "You got any chiva left, homie?"

Chomo: This term refers to a child molester.

Chopping It Up: When inmates talk to each other. For example, "I was chopping it up with Huero, and he said he is going to 'Hit' this weekend at his visit."

Chow Hall: This is where the convicts on each yard eat their breakfast and dinner.

Christian Car: A group of men in prison consisting of all races who repented of their sins and accepted Jesus Christ as their savior in accordance with Romans 10:9-13. They have been released from their gang's "Prison Politics," except if there is a riot. If there is a riot, they must jump with their "People." If they don't participate in a riot with their race, they will get "Checked."

Christmas Tree: An inmate-manufactured weapon shaped like a Christmas Tree. This shape causes more damage when it is removed due to the sharp, angled edges.

Chrono: Some chronos might be an exemption that inmates can get from doctors, so they get special treatment. For example, there are chronos for inmates with bad shoulders, so they can only be handcuffed in the front of their body. I remember a chrono for an inmate in the "Hole" who was allowed a shower every day instead of once every three days.

Chuckies: A nickname for Chuckawalla Valley State Prison.

Chump: A good-for-nothing and "Weak" person who doesn't get any respect from their peers. For example, "Chico is a chump; he doesn't get any respect from the homies."

Chump Out: When an inmate shows fear or cowardice and fails to do what is expected. For example, "I knew that punk would chump out again. He has a 'Jacket' for 'Wolfing.'"

Chump Status: When people in a "Car" ignore a person because of their bad behavior. Their fellow gang members will not associate with them until they redeem themselves. This is usually accomplished by "Putting In Work" by going on a "Mission" and doing a "Clean Up."

Chunk 'em: A person who has a reputation for being able to fight well.

For example, "Taz can chunk 'em; everyone knows that."

Chunken 'em: When people are fighting. For example, "Crazy D spilled some 'Pruno' on the homie's new shoes, so they started chunken 'em."

Church: When a prison gang gathers to discuss gang business.

CIAU: The Criminal Intelligence and Analysis Unit analyzes criminal suspects and criminal organizations inside California's correctional system. The Criminal Intelligence and Analysis Unit is a sub-unit of the "Office of Correctional Safety."

CIM: California Institution For Men, also known as Chino Prison.

Cinqueros: A violent group on the "SNY" prison yards. They are commonly referred to as the "25's."

Civil War: Sometimes gangs fight within their ranks over who will be calling the shots on a particular yard or prison. More often than not, once the dust settles, the soldiers who supported the losing side will be "Removed" by the ones who won the battle. Ultimately, most of these power struggles are over who will control the drug trade on a particular yard or prison. Countless loyal homies have had their "Careers" ended by being on the losing side of a civil war.

Civilian: A person not involved in a gang or "Prison Politics." Another term that's related to this in prison is "Resident."

Clap: A term used for a "Contraband" cell phone in prison. For example, "I have a clap at the 'Pad.'"

Clapper: A term used for a "Contraband" cell phone in prison. For example, "I have a clapper if you need to call your people."

Classification: The California Department of Corrections and Rehabilitation classification system categorizes inmates in two different ways. This system places inmates in their "Housing Security Level" and "Custody Level."

Classification Committee: When an inmate gets into serious trouble in prison, he will go to committee. They will reconsider his program, workgroup, and housing assignment.

Classification Override: When an inmate gains admittance to a program or prison he wouldn't typically qualify for.

Clavo: A term that refers to drugs smuggled into prison. For example, "I was hitting clavo every two weeks at Centinela."

Clean Jacket: This means a convict has a good name among his peers in prison. He has no "Funny Charges," and there is no question about his "Get Down."

Clean Time: An old-school term used to describe when a convict does his time in prison without getting into trouble. For example, "I did clean time my last year so I could go home."

Cleanup: When a convict messes up, he is given an opportunity for a cleanup to make his name good again. A cleanup usually means he must "Blast" someone who has fallen out of favor with their gang.

Cleanup A Yard: When a "Car" goes on a mission to remove all of the "Degenerates" and "Basura" belonging to their race from the yard.

Cleanup Crew: These are the inmates who owe a "Cleanup" to their gang, and they are the ones next "On Deck" to "Blast" someone. In some prison gangs, after a member has been "Deemed No Good," they might be allowed to regain their status and become in "Good Standing." For this to happen, they must "Put In Work" by doing a cleanup.

Cleanup Crew: When an inmate is going to be "Poked," some "Factions" will use three attackers. One inmate will do the poking, then he will quickly walk away and hand off his weapon, and the two other inmates will start physically attacking the victim. These two inmates are the cleanup crew, and their main job is to create a diversion so the other inmate who did the stabbing can get away. The cleanup crew will get caught for the attack and sent to "Administrative Segregation." Since no weapon is discovered, the cleanup crew doesn't get charged for the stabbing; they only get charged for the physical assault.

Cleaner: A convict sent on a "Mission" to "Remove" or "Discipline" other people.

Cleaning House: When a prison gang gets rid of members by "Poking" them or beating them up. Once an inmate is "Smashed" by other gang members, prison officials remove him from the yard and place him in "Protective Custody."

Cleaning The Books: When a prison gang gets rid of members by "Poking" them or beating them up. Once an inmate is "Smashed" by other gang members, prison officials remove him from the yard and place him in "Protective Custody."

Clear The Air: When people resolve their issues and agree to leave their disagreements behind.

Clear Your Paperwork: When a convict "Lands" on a new yard or facility, his "Paperwork" will be gone over by a designated person from their "Car" to see if they have any "Funny Charges."

Clecha: This word means a person's "Schooling" and how they were taught. For example, "As a youngster, I was embraced by some good homies who gave me righteous clecha."

Clerk: An inmate who works in the "Program Office" and performs duties similar to a secretary. They spend their day typing reports and other official documents. Clerks tend to have a good rapport with the officers and get special treatment from them. If someone brings doughnuts or pizza into the office, the clerks will be offered some discreetly. An officer will tell them, "Go ahead and cleanup that mess over there." When the clerk goes over there, he will see a slice of pizza or a doughnut, and he knows that's the green light to eat it.

Clique: Within some gangs, there are numerous cliques determined by the street. For example, a gang claims five streets as their territory, and each street is a clique within the same gang.

Clique Hopping: When a gangster changes cliques within the same gang. A street gang can have several cliques, but they are all under the same umbrella. A huge gang might have numerous streets as its territory, and each street is a different clique, but still the same gang.

Cliqued Up: When two or more groups of people form an alliance. For example, "The Insane and Rolling 20's Crips are clicked up in prison."

Clip His Wings: This means a person will be "Removed" from the prison yard for breaking the "Household Policies." For example, "Diablo said to clip his wings. Casper has to go."

Clipped: When an inmate gets "Blasted" in prison. For example, "Did you hear about Crow? He got clipped coming out of the chow hall."

Close Custody Count: This type of "Count" in prison is for inmates designated as Close Custody for their "Custody Level."

Close The Tier: In the "Hole," the "Shot Caller" will yell out of his cell and say "good night" to each of his comrades in their cells, and they will reply "good night." Once the tier is closed, they can't "Fish" or loudly talk to people in other cells.

Close To The House: When a convict has a short time until he is released from prison. For example, "I'm close to the house dog. I'm trying to stay out of the mix."

Closing The Tier: In the "Hole," the "Shot Caller" will yell out of his cell and say "good night" to each of his comrades in their cells, and they will reply "good night." Once the tier is closed, they can't "Fish" or loudly talk to people in other cells.

Clothed Body Search: When a correctional officer searches a convict with his clothes on. This search consists of patting the convict down in search of "Contraband."

Clothesline: The string convicts tie across their "Cells" to dry the clothes that they hand wash. Clotheslines are prohibited in the cells and are usually taken down during a cell search. The convicts have their laundry done every week, but most choose to wash clothing items more often than that.

Cluck: To sell your possessions to buy drugs. For example, "Why is Dreamer's locker empty? Did he cluck off his stuff to buy more 'Black?'"

Cluck Head: A dope fiend inmate who constantly lies to his family so they send money to pay his drug debts. For example, he will tell them his television broke, and he needs money to buy another one, but he will use the money they send to pay for his drug debts.

If things get desperate and he is about to get "Poked," he will tell his family that he will get killed if they don't send money.

Cluck Their Stuff Off: When a dope fiend inmate sells his possessions to buy drugs in prison. These inmates will "Run Their Family Dry" to get high in prison.

CMC: California Men's Colony is a prison in San Luis Obispo.

CMF: California Medical Facility, also known as Vacaville State Prison.

Co Co County: The nickname inmates use for Contra Costa County.

Co Co County White Boys: A "Peckerwood" "Car" in prison from Contra Costa County In California.

Cosign: To vouch for another person by putting your reputation on the line for them.

CO: A slang term for a correctional officer.

COCF: This stands for California Out Of State Correctional Facilities. In 2006, the California Department of Corrections and Rehabilitation started a program that sent inmates to six out-of-state prisons to do their time. In 2010, at the height of this program, there were 10,400 inmates serving time out of state. This program ended on June 25, 2019.

Cockfights: Between 1989 and 1994, it is alleged that officers at Corcoran State Prison orchestrated confrontations between rival gang members in the Security Housing Unit (SHU). During this period, seven inmates were fatally shot, and 43 others sustained severe injuries due to officers discharging their firearms.

Code: This is the standard guidelines a gangster must follow to remain in good standing with his peers. For example, testifying in court or cooperating with law enforcement goes against the code.

Code Of Conduct: The rules and regulations of a prison gang that all members follow. The code of conduct is also referred to as "Household Policies," "Household Rules," "Constitution," or "Bible."

Code Of Silence: This is the notion that officers in the California Department of Corrections and Rehabilitation will lie for each other and cover up crimes committed against inmates. Inmates call this type of behavior being a member of the "Green Wall Gang."

Coffin: Some inmates use this term for a bed in prison. For example, "I'm going to land this plane homeboy. It's time to hit the coffin."

Coffin Or Court Date: The two places the gang life will take you.

Cold In The Field: This means prison and the streets are a cold game, and you can't trust anyone, not even your comrades. For example, "It's cold in the field out there. You need to watch your back, homeboy."

Cold Issue: When a gang or gang member is ruthless in dealing with another person or gang. For example, "Loko gave Trey a cold issue yesterday. He had that coming, though."

Cold Line: When a gang or gang member is ruthless in dealing with another person or gang. For example, "The Insane Crips and the Rolling Twenties have a complicated relationship; sometimes they push a cold line on each other."

Cold Line Pusher: When a gang member goes to the extreme in gang banging or other issues. For example, "Frosty is a cold line pusher."

Cold Piece: A cold-blooded person. For example, "Dirty D is a cold piece; don't turn your back on him."

Cold Piece Of Work: A cold-blooded person. For example, "When I got sent 'Upstate,' my old lady stopped taking my calls. She is a cold piece of work."

Cold Shoulder: When a prison gang member is investigated by his comrades for wrongdoing. He will be kept to the side, and no gang business or "Politics" will be shared with him until he is cleared of any violations.

Cold Stroll: A convict who walks in a manner that says, "Don't play with me." For example, "Iceman has a cold stroll; he doesn't play around."

Collections: When inmates ask people in their "Car" to donate to help one of their homies out. They often do this to help pay a drug debt and avoid rioting with another race.

Collective: The people one associates with or the gang members from one's county.

College: This refers to serving time in a state prison. Gangsters who go to prison usually gain a higher level of education in criminal activities. For example, "I went to college in 2020 at CDCR."

Come Up: When a person gains money or material items or gets put in a favorable position.

Comfortable: Every convict's goal is to live as comfortable as possible while in prison. It means having plenty of "Canteen" and getting "Packages" regularly, having access to a cell phone, having money on their "Books," and having a woman who will be there and ride out that time with him. For example, "You know how it is homeboy. We are all just trying to live as comfortable as possible in here."

Coming Off: To give your homies something of what you have. For example, "Dude just 'Hit' some 'Black,' and he isn't coming off none of it."

Coming Through: When someone hooks you up with something that you need.

Coming Up: When convicts are involved in a fight amongst themselves. For example, "It was coming up between the 'Woods' and Blacks."

Commando: A more advanced version of a "Burpee."

Commissary: Store on prison grounds where inmates buy food and other supplies. Inmates can purchase a maximum of $240 a month from the commissary. Commissary is also used to describe items from the commissary. For example, "I got a bunch of commissary in my cell, homie."

Commission: The leadership of the "Aryan Brotherhood."

Community Crew: These are groups of several inmates who go into the local communities under a corrections officer's supervision and perform various tasks to improve the community. I supervised a community crew for a couple of weeks, and the inmates constructed brick walls and cleaned several local parks during my brief stay.

Compas: A word that translates to friends. For example, "At Kern Valley Prison, I caught an attempted murder with my compas."

Compassionate Release: This program is available to terminally ill inmates with six months or less to live. The inmates who qualify for this "Medical Parole" must also be deemed no longer a threat to society and have a place to go when released.

Complex Control: Complex Control is inside the prison facility at the entrance of the other yards opposite "Central Control" at Centinela Prison. "Yard Officers" "Chit Out" their equipment from Complex Control with circular brass tokens with their initials on them. Complex Control also controls the access to the two gates that open to their prison yards.

Compound: An old-school word used to describe a prison or prison yard. For example, "When I pulled up to Tracy, I knew almost everyone on the compound."

Compton & Watts Car: In prison, the "Crips" from Compton and Watts are in the same "Car" and ride together. It means they support each other and back the play of one another. This alliance is called the "Hub And The Dub." The Hub refers to Compton, and the Dub stands for Watts.

Comrade: A homie who has remained steadfast through thick and thin, whether on the streets or in prison.

Concrete Status: When a "Southerner" has violated "Household Policies," sometimes as punishment, they might be ordered to do "Burpees" on the yard. They will be directed to go to a concrete patch, do burpees as soon as the yard opens, and keep doing them until it closes. This type of punishment is called concrete status.

Concrete Yard: This is the small concrete exercise area in the "Hole" used for "Group Yard."

Condemned Housing Unit: This housing unit at San Quentin State Prison was for inmates condemned with a death sentence.

Conditions Of Parole: The rules a parolee must follow to stay out of jail or prison.

Confidential Mail: This is mail inmates get from their legal representatives and other official entities. Officers are not allowed to read it. Prison staff inspects and reads all regular mail inmates send or receive.

Confined To Quarters: When new inmates arrive at a prison, they are CTQ (confined to quarters) until going to "Committee." Inmates are stuck in their cells all day for a few weeks until cleared to go to the "Mainline." Inmates can also be confined to quarters for various lengths of time for disciplinary reasons.

Conjugal Visit: When an inmate's wife will stay the night with him on prison grounds at the "Love Shack." The love shack is a small building surrounded by a secure fence. It has a small kitchen, bedroom, and seating area. His wife can bring food to cook in the kitchen during their short stay.

Conjugal Visit: What an inmate will say to his "Cellie" when he wants some "Cell Time." For example, "Check this out, homie, I'm going to a conjugal visit. You need to go to yard."

Conservation Camp: There are approximately 1,500 inmates in the 35 conservation camps across California. These inmates help fight fires, clear brush and fallen trees, and maintain parks.

Constitution: This is the rules and regulations of a prison gang. The constitution is also referred to as "Household Policies," "Household Rules," "Bible," or "Code Of Conduct."

Contact Visit: A visit where inmates can hug, hold hands, eat together, and kiss their visitors. If inmates have a lousy visit, they are prone to violence towards officers or other inmates. A lot of "Contraband" is brought in through contact visits via the visitors. If an inmate gets regular visits from a person, they might be pressured by their "People" to have them bring in drugs during a visit.

Contraband: Forbidden items that inmates are not allowed to possess. Contraband may include drugs, "Pruno," "Bangers," "Clapper," and razors.

Contraband Surveillance Watch: When inmates are suspected of ingesting drugs, they are placed alone in a cell in the "Infirmary" with no running water so their feces can be inspected. This is commonly referred to as "Potty Watch" by officers.

Control Booth: The enclosed command center of a "Housing Unit" at Centinela Prison. The control booth is a 25' by 25' foot two-story secure room with one access point via two locked steel doors. The control booth has several sizeable sliding glass windows covered by steel bars. There is a tiny bathroom in the control booth with privacy windows. A large control panel with hundreds of buttons opens every door in the housing unit. The control booth also manages the telephones, televisions, and the water to the showers. The control booth also has a Mini-14 rifle, the "Floor Officer's" equipment, and the 40 mm launcher that fires various projectiles to break up fights.

Control Booth Officer: The officer assigned to the "Control Booth" in a "Housing Unit."

Controlled Release: When there is "Tension" between races, the administration will do a controlled release to see if things will "Kick Off" between the two groups. It means they will release a small amount of each group at a time to see if they fight each other.

Convenience Bed Move: When an officer puts in the paperwork for a "Bed Move" for inmates in his "Housing Unit" just because the inmate asked. For example, "Hey Superman, me and my cellie aren't getting along. Can you move me in with my homie Trouble in cell 212?"

Convict: A convict honors his word and treats others with respect. A convict won't allow another person to disrespect them unchallenged.

Convict Code: The rules of respect that a "Convict" lives by. A convict honors his word and treats others with respect. A convict won't allow another person to disrespect them unchallenged.

Cook Kit: A hypodermic needle and other supplies used to "Mainline" drugs while in prison.

Cookie Wheels: Inmates smash cookies into small crumbs. They cook syrup and peanut butter to make caramel. They mix the crumbled cookies with the caramel and mold it in a jar lid. They add various toppings like crushed peanuts, caramel, and chocolate. They sell cookie wheels for .50 each.

Cooking: The three-day fermentation process when making "Pruno." For example, "I have some 'Wine' cooking in my cell, homie."

Cool Time: When two people or groups get along, and everything is cool between them. For example, "I used to be on cool time with Big Drew. Now it's 'On-Sight.'"

Cool Your Jets: This is what you say to a person heading for a "Wreck." For example, "Badger, you need to cool your jets and stop using that 'Black.' It's not a good look, comrade."

Cop: A slang term for a correctional officer.

Cop Beater: An inmate with "Priors" for assaulting officers in the California Department of Corrections and Rehabilitation. Cop beaters have "Nothing Coming" from officers who are loyal to their comrades. If any officer treats a cop beater nicely, their fellow officers will shun them.

Cop Shop: The area in a prison where the correctional officer's office is.

Cornball: A good-for-nothing and "Weak" person who doesn't get any respect from their peers. For example, "Bozo is a cornball. He doesn't get any respect from the homies."

Correctional Counselor: Every inmate is assigned a correctional counselor. Their jobs are to interview the inmates, evaluate their program progress, summarize reports from the inmate's files, and assist them with parole suitability.

Cosmetics: The deodorant, toothpaste, mouthwash, lotion, etc., that inmates have. For example, "Comrade, I have lots of cosmetics in my locker. What do you need?"

Count: This is when all convicts in prison are counted to ensure none have escaped and to verify their safety and general welfare. The count is critical in prison, and all "Program" will cease until the count clears and all inmates are accounted for. The California Department of Corrections and Rehabilitation has several different types of counts. These counts are: "Positive Count," "Standing Count," "Out Count," "Informal Count," "Negative Count," "Picture Count," "Emergency Count," and "Close Custody Count."

County: In prison, this refers to the county a convict is from. Most of the time in prison, convicts will separate themselves by counties. Each "Car" will discipline its members. For example, if a "Peckerwood" from "Berdoo" needs to be "Disciplined," only other "Woods" from Berdoo will participate in this process. Gang members don't like people from other counties putting hands on their comrades.

County Born & State Raised: This means the first time an inmate started doing time was in the county jail and they ended up in prison. This phrase means the person saying it wasn't a "YA Baby."

County Lid: A year sentence in the county jail.

Court Fees: The money a "Norteno" must pay after an investigation and background check was done on him after returning from being a "Northern Rider." Northerners are allowing former members who were Northern Riders to return if they want. An investigation into their background will be done, and if it clears, they must pay a court fee and then do a "Cleanup" to be in "Good Standing."

Courted In: The process in which a "Convict" joins a prison gang.

Courted On: When a gang member is initiated into a gang by a beating from several other members. For example, "I was courted on the 'Set' by four 'Reputable' homies."

Courtesy Flush: To turn the water on to an inmate's toilet so he can flush it. Water would have been turned off to the inmate's cell only if he was "Flooding The Tier" using the water from his toilet. Between each cell is a small locked enclosure called a "Chase" containing the shut-off valves for the water.

Courtesy Flush: A courtesy flush means to flush the toilet when your excrement hits the water so your "Cellie" doesn't have to smell your funk.

Cover: This is the person or group acting as security in prison for members of their "Car." The cover will have a "Banger" on him if he needs to "Poke" someone who threatens his comrades. During everyday activities in prison, members of gangs provide cover for each other while they are in vulnerable positions. For example, if a group of "Northerners" are doing "Burpees," a member of their car will be acting as cover while the others work out.

Covers Get Pulled: To call someone's bluff or reveal damaging secrets about them. For example, "I know Lil Wolf is a snitch. I can't wait when his covers get pulled."

Crack: To take something from another person. For example, "I'm going to crack you for all your soups when you lose that bet on the Superbowl."

Crack Your Door: This is a term used when a cell door is opened in prison. For example, "Comrade, have the cop crack your door so I can give you this radio."

Cracked: When an inmate gets busted for a prison rules infraction or caught with some "Contraband." For example, "I got cracked with a 'Chirp' last week."

Cracked: When an inmate can convince an officer or "Free Staff" to bring "Contraband" to prison. For example, "Kilo cracked that cook, and he will bring in five cell phones and some weed."

Cracked: When a person on the streets gets arrested. For example, "I got cracked for a 'Hot One.'"

Cracked: This term is used when a cell door is opened in prison. For example, "I need my door cracked. Get at the tower cop for me."

Cracking: When a prison, yard, or area is violent with battles between different "Cars." For example, "Corcoran was cracking when I was there in 2022."

Cracking Off: This describes a place with constant fights and stabbings. For example, "It was always cracking off on Charlie Yard at Centinela Prison."

Crash Dummy: A "Lame" who is used by his homies to do their dirty work, and as a result, he gets more time in prison.

Crash Him: To violently attack another person. For example, "That fool has been 'Bumping His Gums,' I'm going to crash him."

Crash The Car: When people in a "Car" break "Household Policies,"that results in them getting into a "Wreck." This means a person or group in prison does something scandalous that gets them and their comrades into trouble.

Crashed: When a person gets violently attacked. For example, "That fool got crashed for running his mouth."

Crashed Out: When an inmate "Rolls It Up" and goes "SNY" or "PC." For example, "Hey, homie, what happened to Rowdy? He crashed out?"

CRC: California Rehabilitation Center, also known as "Norco" prison. It was named the Norconian Club before being abandoned in the 1940s and turned into a prison in 1962.

Creative Writing: A common practice among correctional officers of writing an official report to help their cause in an altercation with an inmate.

Credit Gets You Whacked: If you don't have enough in your cell to cover a debt, don't use drugs or gamble. People who don't pay their debts in prison get "Whacked."

Creep: A good-for-nothing and "Weak" person who gets no respect in prison. It can also refer to someone with "Funny Charges."

Crime Partner: A person on the streets with whom a convict committed crimes. For example, "Lee Dog was my crime partner on the streets."

Crimey: A crime partner on the streets. For example, "Homie, do you know Droopy? That's my crimey."

Crip Module: A "Pod" in a county jail where they place "Crip" inmates.

Crip Prayers: Some "Crips" in prison use this name for "Burpees," which is a challenging exercise that builds up a person's stamina.

Crip Tank: A "Pod" in a county jail where they place "Crip" inmates.

Cripism: A Crip's belief on how a true "Crip" should conduct themselves. For example, "Slim is a brotha whose Cripism is on point."

Crips: A street gang formed in Los Angeles, California. The color blue identifies Crips, and they have a rivalry with the "Bloods."

Crisis Bed: Inmates who suffer from severe mental health disorders that an outpatient program cannot treat are usually sent to Mental Health Crisis Beds. Crisis beds provide 24-hour care for the inmates; they cannot stay in one of these beds for more than ten days.

Crisis Response Team: This group of highly trained officers at each prison is available to help in various emergencies, such as riots and active shooter scenarios. This group of officers was formerly named "SERT."

Critical Tools: These are tools that are needed in prison for daily upkeep and operation. Critical tools may include a ladder, rope, bolt cutters, hacksaws, and wire cutters. If a critical tool is missing, the entire prison will go on "Lockdown" until they are found.

Critical Workers: Inmates who must perform essential duties even during "Lockdown."

Crooked CO: A correctional officer who is bringing in drugs and cell phones to inmates. An officer who is "In The Pocket" of a convict or "Faction" in prison. An officer who lies on reports and tries to frame inmates for crimes.

Crossed Out: A gang member who has been "Removed" for breaking their code of conduct. Getting crossed out involves extreme violence, ranging from a severe beating to getting "Poked" numerous times. For example, "I have seen a lot of good homies get crossed out over petty reasons. So just because someone is removed doesn't always mean they deserved it."

Crossed Over: When an inmate "Rolls It Up" and goes "SNY" or "PC." For example, "I heard that Yogi crossed over."

Crossed Up: When a gangster is betrayed by his homies. When a gangster fails to understand "Prison Politics" and falls victim to a savvy comrade looking to move up the ladder in the organization.

CRT: The Crisis Response Teams are a group of highly trained officers at each prison who are available to help in various emergencies such as riots and active shooter scenarios. This group of officers was formerly named "SERT."

Crying The Blues: When people make excuses or try to get out of something they don't want to do. For example, "Rhino was told he was getting transferred to Pelican Bay, and he started crying the blues about why he didn't want to go."

CTF: Correctional Training Facility, also known as Soledad Prison.

CTQ: When new inmates arrive at a prison, they are CTQ (confined to quarters) until going to "Committee." Inmates are stuck in their cells all day for a few weeks until cleared to go to the "Mainline." Inmates can also be confined to quarters for various lengths of time for disciplinary reasons.

Cuerno: This word translates to "Horn," referring to a "Contraband" cellphone in prison. For example, "Hey homie, I need 30 minutes on the cuerno tonight."

Cuff Up: What a correctional officer tells an inmate when he wants to place "Mechanical Restraints" on him.

Culinary: The locked room behind the actual "Dining Hall" where the food for the convicts on the prison yard is prepared.

Culinary Officer: This is the correctional officer who works in the "Dining Hall" and supervises the inmate culinary workers.

Culinary Worker: A convict who works in the "Dining Hall" and helps prepare the food for the 1,100 convicts on that particular prison yard at Centinela Prison.

Cup: This means a cup of "Pruno" or "White Lightning." For example, "Hey, homie, can I get a cup?"

Curfew: This is the amount of time a convict has to get off of a yard that is "No Good." Factions have different amounts of time for their members to attack someone on a yard that is a "No Landing Zone." Usually, they have 48 hours to "Take Off" on someone on that yard. For example, "The curfew is tomorrow to get off of this yard, homie. Let's go do what we have to do."

Curfew Time: In "Dorm" living, the different "Cars" usually agree to times when their people will be quiet. Curfew time is generally between the hours of 2200 hours to 1000 hours.

Curfew Yard: A prison yard that "Mainline" convicts are not allowed to "Program" on by their "Faction." If they are transferred to a curfew yard, they must attack someone so they can be taken off the yard. If a convict programs on a curfew yard, their faction will "Remove" them when it is discovered. For example, "Centinela D Yard, is a curfew yard."

Custody Designation: When an inmate goes to a "Reception Center," he is eventually assigned a custody designation. Six custody designations determine the level of supervision the inmate will require while in prison. These six custody designations are Minimum B, Minimum A, Medium B, Medium A, Close, and Maximum.

Custody Level: When an inmate goes to a "Reception Center," he is eventually assigned a custody level. There are six custody levels, and they determine what level of supervision the inmate will require while in prison. These six custody levels are Minimum B, Minimum A, Medium B, Medium A, Close, and Maximum.

Cut: When a person is quietly observing a situation and waiting to make their move unexpectedly. For example, "Sometimes on the prison yard, you will have a homie waiting in the cut to make a move and take that yard."

Cut A Bunk: This is when a convict will cut out a piece of metal from their bunk so they can fashion it into a weapon. For example, "I'm going to cut my bunk because I need a 'Banger' for that little problem I have."

Cut Loose: When a person gets released from police custody. Sometimes, they are cut loose after making a deal to cooperate with the authorities.

Cutoff: When a gang member breaks "Household Policies," his homies will stop associating with him. They won't talk to or give him drugs, alcohol, tattoos, etc., until he does a "Cleanup" to clear his name. For example, "Bugsy is cutoff, don't kick it with him anymore."

Cut Out: A third party on the streets used for moving money, drugs, and other "Contraband" while an inmate is in prison.

Cut Them Loose: To stop kicking it with certain individuals. For example, "I felt bad because I 'Drove Up' with Listo and Serio, but I had to cut them loose."

Cutter: A device used to cut the metal in the prison to make "Bangers." Inmates will cut metal off of nearly anything to make a knife out of.

Cutter: An inmate-manufactured weapon usually made with a razor to cut others. For example, "I had a cutter when I caught that fool slipping, and it was 'All Bad' for him."

Cutthroat Politics: This is when a "Faction" member has "Crossed Up" a homie for money, power, or other reasons. It's using another homeboy for personal gain and not caring about what happens to him. For example, a "Shot Caller" on the yard orders a homie to keep bringing in drugs from their "Pipeline" even if they are about to get "Cracked" by the "Black Patches."

Cutting Out: An old-school term for when a convict would use a hacksaw blade to cut their cell bars so he could squeeze out and attack an inmate or officer. For example, "It was wild back at San Quentin; dudes were cutting out and butchering fools."

Cuzz: A term that "Crips" call each other. For example, "What's up, Cuzz? I need to holla at you."

CVSP: Chuckawalla Valley State Prison.

D

DA Referral: When a convict commits a serious crime in prison, his case can be referred to the local District Attorney for consideration for prosecution. If the local District Attorney decides to pick up the case, the convict will go to trial. If he loses, he will get more time added to his sentence.

Dago: This is how "Peckerwoods" in prison from San Diego spell it. They don't use the letters I and E in their tattoos because they want to be distinct from the "Woods" out of the Inland Empire. The woods from the Inland Empire use "IE" in their tattoos. These two White "Cars" have a friendly rivalry, so that is why they try to separate in that manner while getting tattoos.

Daily Tier Report: "Norteños" in the "Hole" must complete a daily tier report highlighting their daily observations. These reports must be turned into "Tier Security" by 2000 hours. This report includes enemy and "K-9" interactions, cell movements, yard, enemy conversations, and movement.

Damu: This word means "Blood" in Swahili, and some Black inmates use Swahili words in prison to get back to their cultural heritage.

Dancing Shoes: To gain membership into a prison gang. For example, "Money just got his dancing shoes into the 'Aryan Brotherhood.'"

Date: The specific day an inmate is scheduled to be released. For example, "I am staying out of the mix, homie. I don't want to mess up my date."

Day For Day: When a convict is credited an extra day time served for good behavior.

Dayroom: The area inside "Housing Units" where convicts can watch television, play games, use telephones, talk, and many other social activities.

Dayroom Recall: When "Dayroom" is concluded, dayroom recall is yelled into the microphone by the "Control Booth Officer," and the convicts return to their "Cells." Immediately after dayroom recall, the convicts on the yard return to the "Housing Unit," and they lockup in their cells.

Dead Cell Status: When a prison gang member is placed under investigation by his comrades for wrongdoing. He will be kept to the side, and no gang business or "Politics" will be shared with him until he is cleared of any violations. For example, "Reaper is on dead cell status. Stop going to his door."

Dead Issue: When two inmates or groups agree to stop fighting. For example, "I'm not tripping that Snake double-crossed me. It's a dead issue."

Dead Man Walking: The term describes an inmate with a "Green Light." For example, "You see that dude over there? That's Danny Boy; he is a dead man walking."

Dead Time: Some convicts on "Death Row" refer to their prison sentence as dead time. In the year 2023, it has been determined that the death row inmates currently housed at San Quentin will be relocated to various correctional facilities across the state. The state of California is actively dismantling its death row system, thereby eliminating the practice of segregating inmates who have been sentenced to death.

Dead Time: When inmates are about to parole, they are unassigned from their prison job and placed on "S Time." S Time is also referred to as Dead Time.

Deadly Force: Any use of force by an officer that is likely to result in death.

Deal With Your Time: To do your time through hardships and find a way to endure even though it's hard. For example, "In the 'Hole,' we didn't have a television or personal property. You had to deal with your time."

Death Before Dishonor: A very common tattoo that inmates get. This tattoo means that they would rather die than bring dishonor to themselves, family, and friends.

Death Care: The medical treatment for convicts in California prisons is notoriously bad. Instead of calling it health care, some call it death care.

Death Row: Convicts housed at San Quentin State Prison condemned to death. They have their own section, and in the past, they were given meals of better quality than the "General Population." In the year 2023, it has been determined that the death row inmates currently housed at San Quentin will be relocated to various correctional facilities across the state. The state of California is actively dismantling its death row system, thereby eliminating the practice of segregating inmates who have been sentenced to death.

Debo: To punk someone and take their things. For example, "Lowdown pulled a debo and took all of that dude's 'Canteen.'"

Debrief: Inmates who wish to establish that they are no longer associated with a prison gang must provide information regarding their gang's past activities. The inmate must give names and identify specific criminal activity because this is the only way to establish that they have left a prison gang. The debriefing process can take several months, and when it is complete, the inmate is placed on a "Sensitive Needs Yard."

Debrief Processing Unit: This "Housing Unit" is for inmates who have just started the process to "Debrief."

Debt Cap: Sometimes, "Cars" in prison enforce debt caps for their members. It means convicts have a monetary limit on how much debt they can owe other convicts. For example, $200 is a standard debt cap in prison.

Debt Hanging: A drug debt that still needs to be paid. For example, "Homie, you ain't leaving this yard with that debt hanging. You better get that taken care of before you parole."

Deemed No Good: When a decision is handed down from the "Big Homies" that an inmate is a "No Good."

Deep: When there are large amounts of a "Faction" on a prison yard. For example, "Those 'Peckerwoods' are deep in High Desert Prison."

Degenerate: A "No Good" inmate. Someone who has betrayed his brothers.

Degenerate Gangs: This is one of the terms used by "Mainline" inmates to describe "SNY" gangs.

Departmental Review Board: This board facilitated that process when the courts ordered the California Department of Corrections and Rehabilitation to release convicts from their indefinite "SHU" terms. The release of these inmates to the "Mainline" was started in 2015. The court case that spearheaded this was Ashker v. Brown. Ashker happens to be an "Aryan Brotherhood" member.

Details: The "Nuestra Familia" members have several "Northerners" who follow them around and provide protection.

Determinate Sentence: A prison sentence with a set time frame. For example, a 15-year sentence.

Diaper Sniper: This is a term used for a child molester.

Diesel Therapy: A notorious and painful tactic of keeping convicts on the "Grey Goose" for prolonged periods as punishment. For example, a troublesome inmate will be constantly transferred from various prisons to keep them on the Grey Goose for weeks or even months. Convicts despise being transported because the seats and "Transport Jewelry" used on the bus are uncomfortable on extended trips.

Digging Up Knives: Every "Car" in prison will have knives buried in the yard in different areas. When one car is about to attack another, they will start digging up knives for battle. For example, "The 'Peckerwoods' at Salinas Valley started digging up knives, then they charged us on the basketball court."

Dime: A ten-year prison sentence.

Dining Hall: This is where the convicts on each yard eat their breakfast and dinner.

Dining Officer: The correctional officer who works in the "Dining Hall." They supervise the inmate workers who prepare the meals for the yard.

Dinner & A Show: When inmates are eating at the chow hall, and a fight breaks out.

Director's Rules: A compendium of rules that govern the treatment of convicts, their behavior, discipline, rights, and anything else that might apply to them while they are in prison. The Director's

Rules is also referred to as the "Title 15."

Dirt: Criminal activity that was done for oneself or the gang. For example, murder, robbery, assaults, and selling drugs are all forms of doing dirt.

Dirtbag: A lazy, sloppy, and good-for-nothing person nobody respects in prison. For example, "That fool went to sleep after working out without showering. He is a dirtbag."

Dirty CO: A correctional officer who is bringing in drugs and cell phones to inmates. An officer who is "In The Pocket" of a convict or "Faction" in prison. An officer who lies on reports and tries to frame inmates for crimes.

Dirty Macking: This is when a person spreads damaging or false information about someone else. For example, "Pajarito was dirty macking me after I stopped doing business with him. He is just a 'Punk' who nobody respects."

Dirty Politics: This is when "Faction" members have "Crossed Up" a homie for money, power, or other reasons. Basically, it's using another homeboy for personal gain and not caring about what happens to him. For example, a "Shot Caller" on the yard orders a homie to keep bringing in drugs from their visitor even if they are about to get "Cracked" by the "Black Patches."

Dirty Vato: A dude known for scandalous behavior towards others. This is the type of person you never turn your back on or trust because they are ruthless and only care about themselves. For example, "Kuko is a dirty vato; don't turn your back on him."

Disciplinary Disposition: When a gang member is investigated by his comrades for violating a gang rule, this is the final verdict if found guilty. The punishment for the convict who broke

"Household Policies" can range from writing 1,000-word essays, going on "Bunk Status," going on the "Burpee Line," getting violently attacked by several homies, getting a "Soft Check," to getting "Stabbed Off The Yard."

Discipline: When a prison gang member is disciplined by his comrades for breaking a gang rule. The "Peckerwoods" will "DP" one of their members for minor violations by having two "Woods" assault the rule breaker for 23 seconds. It's 23 seconds because the 23rd letter in the alphabet is a "W," which stands for White. The "Southerners" will DP a member for minor violations for 13 seconds because the 13th letter of the alphabet is an "M," which stands for "Mexican Mafia." Of course, more severe rule violations will result in more serious consequences, up to getting stabbed off the yard. For less severe offenses, gangs will make violators do "Burpees" by the hundreds. Sometimes, they will make the violator stay on their rack for a set period. This is called "Rack Status."

Disciplined: When a prison gang member is disciplined by his comrades for breaking a gang rule. The "Peckerwoods" will "DP" one of their members for minor violations by having two "Woods" assault the rule breaker for 23 seconds. It's 23 seconds because the 23rd letter in the alphabet is a "W," which stands for White. The "Southerners" will DP a member for minor violations for 13 seconds because the 13th letter of the alphabet is an "M," which stands for "Mexican Mafia." Of course, more severe rule violations will result in more serious consequences, up to getting stabbed off the yard. For less severe offenses, gangs will make violators do "Burpees" by the hundreds. Sometimes, they will make the violator stay on their rack for a set period. This is called "Rack Status."

Disneyland: An old-school nickname for California Men's Colony State Prison in San Luis Obispo. This nickname has been used for various soft prisons throughout the years.

Disposition: When a gang member is under investigation by his comrades for violating a gang rule, this is the final verdict. The punishment for the convict who broke "Household Policies" can range from writing 1,000-word essays, going on "Bunk Status," going on the "Burpee Line," getting violently attacked by several homies, getting a "Soft Check," to getting "Stabbed Off The Yard."

Disregard Status: When a prison gang member is investigated by his comrades for wrongdoing. He will be kept to the side, and no gang business or "Politics" will be shared with him until he is cleared of any violations.

Disrespecting My Program: This is when an inmate does things that bother other convicts and disrupts their daily routine. For example, "Crazy Ray is 'Being Loud In The Vent' and disrespecting my program."

Disruptive Group: This class of inmates belongs to street gangs, prison gangs, or other violent organizations such as outlaw motorcycle clubs.

Disturb My Program: This is when an inmate does things that bother other convicts and disrupts their daily routine. For example, "Check this out, don't disturb my program!"

DMS: The Daily Movement Sheet for the prison lists all arrivals, departures, temporary releases, out-to-courts, family visits, changes in housing, work assignments, and custody classifications during the previous 24-hour period.

Do Me Dirty: To betray a comrade. For example, "I can't believe Chili did me dirty like that."

Do My Own Time: When a convict withdraws from "Prison Politics" and refuses to have other gang members running his "Program" and making him do criminal activities.

Do Or Get Done: In some "Factions," a gang member must follow orders from his "Shot Caller," or his gang will "Smash" him for his disobedience. As a result, the phrase "Do or Get Done" reflects this cold, hard fact.

Do Time Standing On My Head: This means it's easy for a person to do prison time. For example, "Homie, I wasn't stressing in prison. I can do time standing on my head."

Do What You Got To Do: This means doing whatever you must to keep your respect as a man. If a person got threatened in prison, the typical response was, "Do what you got to do, and I'll do what I got to do."

Do You Smell Smoke? Because You Are Burnt: What you say to a comrade when he gets played for a fool. For example, "You paid $60 for that? Do you smell smoke? Because you are 'Burnt' homie."

Do Your Homework: This means a gang member must do the proper research before speaking on someone or something due to the seriousness of the situation. For example, "Check this out, youngster, you better do your homework before pushing that issue with the homie."

Do Your Own Time: When a convict withdraws from "Prison Politics" and refuses to have other gang members running his "Program" and making him do criminal activities.

Do Your Time Don't Let Your Time Do You: This means that instead of serving years in prison and becoming hostile, bitter, fat, a drug addict, an alcoholic, or lazy, a convict strives to better himself while incarcerated. This mindset gives a man hope for the future and helps him become a better man while incarcerated.

Dog Biscuit: This is an old-school term used for the "Reduced Food Rations" that some inmates used to get when they were in the "Adjustment Center." The dog biscuit was made by compressing leftover food into a cube and drying it out. This dehydrated mass of former slop was then given to the inmates on reduced food rations.

Dog Cage: The cage in the "SHU" that one inmate is placed in, and they get one hour to get some sun, talk, and exercise.

Dog Kennel: The cage in the "SHU" that one inmate is placed in, and they get one hour to get sun, talk, and exercise.

Dog You Out: Getting physically assaulted violently. For example, "Whenever I see you, it's on! I'm fixing to do you dirty. I'm going to dog you out."

Dogged Him Out: When an inmate punches someone in the face. For example, "Catfish was running his mouth, so I dogged him out."

Doggy Run: The small exercise yard in the Pelican Bay "Security Housing Unit" that convicts can use for one hour daily.

Doggy Walk: The small exercise yard in the Pelican Bay "Security Housing Unit" that convicts can use for one hour daily.

Doing Dirt: Criminal actions carried out for one's benefit or in the interest of a gang. Some examples include murder, robbery, assaults, and selling drugs.

Doing Life On The Installment Plan: An inmate who does decades in prison on several different prison terms.

Doing My Own Number: When a convict withdraws from "Prison Politics" and refuses to have other gang members running his "Program" and making him do criminal activities. For example, "I'm not in the mix. I'm doing my own number."

Doing My Own Time: When a convict withdraws from "Prison Politics" and refuses to have other gang members running his "Program" and making him do criminal activities.

Doing The Family Thing: When a gang member stops gang banging and lays down his "Flag" so he can raise a family. For this reason, gang members will let a respected member walk away from them.

Doing Way Too Much: An inmate acting too rambunctious and drawing too much attention to himself and his "Car." For example, "Goofy, you are doing way too much. You need to 'Pump Your Brakes' homie."

DOM: The Department Operations Manual for the California Department of Corrections and Rehabilitation.

Don't Drop The Soap: Convicts sometimes say this to young homies new to "The System" as a joke.

Don't Get Between A Tecato & His High: Those "Tecato" homies with "Status" only care about their high and nothing else at the end of the day. So many righteous homies have been done dirty and "Crossed Up" by tecatos in prison who only care about their next fix. A gangster can give his freedom and loyalty to his organization, yet in the end, he is thrown away like trash just because some tecato only cares about his next high.

Don't Get Between The Needle & Vein Of A Tecato: Those

"Tecato" homies with "Status" only care about their high and nothing else at the end of the day. So many righteous homies have been done dirty and "Crossed Up" by tecatos in prison who only care about their next fix. A gangster can give his freedom and loyalty to his organization, yet in the end, he is thrown away like trash just because some tecato only cares about his next high.

Don't Get Down Like That: A particular activity beneath a person or something you won't put up with. For example, "I'm not a thief; I don't get down like that," or "I know you ain't talking to me because I don't get down like that!"

Don't Mess With The House: This means to pay your "Taxes" to the "Big Homies" because they don't play around. It also means if you owe any "Hot Money," you better pay it. Don't mess with the house means don't play with anything that belongs to the big homies.

Don't Talk About It, Be About It: This means to do what you say and say what you do. If you say something, stand on it. For example, "You have an issue with that dude? Don't talk about it, be about it. Handle your business."

Door Policy: In the past, if a cell door was "mistakenly" opened in the "SHU" while a gang member was on the tier, they were obligated to attack if it was their enemy. The "Northerner" and "Southerner" leadership determined they were being used as a "Crash Dummy" by crooked officers, so they stopped requiring their "People" to attack under these circumstances. Instead of immediately attacking when a door was "Popped," they were told by their people to stand their ground and observe.

Door Pops: When an inmate rigs his cell door so that it closes, but it does not lock, thus deceiving correctional officers into thinking his cell door is secured. The inmate can open his door anytime and attack officers or other inmates. There were several assaults at my prison committed by inmates using this method.

Doorstep: Inmates will roll up an old newspaper or magazine and place it under their cell door. Sometimes, they will use a towel if that is all they have. The purpose of the doorstep is to keep dirt, bugs, noise, and rodents out of the cell. For example, "I need to make a new doorstep because dust is getting in my cell."

Dope Fiend: A drug-addicted inmate who constantly lies to his family, so they send money, and he uses it to pay his drug debts. For example, he will tell them his television broke and he needs money to buy another one. He will use the money to pay for his drug debts when he gets it. If things get desperate and he is about to get "Poked" for owing cash for drugs, he will tell his family that he will be killed if they don't send money.

Dope Fiend: To sucker punch someone. For example, "Did you see Thumper dope fiend that vato?"

Dope Fiend Move: A scandalous action against another person that only a dope fiend would do. For example, "Lowdown did a dope fiend move. I have no respect for that dude."

Dope Game: A convict who is "Hitting" and selling drugs in prison is involved in the dope game. The dope game is the marketplace of drugs in the penitentiary.

Dope Sick: When a "Dope Fiend" goes through withdrawal because they can't get any dope. For example, "That 'Tecato' is dope sick; he is sleeping all day and dripping sweat all over the cell."

Dope Wreck: A person who causes problems with others whenever they get high on drugs. Similar to a person who can't handle their alcohol, a dope wreck is someone that others avoid when they are under the influence of drugs. For example, "Kilo is a dope wreck. That fool always causes issues when he is loaded."

Dope Wreck: A snitch whom the administration sends to particular yards to find out who is selling the drugs. Once the dope wreck finds out who the "Plug" is, they report it to the administration. The administration will remove the dope wreck from the yard before taking down the "Pipeline."

Dorm: A building where inmates are housed in an open-air environment and sleep in two-man bunks. Inmates in a dorm setting, must have their "Points" below Level IV.

Dormie: This term refers to a person who lives in the same "Dorm" on the prison yard. For example, "Crook was my dormie at Avenal State Prison."

Double Bunk: In "Dorm" settings, this refers to when a bed is placed on top of another. A "Cadillac Rack" is a bed without another bed on top of it in a dorm setting, and inmates highly prize them.

Double Cell: Housing two inmates in a cell designed for only one.

Double Lock: Convicts will rig their cell doors so that if the "Control Booth Officer" presses the button to open it, the door won't open. The main reason convicts do this is to prevent an officer from opening their cell door when their enemies are on the tier. I have heard numerous stories from convicts who claimed their cell doors were intentionally opened while their enemies were on the tier near their cells.

Double Up: Some gangs will double the owed price after two weeks when a drug payment is late in prison. Once the debt gets to $1,000, they get "Removed."

Doughnut: A rolled-up piece of toilet paper shaped like a doughnut. They are set on fire, and the inmates use them to cook food or heat water in their cells. Inmates are allowed "Hot Pots" for this very purpose, but "Indigent" inmates can't afford one, so they use this primitive method to heat their food or water.

Down For Your Crown: When a person won't let anyone disrespect them. They won't run from a fight or bend to any pressure. For example, "You have to be down for your crown. There is no other way to go about it behind these walls, homeboy."

Down One, Drown One: As soon as a convict pinches off a turd in the toilet, he flushes it so his "Cellie" doesn't have to smell his funk.

Down Status: When people in your "Car" ignore you because of your bad behavior. Your fellow gang members will not associate with you until you redeem yourself, and that is usually accomplished by "Putting in Work" by doing a "Clean Up."

Downed Him: A term used to describe a violent attack. For example, "We were walking the yard and came across a Blood, so we downed him."

Downtown: These are opiates in prison, chiefly "Black." For example, "I got some downtown homie!"

DP: When a prison gang member is disciplined by his comrades for breaking "Household Policies." The "Peckerwoods" will DP one of their members for minor violations by having two "Woods" assault them for 23 seconds. It's 23 seconds because the 23rd letter in the alphabet is a "W," which stands for White. The "Southerners" will DP a member for minor violations for 13 seconds because the 13th letter of the alphabet is an "M," which stands for "Mexican Mafia." Of course, more serious rule violations will result in severe consequences like getting "Stabbed Off The Yard." For less serious violations, gangs will make violators do "Burpees" by the hundreds. Sometimes, they will make the violator stay on their rack for a set period; this is called "Rack Status."

Draft: When a prison gang "Opens Their Books" and picks new members to join their gang. For example, "In 2009, the 'Brand' had a draft and made Beast."

Drag: A false story used to take advantage of someone or to manipulate them. For example, "Stop running that drag on me, fool. T-Bone already told me what happened."

Dragon: The high given by doing drugs. For example, "Pee Wee is no good because all he does is 'Chase the Dragon.'"

Drama: Conflict or "Tension" with other people. For example, "I'm not even going to say anything to him because I don't want any drama."

Draw: This refers to how much "Canteen" an inmate can purchase monthly. Inmates can purchase a maximum of $240.00 a month. When an inmate spends the maximum amount, it is called a "Cadillac Draw."

Draw: The prison that the inmates at the "Reception Center" are assigned to before being transported on the "Grey Goose." For example, "What did you draw, homie?" The answer is, "I'm going to Salinas Valley."

Dress Outs: The civilian clothes given to a convict in "Receiving and Release" just moments before his release.

Drills: "Northerners" in prison practice drills to be ready for battle with another person or "Car." Each Northerner has a specific place they need to be "Posted Up" at on the yard or "Building" during this drill.

Drink A Lot Of Water & Walk Real Slow: Old-school advice given to "Fish" inmates new to prison life. It means this is a dangerous place, so watch yourself and don't step on anyone's toes.

Drive-by: When a person walks by your bed or cell, "Mean Mugging" or "Mad Dogging" you. For example, "Dasher just did a drive-by. Why does he keep looking in our cell?"

Driver's License: The "128 G" is an official piece of paper that lists an inmate's crimes, history, and other significant information that other gang members use to determine if someone is "No Good."

Drives Up: When a convict arrives at a new prison. For example, "Stomper drives up to our yard and starts 'Name Dropping,' and some of the homies didn't like that."

Driveway: The concrete walkway in front of the prison cells in a "Housing Unit" or "Bunks" in a "Dorm."

Driving Iron: When CDCR still had the "Weight Pile," this term was used for working out with weights. For example, "Hulk is at the 'Weight Pile' driving iron."

Driving Partners: When CDCR still had the "Weight Pile," this term was used for your workout partners. For example, "Big Joe and Lumpy are driving partners."

Drone Drops: Associates of inmates use drones to deliver "Contraband" into prison yards under darkness. These drone drops have been going on at numerous California state prisons in the recent past.

Drop It: This is when a convict drops the "Banger" from his anus when it's "Hooped." For example, "Check this out, little homie, if things 'Kick Off' with the 'Woods,' you need to drop it and 'Put In Work.'"

Drop One & Flush One: As soon as a convict pinches off a turd in the toilet, he flushes it so his "Cellie" doesn't have to smell his funk.

Dropout: When a prison gang member decides to quit their gang and enter "Protective Custody."

Dropout List: Every prison gang has a ledger of "No Good" former members who will be "Poked" whenever possible. Every prison will have a copy of this list, usually kept in the "Hole." These lists are very extensive and can have hundreds of names on them. The dropout list is usually "Hooped" for safekeeping.

Drop Points: When an inmate's "Points" drop because of good behavior, and as a result, he gets to go to a lower-level prison. Lower-level prisons are easier to do time in if living in an open "Dorm" doesn't bother you too much. Level I and II yards, the lowest in the California Department of Corrections and Rehabilitation, are dorm living, which is hard to get used to when you have been in a cell on Level III and Level IV yards.

Dropped A Piece: When an inmate has a "Banger" in his anal cavity and pushes it out quickly so he can use it on an enemy. For example, "Those seven 'Bulldogs' rushed those three 'Woods.' One of them dropped a piece, and he started poking those Bulldogs."

Dropping Procedures: These steps make it easier for a convict to drop the "Banger" from his anus when it's "Hooped." New arrivals to prison yards are "Schooled" on these things by their "Car" during their training period.

Dropping A Kite: When a "Snitch" drops a "Note" in the outgoing mailbox or places where officers will find it. For example, "I saw Mouth dropping a kite last night."

Dropping A Note: When a "Snitch" drops a "Note" in the outgoing mailbox or places where officers will find it.

Dropping Knives: When an inmate moves into a "Pod," "Building," "Tier," or "Row" in prison or jail, and his enemies start to drop their metal knives on the concrete floor. They do this to let him know he is about to get "Poked" during the next "Unlock." This is psychological warfare of the highest order. Metal knives hitting a concrete floor in that environment make a loud and distinctive sound.

Drove Up: When a convict arrives at a new prison. For example, "Hey, Bandit, guess who just drove up?"

Drum: An old-school term for a "Cell."

Dry: When no convicts on the yard are "Hitting." It means there aren't any drugs on the yard because no visitors, "Free Staff," or officers are bringing any in. For example, "It's been dry on this yard for too long, comrade."

Dry Snitching: To inform on someone indirectly by talking loudly or performing suspicious actions when others are in the area.

Ducat: A pass convicts use to attend an appointment or visit. It is also a piece of paper or token redeemable for specific services in prison, such as a car wash or haircut.

Ducat To The Chapel: Old-school term used to describe a plot to murder an inmate. For example, "Give Sinner a ducat to the chapel."

Ducking: To hide from someone or something out of fear or to avoid an issue. For example, "Big Russ owes me money after losing a bet on the Super Bowl. Now that fool is ducking me."

Duds: This term refers to clothes.

Duel Vocational Institution: This prison has a storied history in the California Department of Corrections and Rehabilitation. It was shut down on September 30, 2021.

Dummy Up: This means to play dumb when a person is trying to get information out of you. For example, "I told the little homie to dummy up if anyone asks him about what happened to Crazy Ray."

Dump Truck: A lazy, sloppy, and good-for-nothing person nobody respects in prison.

Dungeon: This is another term for "Administration Segregation." This is where inmates are sent for committing crimes within their prison sentence. It is a prison within a prison. The inmates are in their cells for 23 hours a day. They have limited personal items due to security reasons. The inmates are allowed a shower once every three days. They have an option to exercise on a small yard behind the "Housing Unit" with "Gun Coverage."

Duty Belt: The thick leather belt officers wear carrying all of their equipment.

DVI: This is the nickname for the prison Duel Vocational Institution. This prison has a storied history in the California Department of Corrections and Rehabilitation. It was shut down on September 30, 2021.

E

Eagle Warrior: This is a tattoo of an Aztec Eagle Warrior that a "Camarada" earns by "Putting In Work."

Ear Hustling: This means trying to listen to a private conversation between other people. I vividly recall the first time I ever heard this term in prison, and I laugh every time I think about it. I was talking to a female officer in front of the chow hall, and an inmate stopped by us and just stood there looking around like he was lost. The officer I was talking to looked at him in disgust and said loudly, "Why are you ear hustling? Kick rocks." I laughed after she said that, and the inmate just walked away, mumbling to himself.

Early Discharge: When an inmate dies or is killed in prison. For example, "The homies' 'Cleaned House' yesterday, and they gave Grumpy an early discharge."

Earn Your Area Code: For a convict to get a tattoo with his area code in prison, he has to earn it by "Putting In Work." Putting in work in prison can range from physically beating another person to "Blasting" them.

Earn Your Bed: This means as a convict in a "Faction," you have to "Put In Work" for the "Cause" while in prison. For example, "Listen up, little homie, you need to earn your bed. There ain't no free rides in here."

Earn Your Cell: This means as a convict in a "Faction," you have to "Put In Work" for the "Cause" while in prison. For example, "Check this out, youngster, you need to earn your cell around here. Get with the 'Program.'"

Earn Your Clover: This means to earn your shamrock (Clover Leaf) tattoo. This is when a convict murders another person to become a member of the "Aryan Brotherhood."

Earn Your Jersey: This is when a convict earns his membership into a gang by "Putting In Work." Putting in work in prison can range from physically beating another person to "Blasting" them.

Earn Your Jersey Back: In some prison gangs such as the "25's," after a member has been "Deemed No Good," they might be allowed to redeem themselves and become in "Good Standing." For this to happen, they must "Put In Work" by doing a "Clean Up." After they put in work, they will be accepted with no restrictions.

Earn Your Letters: For a convict to get a tattoo with the letters of his city in prison, he has to earn it by "Putting In Work." Putting in work in prison can range from physically beating another person to "Blasting" them.

Earn Your Red Star: For a convict to gain membership into the "Zapatista" "SNY" prison gang, he has to earn it by "Putting In Work." Putting in work in prison can range from physically beating another person to "Blasting" them. The Zapatistas use the red star as a symbol for their movement.

Earn Your Rock: This means to earn your shamrock (Clover Leaf) tattoo. This is when a convict murders another person to become a member of the "Aryan Brotherhood." For example, "Bloodhound earned his rock when he killed Yogi at Folsom in 2015."

Earn Your Town: For a convict to get a tattoo with his city in prison, he has to earn it by "Putting In Work." Putting in work in prison can range from physically beating another person to "Blasting" them.

Earned His Date: When a convict does his time and gets a parole date. For example, "Baby Face earned his date; I hope he sees her."

Earned His Stripes: To push a "Hardline" in prison and gain the respect of your peers. For example, "Wildman earned his stripes at Folsom."

Earning Your Bones: "Putting in Work" for your gang and gaining respect from other members. It can also be the "Mission" a gang associate is given to gain membership into the prison gang.

Earning Your Stripes: "Putting in Work" for your gang and gaining respect from other members.

East Hall: It refers to the "Orientation Building" at Tracy Prison back in the day.

Educated: When an older convict gives knowledge to a young "First Termer" to help him navigate the treacherous waters of the penal system. This process helps the youngster stay away from trouble and getting himself into a "Wreck." Some of this education might include how to make a knife. The "Big Homie" will tell the "Fish" to make a knife, and he will grade it. If the knife isn't good enough, he will have him make it again. He might also teach him how to make a "Bomb" to melt plastic for a knife if he has no metal. He will instruct him on how to defend himself and on various exercises.

Eight & Hit The Gate: This is when a correctional officer goes to work and does his eight hours without harassing the convicts. This officer does not bring his problems from home and takes them out on the convicts under his care. In other words, they are fair, firm, and consistent. For example, "You know how I get down, I do my eight and hit the gate. I'm not here to play games with you and make your time harder. I give you respect as a man and expect the same in return."

Elbows: An elbow is a life sentence in prison. For example,"Orange County don't play. They are handing out elbows to the homies."

EME: EME is the pronunciation of the letter M in Spanish. The letter stands for "Mexican Mafia." "Southerner" street gangs follow the orders from the Mexican Mafia on the streets and in prison. M is the 13th letter of the alphabet, and Southerners use the number 13 in graffiti and tattoos to show allegiance.

Emergency Count: This type of "Count" in prison is a "Positive Count" of inmates during an emergency, riot, natural disaster, major incident, or escape.

Emero: A term used by "Southerners" for a member of the "Mexican Mafia."

Employee Assistance Program: It is a service provided by the State of California to promote health and well-being and help employees deal with stress, money worries, family concerns, and other problems. The Employee Assistance Program's placards were displayed prominently throughout the prison. One night in the "Program Office," I was talking to the "Program Sergeant" about an issue I was having in my "Housing Unit." When I finished talking, he pointed to a poster on the wall and bluntly stated, "Why don't you call them?" I looked at the poster, and it was for the Employee Assistance Program. We both laughed, and I handled that issue myself the next day.

End His Career: When a convict does something his homie thinks makes him "No Good," and goes on a campaign to "Wash Him Up." For example, "Brains was pushing the issue on Numbers, and he was trying to wash him up and end his career."

End Of Hostilities: This is the end of the war between "Northerners" and "Southerners." This bloody prison and street war lasted from approximately 1968 to 2012.

End Of The Line: Old-school nickname for Folsom State Prison.

Ended His Career: When a "Mainline" inmate does something that his "Big Homie" thinks makes him "No Good." For example, "Bullet 'Pulled up' to a 'No Landing Zone' and he 'Programmed' until his parole. He ended his career. He is no good."

Endorsement: When the administration clears an inmate for transfer to another prison. For example, "I got my endorsement to San Quentin."

Enemigo: This word translates to enemy.

Enforcer: A gang member that physically enforces the "Household Policies" of his gang among other members. For example, sometimes, if a gang member breaks a minor rule, the enforcer will assault him without leaving marks on his face so that the beating won't catch the officer's attention. If the infraction is serious enough, the enforcer will be sent on a "Mission" to "Blast" the disgraced prison gang member.

Enhanced Outpatient Program: This program is similar to a medical day treatment program, but it is offered within a prison setting. This program is designed for inmates participating in the mental health program within the California Department of Corrections and Rehabilitation.

Entourage: "Mexican Mafia" members on the "Line" have several "Southerners" shadow them and provide security.

EOP: The Enhanced Outpatient Program is similar to a medical day treatment program but in prison. This program is for inmates in the mental health program at the California Department of Corrections and Rehabilitation.

EOU: The Emergency Operation Unit supervises departmental operations such as hostage rescues, special transports, and riot suppression. The Emergency Operations Unit is a sub-unit of the "Office of Correctional Safety."

EOP RHU: This acronym stands for Enhanced Outpatient Restricted Housing Unit. This is for inmates in the Enhanced Outpatient Program who require restricted housing. The Enhanced Outpatient Program is similar to a medical day treatment program, but it is offered within a prison setting. This program is designed for inmates participating in the mental health program within the California Department of Corrections and Rehabilitation.

EPRD: Earliest Possible Release Date for a convict if they do not get into trouble while in prison and get more time added to their sentence.

Erring & Slurring: When the "Independent Riders" greet each other on the yard, they call each other ER. For example, "What's up ER?" They say ER because Rider ends in ER. This greeting is called Erring and Slurring. The ER in their greeting rhymes with the UR in the word slur.

Escort: Some "Factions" require witnesses for all dealings with officers and other prison officials on high-level yards. They have this requirement to document what was said and verify a homie isn't snitching. This witness is called an escort.

Ese: A word that translates to dude, bro, or homie.

Established: When a gang or individual has an area under their complete control. For example, "When I 'Drove Up' to Old Folsom, the homies were already well established."

Estilo: A word that translates to style. For example, "I like your estilo, big dog."

Every Car Must Crash: This means every "Car" on a prison yard will eventually lose its power to another group or "Faction."

Every Time I Ate He Ate: This means whenever a homie made some food in his cell, he always offered some to his "Cellie." For example, "To keep it 100, it hurt me when Bolo 'Took Off' on me. Every time I ate, he ate. It just messed me up that the homie would 'Do Me Dirty' like that."

Everyone Will Mind Someone: This fact of prison means a "Faction" will enforce their "Code Of Conduct," and everyone will fall in line one way or another. For example, "Renegade thinks he can keep going 'Against The Grain.' Everyone will mind someone. He is about to learn the 'Fellas' don't play."

Everything's Gravy: This saying means there aren't any problems, and things are going well. For example, "On second thought, homeboy, don't worry about that money you owe me. Everything's gravy. I'm good, brother."

Excessive Force: This means using more force than is reasonable to accomplish a lawful purpose.

Excuse Me On The Tier: This is what some convicts yell out of their cell before they loudly communicate with a homie in another cell.

This shows respect to others who might want to talk on the tier.

Eye Buster: An eye buster is a tattoo of a convict's hood that's visible to others.

F

Face The Music: When people face repercussions for something they did. For example, "Woody messed up; now he must face the music."

Faction: This refers to the people you associate with or the gang members from your county.

Fade: To fight with another person. For example, "You don't want that fade with me."

Fair One: To treat an adversary respectfully and give them a fair fight. For example, "I will give you a fair one, homie. What you wanna do?"

Fake, Fraud, Or Part-Time Broad: An old-school saying regarding reading people in prison and knowing what they are really about. For example, "You never know who you are dealing with in prison. I got pretty good at realizing what kind of dude I was dealing with, who is a fake, fraud, or part-time broad."

Faking The Funk: A person who acts like they are "With The Business," but in reality, they are just a "Lame." For example, "Lots of cats on this yard are just faking the funk; they aren't with the business."

Fall In Line: In prison, things are what they are; if you go "Against The Grain," you will end up in a "Wreck."

Fall Out: When an inmate passes out. For example, "I'm about to fall out! It's too hot out on this yard."

Falls In Your Lap: When something out of your control becomes your problem, and you must deal with it. For example, "I was doing my time and going with the 'Program' when this cat with

'Bad Paperwork' 'Pulled Up.' The 'Big Homie' told me I had to handle it. The drama just falls in your lap in prison, so I 'Poked' that fool because I had no choice."

False Jacket: This is when an adversary spreads lies about another person in prison to "Smut Up" their name. This is done by someone who is "Politicking" against them.

Familiano: A member of the "Nuestra Familia" prison gang.

Family Visit: When an inmate's wife or family member stays the night with him on prison grounds. They stay in a small building surrounded by a secure fence with a small kitchen, bedroom, and seating area. The visitors can bring food to cook in the kitchen during their short stay.

Family Visit: What an inmate will say to his "Cellie" when he wants some "Cell Time." For example, "Check this out, homie, I'm going to a family visit. You need to go to the yard."

Farewell Party: Sometimes, before an inmate is released, his homies will celebrate by pranking him. They might put toilet paper all over his cell or throw a bucket of water on him. It's all in good fun. They genuinely are happy their homie is getting out.

Farmers: A derogatory name used for the "Northerners" because agricultural farms and fields enclose their geographical vicinity.

Fat Mouth: To disrespect another person with your words. For example, "I didn't like that 'Lame,' so I would fat mouth him every time I saw him."

Fat Mouthing: To disrespect another person with your words. For example, "That pig kept fat mouthing me. That's why I 'Took Off' on him."

FAT: The Fugitive Apprehension Team arrests high-risk parolee violators. The Fugitive Apprehension Team is a sub-unit of the "Office of Correctional Safety."

Father's Day Massacre: At Corcoran Prison on Father's Day in 2009, the "Southerners" viciously attacked the "Northerners." This coordinated attack was in retaliation to the Northerner's attacks on the Southerners at New Delano and Pelican Bay Prisons.

Faulty: A belief that turns out to be false and detrimental to a person or "Cause." For example, "One of the faulty beliefs that we realized in prison was we were enemies on the streets and killing each other, but in prison, we had to call a truce. It made no sense."

Featherwood: A White woman who associates with "Peckerwoods."

Federal AB: This refers to the "Aryan Brotherhood" that runs the Federal prison system in America for White inmates. They are allies with the "California AB," which has a different "Commission" and runs the California prison system for the White inmates.

Federal Crack: This refers to a person getting convicted of a federal crime and going to federal prison. For example, "Colorado got a federal crack for bank robbery."

Feeding His Arm: An inmate who is always doing heroin in prison. For example, "That 'Tecato' is always feeding his arm."

Feel Good: Something that a person finds really pleasurable. For example, "Hitting the 'Weight Pile' is my feel good."

Fell Off: A person who has stopped living up to ideals they once pushed a "Hardline" on. Someone who has disappeared from the frontlines, and you don't see or hear about them anymore. For example, "Did you hear about Diamond? That cat fell off! I can't believe he went out like that."

Fell Out: When an inmate passes out. For example, "Superman, hit your alarm! My 'Cellie' just fell out."

Fellas: The leaders of a prison gang or "Car" who wield significant influence over their comrades. Officers with a persistent problem with a convict usually talk to the fellas to resolve the issue. The fellas help keep things in order in prison.

Fence Parole: When an inmate escapes from a correctional facility by climbing the fence. For example, "Did you hear about Speedy? He got that fence parole and was out for three days."

Feria: A word that translates to money. For example, "Where is that feria you owe me?"

Field House: A large gymnasium for the inmates at "Tracy" prison. Various team sports and other activities were available there for the inmates. Tracy prison was shut down on September 30, 2021.

Fierro: In prison, this word is used for an inmate-manufactured weapon. For example, "Hey fool, slide me that fierro."

Fifi: A tightly wrapped towel or sock with a plastic bag or latex glove inside. The inmate will put lotion inside the plastic and use the Fifi to masturbate. For example, "Fifi is coming over for a 'Conjugal Visit,' so you need to go to yard homie."

Filero: In prison, this word is used for an inmate-manufactured weapon. For example, "I have a real nice filero. Let's go handle that issue."

Filter: A message between gang members. For example, "A filter went out that Silent was 'No Good' and that he was on 'Disregard Status.'"

Fine: Some prison gangs fine their members for getting caught with or losing a "Kite." A "Mexican Mafia" member once instituted a $500 fine for any homies who lost a "Wila."

Finessed: When a person uses their abilities to get over on someone. For example, "I finessed an extra tray of chicken at the chow hall."

Fire Camp: There are approximately 1,500 inmates in the 35 fire camps across California. These inmates help fight fires, clear brush and fallen trees, and maintain parks.

Fire On Him: To physically attack someone. For example, "If that fat officer ever trashes our cell again, I'm going to fire on him."

Firme: This word means something is cool. For example, "Stalker 'Hit' at his visit, that's firme."

Firme Raza: This refers to a group of high-ranking "Southsiders" in "YA" who got the utmost respect from their peers. To attain the rank of firme raza, a person must have put in a lot of work fighting others in YA. For example, "That's Batman, homie, he is firme raza. So watch what you say around him."

First Termer: An inmate doing his first prison term. For example, "Yeah, my cellie is just a youngster. He is a first termer."

First Time Down: An inmate doing his first prison term. For example, "This is my first time down; you need to work with me a little bit, homeboy."

Fish: A new person in prison who is clueless about how things are.

Fish Kit: Toiletry items a "Fish" inmate receives from correctional officers when they first arrive. These items include powdered toothpaste, toilet paper, a comb, a "Bed Roll," a toothbrush, a bar of soap, a razor, a cup, a spoon, etc.

Fish On A Line: A group of "Fish" inmates walking into prison for the first time.

Fish Row: A bunch of "Fish" inmates in cells next to each other in a "Building."

Fish Tank: This term refers to the "Orientation Building" on the prison yard where the "Fish" inmates are housed for approximately two weeks until all of their paperwork is ready.

Fishing: When inmates are in their cells, they pass things to each other using a "Fishing Line." They forcefully slide the fishing line under their cell door, and their comrade in another cell will use his fishing line to grab it. He will then pull it into his cell, attach whatever he is giving him, and tell his comrade to pull back his line.

Fishing Line: This is a torn-up sheet or the elastic from a pair of boxers, tightly wound together, that inmates use to pass things to each other. They forcefully slide the fishing line under their cell door, and their comrade from another cell will use his fishing line to grab it and pull it into his cell. Inmates attach messages or items and pass them back and forth using fishing lines.

Fishing Pole: An item such as a rolled-up newspaper that an inmate uses to help while he is "Fishing."

Flag: A colored bandanna that inmates wear to represent their gang. For example, "Frog had his red flag out in the 'Dayroom.'"

Flag: A movement, organization, or ideal a convict represents in prison. This flag can be anything a convict pushes and is willing to fight for.

Flamed Up: A "Blood" gangster wearing a lot of red clothing and their "Flag" is out to represent his gang.

Flat: A flat piece of prison steel shaped like a knife.

Flat Back: An inmate-manufactured weapon.

Flex: To act aggressively towards someone else with the implication of physical violence if they don't bow down to you. Sometimes, people flex, but they aren't about the business, so they have no intention of backing up their words with action. For example, "That fool Hulk was trying to flex on me at the chow hall."

Flip–Flop: To switch cells with one of your homies. For example, "Clever, I need you to flip-flop with Cricket."

Flipped: When an inmate convinces an officer or "Free Staff" to bring "Contraband" to prison. For example, "Crafty flipped that officer, and he is going to bring in four cell phones and some 'Black.'"

Flipped: When people under investigation cooperate with the authorities and they get a lighter punishment.

Flipped That Cell: When officers aggressively search an area or cell for "Contraband." For example, "Someone 'Dropped A Kite' saying the homie had a cell phone, so the officers flipped that cell."

Flipped That Place: When officers aggressively search an area or cell for "Contraband." For example, "Someone 'Dropped A Kite' saying there were a bunch of cell phones in the 'Gym,' so the officers flipped that place."

Flipping A Yard: Occasionally, in the California Department of Corrections and Rehabilitation, a prison will transfer the inmates presently on the yard and bring in new inmates. This will often happen when the administration changes the "Security Level" of the prison. This process is called flipping a yard by the convicts.

When this happens, all of the "Factions" fight over who gets what bench, bleacher, good jobs, etc. Every group wants the most advantageous area to call their own and the best inmate jobs. Wars will be waged over who gets what. A new yard is notorious for violence as these essential issues get settled. For example, "I got to Calipat, and I was on the first bus there. We were flipping C-Yard to a Level IV."

Floater: A cover for a knife that prevents the metal detector from pinging on it.

Floater: A term used for a radio, television, or other electronic device that does not belong to a convict. All radios and televisions are logged into the convict's "Property Card" in "Receiving and Release," and they are etched with the convict's "CDC Number." These radios and televisions will frequently be used to pay off drug debts, be stolen, or given to other convicts by their rightful owners. Only the convict that television or radio was first assigned to can keep it in their possession. If another convict is caught with it, officers are authorized to confiscate it. A convict often tried to change the CDC number on the floater to his own, but it was easy to spot this type of deception.

Flooded: When a prison yard is full of illicit drugs, numerous inmates are getting high, and some are into serious drug debts that endanger their lives. For example, "Those Level II yards are so flooded that they are always 'Cracking Off.'"

Flooding The Gates: When a prison yard is full of illicit drugs, numerous inmates are getting high, and some are into serious drug debts that endanger their lives. For example, "I heard the homies at Soledad are flooding the gates."

Flooding The Tier: When inmates plug their cell toilet with towels or other objects and repeatedly flush their toilets to flood the tier. This was done quite often by the inmates in the "Hole" when they wanted to give the officers working there a hard time. They would laugh at us while we cleaned the water with mops. The amount of water they put on the tier while doing this was impressive.

Floor Officer: One of two correctional officers who work in a "Housing Unit" or "Dorm" setting.

Floor Time: Since prison cells are so small, inmates will get designated floor time to exercise or do whatever they want while their "Cellie" stays out of their way on their bunk. Floor time is significant during "Lockdowns" as tensions can rise while being stuck in a cell with another man for extended periods.

Flushing: There were claims that other prisons sent their "Problem Children" to High Desert State Prison, which they call flushing. In other words, they are flushing their toilets and sending it to them.

Flying A Lame Flag: This means a person acts like a "Lame," and they get no respect from the homies. For example, "How is that punk still walking this yard? He is flying a lame flag."

Folsom Museum: This museum is located near the entrance of Folsom State Prison and is filled with many artifacts about its legendary history.

Folsom Prison Blues: This refers to a song by Johnny Cash about Folsom State Prison. Johnny Cash played this song live at Folsom Prison on January 13, 1968.

Food On The Shelves: This phrase describes a person who has lots of "Canteen" items in their cell or locker. For example, "G-

Money is living large. He has plenty of food on the shelves."

Food Port: The small opening in the cell door or wall whereby food is given to the inmates. Inmates are also cuffed through this opening while still inside their cells.

Food Port Officer: The correctional officer in the "Dining Hall" who stands by the "Food Port" during breakfast and dinner. They ensure the convicts do not get more than their allotted food servings.

Food Sale: When inmates can buy food from outside restaurants such as Domino's Pizza, Burger King, Kentucky Fried Chicken, etc. The food is delivered to the prisons and brought to each inmate in their "Housing Units." Inmates love to post pictures of giant stacks of food from these places to their Facebook, TikTok, and Instagram accounts via their "Contraband" cell phones.

Food Strike: When inmates get together and refuse to eat because of specific grievances. The Pelican Bay "SHU" inmates had a food strike, protesting being locked down indefinitely. This brought attention to their situation, and they had a favorable court decision regarding that issue.

Foot Soldiers: These are the lowest level gang members in prison who are the muscle for their "Car." They are the pawns of the "Big Homies" who use them to further their agenda.

Football Numbers: This term describes any lengthy prison sentence. For example, "Bronco got football numbers, homie."

Foothold: A prison or prison yard where a particular "Faction" has a small amount of power and wants to get more and turn it into a "Stronghold." For example, "We just arrived on the yard and were trying to get a foothold. We started pressing dudes and had to 'Smash' some."

For The Birds: This refers to something that is a waste of time and effort. For example, "Check this out, youngster, this prison life is for the birds. Get out to the streets and be there for your children. Don't come back here, young homie."

Forced Back: When gang members "Remove" someone for breaking their "Household Policies." Being forced back involves extreme violence, ranging from a severe beating to getting "Poked" numerous times. For example, "Porky got forced back at Lancaster. He is 'No Good.'"

Forever And A Day: A life sentence with no possibility of parole.

Form 812: This is the paperwork submitted by an inmate who claims other inmates on the yard are his enemies and members of a "Security Threat Group."

Format: A 700-word document detailing the philosophy of the "Norteño" cause.

Foul Charges: When an inmate has any of the following on their "Paperwork;" rape, snitching, molestation, abusing women or the elderly, etc. Most prison gangs will violently attack inmates with these things on their "Black & Whites" and "Remove" them from the yard.

Found Suitable: When an inmate goes to the parole board, they find him suitable for parole. For example, "I went to the board, and I was found suitable."

Frajos: A slang term for cigarettes.

Free Staff: People who work at the prison but are not peace officers. For example, clerks, plumbers, cooks, electricians, nurses, and teachers are considered free staff.

Free World: This refers to the communities outside of prison. For example, "When you parole to the free world, there are some things I need you to do for me, homeboy."

Free World Soldier: When prison gang members are released from prison and continue to perform gang business on the streets.

Freelancing: This is a highly frowned upon activity when gang members make money on the streets or in prison but hide the proceeds from the "Fellas." The Fellas require a "Tribute" of 1/3 of all proceeds of illegal activity from their members. Some members hide earnings so they don't have to pay "Taxes" to the "Big Homies."

Freeway: The concrete walkway in front of the prison cells in a "Housing Unit" or "Bunks" in a "Dorm."

Freeway Freddy: This is the name for the mice at L.A. County Jail. Freeway Freddy was always trying to get the inmate's food. I heard a story about Freeway Freddy carrying a soup down the tier.

Freeway Sleeper: Many years ago in L.A. County jail, sometimes inmates had to sleep on the tiers because of overcrowding. The tier is called the "Freeway," hence the name freeway sleeper.

Freeway Time: The time spent by inmates walking the "Tier" and talking to their homies. During this time, they will also pass things from cell to cell for their "People."

Freeze: When a prison gang member is investigated by his comrades for wrongdoing. He will be kept to the side, and no gang business or "Politics" will be shared with him until he is cleared of any violations.

Freeze: When an inmate tells a person to stop doing something. For example, "Check this out: I just talked to some people who say they have never heard of you. You are going to freeze on claiming that, and if you don't, you are going to have 'Problems.'"

Fresh Blood: The term used when prison gangs "Open The Books" and recruit new members into their organization. For example, "I heard 'The Brand' plans on making fresh blood."

Fresh In: An inmate who is at the beginning of their prison journey. For example, "That youngster is fresh in, so I gave him some 'Schooling' on what is expected of him."

Fresh Out: An inmate who was recently released from prison. For example, "Crispy is fresh out. The homies are putting together a care package for him."

Fresnecks: A "Peckerwood" "Car" in prison from Fresno.

Fresno Bulldogs: The Fresno Bulldogs are a prison gang from Fresno, and unlike most gangs, they do not have "Shot Callers." Due to the fact the Fresno Bulldogs don't have shot callers, they are harder to manage in a prison setting because they do whatever they want without a leader keeping them in check.

Fridge: This is when an inmate places food or a soda can in a wet sock and hangs it from the A.C. vent. This is how inmates keep their food cold in a prison cell. For example, "Grab me a soda from the fridge."

From The Gate: The very beginning of something. For example, "Say Blood, right from the gate, you know I got love for you. But I don't like your little homie, Red."

From The Shoulders: A "Squabble" between two people using hands with no wrestling allowed.

Front: Pretending to be someone you're not or fabricating details to make an impression on your peers. For example, "You don't have to front, homie. Ace told me all about it."

Front: This refers to the "Mainline" convicts who do the bidding of the "Big Homies" in the "Back." For example, "In the old days, the 'NLR' was in the front, and did the bidding of the 'Brand' who were in the back."

Front: To give a person drugs, and they agree to pay you at a future date when they have money. In prison, an inmate usually has a $200 debt limit to drugs, and if they go over that limit or don't pay their debt, they will be "Removed."

Front Line: An inmate pushing a "Hardline" in prison. He is always in the mix "Kicking Up Dust."

Front Lining: An inmate pushing a "Hardline" in prison. He is always in the mix "Kicking Up Dust."

Front Me Off: To disrespect someone or reveal secrets about them. For example, an officer might tell an inmate, "Why did you front me off by running around when the sergeant was in here?"

Front Street: To disrespect someone or reveal secrets about them. For example, "That dirty officer switched my outgoing mail and put me on front street because my wife got the letter to my side chick."

Front To Back Charlie Row: Charlie Row is a section in the L.A. County Jail. The inmates on either end of Charlie Row are tasked with being "On Point" for their "People." When the inmates in the front hear the officers' keys coming towards them, they yell, "Front to back, Charlie Row." This verbal warning would notify the homies to stash any "Contraband" and stop illegal activities.

Front Yard: The concrete walkway in front of the prison cells in a

"Housing Unit" or "Bunks" in a "Dorm."

Fronting: Pretending to be someone you're not or fabricating details to make an impression on your peers. For example, "Stop fronting Dreamer. I was there, that didn't happen."

FSP: Folsom State Prison.

FTB: FTB means, F**k The "Brand." The "Wolfpack Skinheads" was a White "Faction" who believed in FTB. These two groups had a violent war amongst themselves in prison. The Brand came out on top and ran the Wolfpack off the "Mainline."

FTW: A tattoo that inmates get that means: F**k The World. This tattoo means they live an outlaw lifestyle and don't respect society's laws.

Full 60: This is when "Northerners" are put on high alert by their "Shot Callers," and they are ordered to be ready for any situation that could put their "Household" at risk.

Full Blast: To go the extra mile when doing something. For example, "When that 'Chomo' comes out to yard, you need to handle that full blast homeboy."

Full Linen: This refers to the total number of t-shirts, socks, pants, shirts, boxers, sheets, towels, and pillowcases an inmate is issued in prison. For example, in "Old Folsom" prison unit 5 in 1988, a Full Linen consisted of four t-shirts, four boxers, six socks, three pants, three shirts, one jacket, two sheets, two towels, and two pillowcases.

Full Shirt: When a convict's upper body is completely covered in tattoos. For example, "Crazy Blue is 'Blasted' with a full shirt of the best tattoos I have ever seen."

Function: How an inmate or group gets along with other people or groups. For example, "You know we don't function with those 'lames,' homie. It's 'On Sight' with those 'Punks.'"

Funk: This means a convict is looking to push a "Hardline" on someone. For example, "If you want the funk, then do what you gotta do."

Funking: To have an active "Beef" with another person or "Car." For example, "We were funking with those 'Peckerwoods' at Calipat."

Funny Charges: When an inmate has any of the following on their "Paperwork;" rape, snitching, molestation, abusing women or the elderly, etc. Most prison gangs will violently attack inmates with these kinds of things on their "Black & Whites" and "Remove" them from the yard.

Funny Money: Old-school term used for prison "Ducats."

Funny Style: To act suspiciously, goofy, or out of character. For example, "Ever since Baby Face 'Cracked' that female officer who works in visiting, he has been acting funny style."

Funny Yard: This is another term for a "Sensitive Needs Yard," they are the majority of yards in CDCR now. These yards are considered "No Good" by the "General Population" convicts. Most inmates on "SNY" yards are there for drug or gambling debts. SNY yards tend to be more chaotic and violent than the "Mainline" because the gang structure is less rigid than the general population gangs.

G

G Homie: A respected "OG" who usually has the "Keys" for his "Car." For example, "Yeah, Neckbone is the G Homie."

G Shield: This is a tattoo of an Aztec "War Shield" that a"Camarada" earns by "Putting In Work" for a member of the "Mexican Mafia." It is also called the "3-Step Shield," and it has three steps to it. Each step is earned by committing an act of violence for a "Pilli."

G'D Up: A gangster dressed in gang attire pushing a "Hardline" on anyone they come across. For example, "Smurf has always been G'd up."

Gaba: A slang term that means White man. For example, "That gaba owes me $100. He has until Friday to get my money right."

Gabacho: A slang term that means White man. For example, "We were at war with the gabachos over a drug debt."

Gain Your Citizenship: When a person earns their membership in a gang or is promoted to a leadership position. For example, "It takes a long time to earn your citizenship as a 'Carnal.'"

Gallo: The means "Roll Call." In the "Hole," the "Shot Caller" will yell out of his cell and speak to each of his people by their "Street Name." He does this in the morning and night. He will "Open The Tier" in the morning and "Close The Tier" at night. Only members in good standing are allowed to participate in roll call.

Gambling Tables: When certain "Factions" have a gambling table in prison, they must pay one-third of the proceeds to the "Big Homies." In other words, these tables are taxed, and if they don't pay, their tables will be shut down.

Game Face: The unique process when an officer or convict gets into the prison mindset to survive. For example, an officer on their way to work must get their game face on before they walk through the "Staff Entrance." After an inmate visits with his friends and family, he must put his game face on before returning to the "Mainline."

Gang Hopping: When a gangster drops out of one gang and joins another. Some "Factions" highly frown upon this behavior.

Gang Jacket: When an inmate is "Validated" as a gang member by the prison administration. For example, "Those lames just gave me a gang jacket."

Gang Module: A "Pod" in a county jail full of gang members.

Gang Of Time: This term describes any lengthy prison sentence. For example, "My boy Max just caught a gang of time for that 'Hot One' I told you about."

Gangsta Car: The Gangsta "Car" in prison is mainly composed of "Crips" from the Eight Tray (83) Gangsta Crips and some other Crip hoods, such as the Avalon Gangsta Crips.

Gangsterism: The way a gangster conducts themselves. For example, "We let those punks know that gangsterism was still in effect here."

Gas Him Up: To instigate a beef by challenging a homie's manhood. For example, "You are going to let Kiki 'Smut' you up like that? On hood, bro, I can't believe what he said about you. The streets are talking about this, and it's not a good look for you."

Gassed: When an inmate throws a putrid mixture of feces, urine, blood, puss, seamen, and insect guts into an officer's face when they walk by their cell. This unholy concoction is usually left to ferment for a few days before so it can grow bacteria to make the officer sick. When gassing an officer, the inmate will aim for the officer's eyes and mouth, ensuring the mixture enters their body. Sometimes, they won't let their concoction sit before gassing an officer because it has fresh HIV and hepatitis-infected blood in the container.

Gassed Out: When a convict gets winded from physical activity. For example, "I kept hitting that fool until I was gassed out."

Gasser: This inmate has "Priors" for "Gassing" officers. For example, "Watch out when you go by cell 134, that 'J-Cat' is a gasser."

Gasser's Alley: This is an area of a prison or jail where inmates who have "Priors" for "Gassing" officers. For example, "Watch out for C-section. That's gasser's alley."

Gassing: When an inmate throws a putrid mixture of feces, urine, blood, puss, seamen, and insect guts into an officer's face when they walk by their cell. This unholy concoction is usually left to ferment for a few days before so it can grow bacteria to make the officer sick. When gassing an officer, the inmate will aim for the officer's eyes and mouth, ensuring the mixture enters their body. Sometimes, they won't let their concoction sit before gassing an officer because it has fresh HIV and hepatitis-infected blood in the container.

Gate Money: The amount of money (approximately $200) given to a convict by "Receiving and Release" when they are released from prison.

Gated Out: When a convict is released from prison.

Gave Him The Business: When a person violently attacks someone. For example, "Lefty was bumping his gums again, and Playboy gave him the business."

Gay Boy Gangsters: This is a violent group on the "SNY" prison yards.

Gay For The Stay, Straight At The Gate: This expression means exactly what it implies.

GBI: This acronym stands for great bodily injury, and it is a charge in prison when an inmate causes severe injuries to another person. A great bodily injury charge will probably lead to the prison forwarding the case to the local district attorney for prosecution.

General Chrono: This is the CDCR Form 128-B used to document information about inmates and their behavior.

General Council: This is the current leadership structure of the "Nuestra Familia." The General Council comprises seven members: three Generals and a four-member "Inner Council."

General Of The Prisons: This person oversees all of the "Nuestra Familia's" prison functions.

General Population: The general population of convicts with minimal restrictions placed on their activities and privileges as opposed to inmates in the "SHU" or "Hole."

General Population Restricted Housing Unit: Under a new policy in 2024, the California Department of Corrections and Rehabilitation renamed the "Administration Segregation" and "Security Housing Unit." Both of those longstanding segregated housing facilities have been renamed to "Restrictive Housing Units." Only inmates who have engaged in violence or have serious safety concerns are placed in restricted housing under this new policy.

Get A Pass: When a gang member chooses not to harm or attack another person despite having the capability to do so. For example, "Dreamer thinks he will get a pass for losing that 'Clavo,' but it doesn't work that way around here, homie."

Get At Him On Paper: To send a "Kite" to another person so you can resolve an issue. For example, "I have a good rapport with Redwood. I will get at him on paper to resolve this issue."

Get Back: To get revenge on a person who has wronged you. For example, "Officer Gomez has been coming at me sideways lately, so during the riot yesterday, I got some get back when I 'Poked' him."

Get Back: To respond to a message from another person. For example, "I shot you a 'Kite' homeboy. Why no get back?"

Get Called On: When a "Big Homie" or your "Car" orders you to go on a "Mission" or do something for them in prison. For example, "Check this out, little homie; if you start getting in the mix and bumping your gums, you will get called on. All of that 'High Power' talk in prison will get you in a 'Wreck.'"

Get Down: The way a convict carries himself in prison. For example, "You know my get down homie, I wasn't going to let that slide."

Get Down: How a prison, yard, or area functions. For example, "When I got to the Level IV yard, it was a whole different get down than those Level III yards."

Get Down: This is what the "Tower Officer" yells to the inmates on the yard over the public address system during an alarm.

Get Down: When inmates get into a fight. For example, "Big Herm came out me sideways, so I told him we need to get down. We went to the stall and got our 'Squabble' on."

Get Down Like That: This describes how a convict conducts himself daily. For example, "I don't get down like that homeboy. You better 'Check My File!'"

Get Him Out The Way: This is an order to "Remove" someone. For example, "Bugsy isn't going with the program? Get him out the way next yard."

Get His Issue: This is the punishment when someone has broken "Household Policies" or disrespected someone. For example, "Books will get his issue today during evening yard. That punk has got to go."

Get His Wings Back: When a person is stripped of their "Status" in a gang and given it back at a later time. For example, "Casper is going to get his wings back."

Get In The Right People's Ears: This is when a convict puts in work for the "Cause" and the "Big Homies" hear about it. The person who keeps "Doing Dirt" for his "Faction" will have his name start "Ringing Bells," and he will gain "Status" in his "Car." For example, "I wanted to get in the right people's ears, so I kept putting in work. I wanted the 'Brass' always hearing my name."

Get Off: To physically attack someone. For example, "If Rowdy slams his locker one more time, I'm going to get off on him."

Get Off My Door: An expression used to ask another person to get away from their cell door. For example, "So the sergeant comes to my door and asks me if everything is okay. I told him, kick rocks, punk! Get off my door!"

Get Off The Door: This is an order for your "Car" or homie to get away from their cell door and stop talking on the tier to other people. For example, "We'll talk about that in the morning;

everybody get off the door."

Get Off Where I'm Mad At: This means if a person is disrespected, they immediately "Take Off" without asking questions. For example, "If someone ever comes at me 'Sideways,' I'm going to get off where I'm mad at."

Get Off Your Chest: This saying is used when confronting another person in anticipation of a fight. For example, "What's up with your attitude? Is there something you need to get off your chest?"

Get On His Head: When a person physically assaults someone else violently. For example, "If Pookie doesn't get my money right, I will get on his head."

Get On The Dummy: This refers to pretending ignorance when someone is attempting to extract information from you. For example, "I had to get on the dummy when the Lieutenant asked me questions."

Get Our Money: To fight with another inmate. For example, "You talk too much, homie. Let's get our money in my cell."

Get Our Money: This means a person or group will work out. For example, "It's time to get our money, homie. Can't stop, won't stop."

Get Out The Way: When people realize their time has passed and it's time to lay their flag down. For example, "I realized that the game had changed, so it was time to get out the way."

Get Their Feelings Hurt: When people get in their emotions about certain situations. For example, "Dudes get their feelings hurt when they get 'Poked.' It's no wonder they snitch, homie."

Get Theirs In: To get payback on someone if they do something to you. For example, "If you attack an officer, they are going to put their boots on you and get theirs in."

Get Your Knuckles Dirty: This means to get into a fight. For example, "Are you ready to get your knuckles dirty, homie?"

Getting Married: When a convict joins a prison gang. For example, "Joker is getting married today."

Getting Off: To physically attack someone. For example, "The cats at Salinas Valley Prison didn't have a problem with getting off on the police. It seemed like they enjoyed smashing them."

Getting Well: When a drug addict gets a fix so they don't go through withdrawals. For example, "I shot Dopey a 'Moco,' and he is getting well."

Ghetto Superstar: A gangster of notable recognition and profound respect, even among their adversaries. For example, "Hustla is a ghetto superstar. His name rings bells, homeboy."

Ghost: A member or associate of the "Mexican Mafia" whose gang affiliation is unknown to those around them. For example, "Casper is a ghost. The 'Camarada' likes to stay in the shadows."

Give A Blessing: When a "Shot Caller" delivers this encoded "Carnival Talk" message, it means to take someone's life. For example, "Give Diablo a blessing for me."

Give A Ducat To The Chapel: When a "Shot Caller" delivers this encoded "Carnival Talk" message, it means to take someone's life. For example, "Give Demon a ducat to the chapel."

Give A Pass: When a gang member chooses not to harm or attack another person despite having the capability to do so. For example, "Snoopy never paid that gambling debt. I'm going to give a pass on that because we go way back."

Give A Ride: When a "Shot Caller" delivers this encoded "Carnival Talk" message, it means to take someone's life. For example, "Give Mustang a ride for me."

Give A Tray Away: When a convict isn't going to eat any "State Food," sometimes they will go to the "Chow Hall" anyway to give the food to their comrade. For example, "I'm not going to eat tonight, but I'm still going to the chow hall to give a tray away."

Give An Early Parole: When a "Shot Caller" delivers this encoded "Carnival Talk" message, it means to take someone's life. For example, "Give an early parole to Big Bird."

Give My Regards: When a "Shot Caller" delivers this encoded "Carnival Talk" message, it means to take someone's life. For example, "Give my regards to Broadway."

Give That Jersey Back: When a "25" member wants to renounce his affiliation. For example, "If you want to leave, you got to give that jersey back."

Gives Up The House: When an officer avoids saying "no" to inmates because they are afraid of a confrontation. For example, "Officer Lopez is a punk because he gives up the house to the inmates."

Giving Up Game: To reveal the secret workings of the criminal underworld. For example, "Scarecrow, I heard you talking to that officer about how we make 'Pruno.' Why are you giving up game, homeboy?"

Gladiator: A young inmate who is determined to establish a reputation for himself by taking on every available "Mission" to assault others.

Gladiator Days: Between 1989 and 1994, it is alleged that officers at Corcoran State Prison orchestrated confrontations between rival gang members in the Security Housing Unit (SHU). During this period, seven inmates were fatally shot, and 43 others sustained severe injuries due to officers discharging their firearms.

Gladiator Dome: The nickname for Corcoran prison where they had the "Gladiator Fights" from 1989-1994.

Gladiator Fights: Between 1989 and 1994, it is alleged that officers at Corcoran State Prison orchestrated confrontations between rival gang members in the "Security Housing Unit." During this period, seven inmates were fatally shot, and 43 others sustained severe injuries due to officers discharging firearms.

Gladiator School: This is the nickname for the prison Duel Vocational Institution. This prison has a storied history in the California Department of Corrections and Rehabilitation. It was shut down on September 30, 2021.

Gladiator School: This moniker attributed to the "California Youth Authority" stems from young individuals being sent there and frequently engaging in ongoing conflicts with their rivals.

Go Between: This person helps their homie who is "Fishing" a long distance down a tier. They will pull the "Fishing Line" into their cell and then shoot it down the tier to help it get to its intended destination.

Go Chest: This is when two inmates will fight each other, but they will only hit each other in the chest. For example, "I'm about to go chest with that fool."

Go For What You Know: It means to handle your business like a "Soldier." For example, "Bolo, when it 'Jumps Off' tonight, go for what you know, comrade."

Go The Distance: When a convict feels so strongly about an issue that he is willing to fight to the death. For example, "Mack was tripping over my dirty socks in the cell. He was ready to go the distance over it."

Go Through: A cover for a knife that prevents the metal detector from pinging on it. For example, "Homie, I got the go through, so I won't have any problems getting the 'Banger' to the homie."

Go To The Elbow: This means to use intravenous drugs. For example, "Have you ever gone to the elbow?"

Go To The Neck With It: This means to put something in your mouth. For example, "I am so hungry I am going to the neck with that sandwich."

Go Up: When things get violent. For example, "I was young and reckless. I believed it had to go up for anything and everything. I was looking for a reason to 'Take Off' on someone."

God Complex: This is an attitude some senior correctional officers get when they have several years in the department and get all of the best positions. Officers select jobs based on their seniority, so they take all of the good jobs with favorable days off. In my experience, the more years an officer has in the department, the worse their attitude is.

Going Out Backwards: When an inmate can't take the pressure on a prison yard and tells the officers they need "Protective Custody." For example, "I am never going out backwards. They are going to have to stab me off of this yard."

Going Out Bad: When an inmate can't take the pressure on a prison yard and tells the officers they need "Protective Custody." For example, "I am never going out bad. They are going to have to take me off of this yard feet first before that ever happens."

Going Up: When things get violent. For example, "If you tell the homies what happened, you know it's going up. They won't let that slide."

Good Con: This is short for good convict, and it simply means a man in prison who carries himself with honor and respect. For example, "I like you, comrade. You're a good con."

Good Earner: A convict who makes good money for their "Faction" by various means. For example, "Felony is a good earner. He has the ear on the 'Big Homie.'"

Good Guy Chrono: This is the CDCR form "128-B" given to an inmate who completes a program or does something worthy of recognition. A Good Guy Chrono goes into the inmate's "C-File." A Good Guy Chrono is also called a "Laudatory Chrono."

Good Looking Out: The preferred way to say "thank you" in prison. For example, "Good looking out on that soup, homie."

Good Standing: This means a convict has no issues he needs to "Clean Up."

Good Time: Good time credits are awarded to inmates who remain disciplinary-free.

Goofy: A good-for-nothing person who doesn't get any respect in prison. For example, "Bulldog is a goofy. He gets no respect from the homies."

Goon Squad: The Goon Squad is similar to the detectives of the prison, and they investigate inmates and officers alike for alleged nefarious activities. Their uniforms have distinct black patches that set them apart from regular officers.

Gooner: A correctional officer who is a member of the "Goon

Squad."

Got A Ticket: This is when a convict receives a transfer to another prison. For example, "Speedy just got a ticket to Calipatria."

Got At: This indicates that you have recently had a conversation with someone. For example, "I just got at Bandit about that issue we are having with him. He said he will handle it."

Got At Him On Paper: This implies that you've communicated a specific matter by sending a "Kite" to someone. For example, "I got at him on paper about that issue we had. He said he will handle it."

Got At Me Foul: When someone comes at you "Sideways" and disrespects you. For example, "Looney got at me foul, so I 'Took Off' on him."

Got Beaters: Someone who can fight well. For example, "Shrek got beaters. Don't play with him, little homie."

Got Down: When inmates get into a fight. For example, "Me and Ray Ray went into his cell and got down. I hit him so hard his ancestors felt it."

Got Hands: Someone who can fight well. For example, "Mad Mike got hands."

Got His Ticket: When a convict gets transferred to another prison or program. For example, "Crazy Rick got his ticket to High Desert."

Got His Wings Back: When a convict who was once in "Bad Standing" does a "Clean Up" or pays a fine to get in "Good Standing." For example, "Chino got his wings back."

Got In His Feelings: When someone gets angry over something you said or did. For example, "Snoop got in his feelings because I disrespected him."

Got It Cracking: To attack another person without hesitation. For example, "My cellie was with the business. He didn't leave me on the tier hanging. He got it cracking with the 'Peckerwoods.'"

Got Made: When a convict gets promoted to be a "Big Homie" of his gang. For example, "Risky just got made. He told me he has big plans for our crew."

Got Mitts: Someone who can fight well. For example, "Big Rob got mitts. I saw the homie sleep lots of dudes at county."

Got More Nerve Than A Toothache: To express or engage in behavior significantly beyond acceptable norms or boundaries. For example, "You got more nerve than a toothache, homeboy. Go 'Rest Your Neck.'"

Got Your Back Like A Bra Strap: This means you will always be there for your homies. For example, "You really came through for me, homeboy. I got your back like a bra strap."

Government Assigned Quarters: Some inmates refuse to refer to their cell as a house, cell, or where they live. They call it their government assigned quarters. I vividly recall one night as a "Fish" on the Level IV Yard at Centinela Prison during "Dayroom Recall." I told an inmate, "Take It Home," and he replied, "My home is in Compton; this cell isn't my home." His reply left me speechless as I stood there and thought about it. From that night forward, I stopped telling inmates to take it home, and I started saying, "Lock It Up."

GP: The "General Population" of convicts who have minimal restrictions placed on their activities and privileges as opposed to inmates in the "SHU" or "Hole."

Grand Slam: The highly coveted Sunday breakfast tray, which consists of eggs, potatoes, sausage, and bacon.

Gravy Train: This breakfast years ago consisted of gravy with small pieces of meat and some toast. These days, it doesn't even come with bread or real meat, but some soy product.

Grease The Tracks: The term convicts use when they grease their anus with a lubricant so the "Banger" will enter more readily. For example, "You are gonna have to grease the tracks if you are going to want to 'Hoop' that 'Piece.'"

Green Light: When a "Shot Caller" in a prison gang orders his "Soldiers" to assault or kill somebody. These inmates, "Put In The Hat," are usually put on a "List" that is "Hooped" and then transported from prison to prison.

Green Light Gang: An entire gang that the "Mexican Mafia" puts a "Green Light" on. This means that if any "Southerner" comes across a member of these gangs on the streets or in prison, they have permission to attack them.

Green Light Yard: This is another term for a "Sensitive Needs Yard." Sensitive needs yards are the majority of yards in CDCR now. These yards are considered "No Good" by the "General Population" convicts. Most inmates on "SNY" yards are there for drug or gambling debts. SNY yards tend to be more chaotic and violent than the "Mainline" because the gang structure is less rigid than the general population gangs.

Green Wall Gang: Alleged groups of officers at California State Prisons who carry themselves like gangsters. These groups of officers are accused of lying on official reports and planting evidence to frame inmates, among other nefarious activities.

Greet The Bus: It is alleged that officers at Corcoran State Prison in the 1990s would have shackled inmates who just exited the "Grey Goose" stand and face the bus. The inmates would then be told what is expected of them at Corcoran, and the officers would beat some.

Greenlighted: This is when a "Shot Caller" gives a "Green Light" for their "Soldiers" to assault or kill somebody. This "List" is "Hooped" and then transported from prison to prison.

Grey Goose: The nickname for the bus that transports convicts between prisons in the California Prison System.

Greyhound: The nickname for the bus that transports convicts between prisons in the California Prison System.

Greystone Chapel: The iconic "Chapel" at Folsom Prison. Each granite stone used to construct the Greystone Chapel was cut by hand.

Grill Gate: The innermost locking bar door in a "Housing Unit" at Centinela Prison that leads to the main door and then to the prison yard. When an officer uses the restroom in a housing unit, which is located in the "Sally Port" between the grill gate and the outside door, the "Control Booth Officer" will lock the grill gate so no inmates can enter. Shower stalls in the "Hole" and Level IV Yards have a grill gate that must be locked when occupied by an inmate.

Groceries: A term used to describe various items from the "Canteen." For example, "Hey Colorado, I just got some groceries from the canteen."

Grooming Standards: Guidelines for personal grooming that all inmates must follow. For example, an inmate's hair and facial hair must be clean and neatly styled. Inmate grooming standards are found in the "Title 15" in section 3062.

Ground Work: Doing criminal activity for your gang. For example, murder, robbery, assaults, etc.

Group Up: When inmates in prison group up by race in anticipation of a riot. Seeing an entire Level III or Level IV prison yard group up is an eerie scene. The "Tension" is so thick you could cut it with a "Tomahawk."

Group Yard: When inmates in "ASU" or the "SHU" get placed in a small concrete exercise yard with other inmates.

Groups: Inmates engage in various self-help groups to improve themselves. Some of these groups are AA (Alcoholics Anonymous) and NA (Narcotics Anonymous). These groups provide a community of support for the inmates as they journey through recovery.

Guard One Security Check: This is a required twice-hourly electronic security check done in "Administrative Segregation" units. These security checks became required in the California Department of Corrections and Rehabilitation in 2014. The officer must go in front of each cell and wave a Guard One wand next to a device that logs what time the officer was there. The officer then must press a button on another device describing what the inmate in the cell is doing. Because of the officers' twice-hourly checks done around the clock, some inmates complain that they can't sleep.

Guidelines: The rules and regulations of a prison gang that all of its members must follow. The guidelines are also referred to as "Household Policies," "Household Rules," "Bible," or "Code Of

Conduct."

Gun Coverage: When a correctional officer is watching inmates on the yard with a Mini-14 and other less lethal weapons such as a 40mm block gun. Gun Coverage usually refers to Level IV yards, or yards in the "Hole," "SHU," or "Adjustment Center."

Gun Tower: In each yard, a designated "Tower" houses an officer overseeing inmates outside their respective "Housing Units." This officer uses the public address system to summon inmates to the yard or for appointments as necessary. In the event of an emergency, the tower officer will instruct inmates to take cover by shouting, "Get Down." Additionally, a "Mini-14" rifle is present in the tower, intended solely to protect lives during violent assault.

Gunner: A correctional officer watching the convicts with a Mini-14 223 rifle and other less lethal weapons.

Gunner: An inmate who likes to masturbate while watching female correctional officers or "Free Staff." For example, "Cuete is a gunner. He is 'No Good.'"

Gunning: An inmate masturbating while watching female correctional officers or "Free Staff."

Gunslinger: An inmate who likes to masturbate while watching female correctional officers or "Free Staff." For example, "Cowboy is a gunslinger. He has no respect."

Gym: An inmate living area in most newer prisons that used to be an actual gym. Due to overcrowding, they shut down the gym and used it to hold 100 inmates at many prisons. These days, they are returning to using it as a gym instead of a "Dorm."

H

Habeas Corpus: A legal procedure that requires a person under arrest to be physically brought into court or before a judge.

Hack: An old-school term for a correctional officer.

Had It Coming: When a person gets what they deserve. For example, "Bugs just got 'Smashed.' He had it coming."

Had The Keys: This means a person was the "Shot Caller" for their "Faction." For example, "Lockpick had the keys when I was on Bravo Yard at Calipat."

Had The Pad: This means a person was the "Shot Caller" for their "Faction." For example, "Scratch had the pad when I was in five block at Centinela."

Had The Spot: This means a person was the "Shot Caller" for their "Faction." For example, "C-Dog had the spot when I was at Folsom."

Half-Time: Half-time credits are awarded to inmates who remain disciplinary-free.

Halfway: When a "Floor Officer" in a "Housing Unit" wants to use the restroom, they will tell the "Control Booth Officer," "I'm going halfway." Halfway refers to the staff restroom being halfway between the "Grill Gate" and the back door in the "Sally Port." Floor officers will also raise one arm at an angle in front of their chest, like half of an X, to let the control booth officer know they are going halfway.

Hall Of Shame: In the "L.A. County Jail" in the gang module, the homies had what they call a hall of shame. When a girl they have been talking to messes up, they throw her picture in a big pile with her name, phone number, and address. They also write on the back of the picture what the girl will do for you in jail. Some homies have met their wives from the hall of shame. Of course, they never told the woman how they got her "Hook Up."

Hammer: An inmate-manufactured weapon made of metal, melted plastic, or any other hard material that can be sharpened to a point.

Hand Raised: When a convict is ready and willing to go on a "Mission" and to "Put In Work" for the "Cause." For example, "In prison, I kept my hand raised because I was trying to make a name for myself."

Hand Shook & Your Money Took: This means a person is known for manipulating and taking advantage of people. For example, "Watch out for Sneaky. You will get your hand shook, and your money took."

Handing Out Wolf Tickets: To speak aggressively to someone without intending to back it up with violence. For example, "Fangs was handing out wolf tickets, so I let him have it."

Handing Out Woof Tickets: To speak aggressively to someone without intending to back it up with violence. For example, "Stutter was handing out woof tickets, so I let him have it."

Handle It: If there is a personal problem or issue, handle it. For example, "Joker came at you sideways? Why are you telling me? Handle it."

Handle Your Business & Everyone Won't Get In Your Business: If a "Faction" in prison disciplines their members for "Stepping On Toes" of members of other cars, they won't have issues. If a faction doesn't keep their people in line, other cars will retaliate for the disrespect, and this will cause riots. If factions police their own, there will be relative peace among other groups.

Handle Your Scandal: This is what you tell a person talking to you about what they will do in a particular situation. For example, "Sounds good. Handle your scandal, comrade."

Hands Off: When a "Shot Caller" issues a directive stating that a specific person or group of individuals will not be targeted for attack.

Hands-On: This describes a person unafraid to get physical with others. For example, "Officer Jones is hands-on, and the convicts respect him for that."

Hands On: To put your hands on another person in an aggressive manner. For example, "Trigger came at me 'Sideways,' so I put hands on him."

Hang A Jacket: To spread false or damaging information about another person. This is usually done when "Politicking" against someone. For example, "Those fools are trying to hang a jacket on the homie."

Hang Around: A person who hangs around gangs and even does things of a criminal nature with them, but they aren't a bonafide member.

Hang Up The Gloves: When a person retires from gang life. For example, "I had to hang up the gloves once I realized there is no future in the gang life."

Happy Cards: These are greeting cards sent to inmates that are laced with drugs. These cards will have sections soaked in drugs that can be ingested to get high.

Hard 19: A term used to describe the situation where an inmate is ineligible to be assigned to a prison yard below level II. The 19 refers to the inmate's "Points," and to be designated to a level 1 prison yard, their total points must not exceed 18. This condition is also known as a "P Code."

Hard 36: This term denotes a situation where an inmate is not eligible to be assigned to a prison yard below Level III. The 36 refers to the inmate's "Points." In order to be designated to a Level II prison yard, the inmate's total points must not exceed 35.

Hard & Soft Count: When doing "Burpees" in prison, there are two counts while performing this exercise. The soft count is the movements within the set, and the hard count is the number of burpees performed. When two comrades are doing burpees together, one will yell out the soft count, and the other will yell out the hard count until they have finished.

Hard As A Rock & Twice As Solid: A saying to describe a convict who is quick to "Put In Work." For example, "Diamond is hard as a rock and twice as solid."

Hard Candy: When a person has a "Green Light" on them and they are going to get "Booked." This phrase is rumored to have started because the "Banger" looks like a candy bar when it is removed from the convict's anal cavity.

Hard Case: This is an inmate who is always causing problems and doing whatever they want, regardless of the consequences. For example, "Anvil is a hard case."

Hard Chequeada: This is when an inmate has violated the "Reglas" of his gang, and for punishment, his homies will assault him for 13 seconds. Face shots are allowed during a hard chequeada. For example, "When Chuco gets to the 'Back,' the homies will give him a hard chequeada."

Hard Move: This term refers to a situation in which an inmate assaults another person using weapons intending to "Take His Wind." For example, "Lazy is going to get his issue today, and it's going to be a hard move."

Hard On The Yard: This means difficult issues are going on in a given situation. For example, "It's hard on the yard, comrade; my old lady isn't accepting my phone calls anymore."

Hardcoring: An inmate always acting hardcore and ready to fight over situations where they think they were disrespected. For example, "Crazy Ray is hardcoring. He is doing way too much. He needs to take a little off that."

Hardline: When a gangster goes to the extreme in gang banging or other issues. For example, "Woody pushes a hardline."

Hardline Presser: When a gang member goes to the extreme in gang banging or other issues. For example, "Killer Mike was a hardline presser."

Hardliner: When a gangster goes to the extreme in gang banging or other issues. For example, "Sporty is a hardliner. He is 'Kicking Up Dust.'"

Hard-Timer: A term used to describe an inmate who, due to the challenges and stress of being incarcerated, begins to behave in ways that are unusual or uncharacteristic. Common triggers for becoming a hard-timer include issues with a girlfriend or wife, legal battles, family illnesses, or receiving a lengthy prison sentence. For example, "Sad Boy is a hard-timer because his old lady left him for his homie on the streets."

Hard Timing: A term used to describe an inmate who, due to the challenges and stress of being incarcerated, begins to behave in ways that are unusual or uncharacteristic. Common triggers for becoming a hard-timer include issues with a girlfriend or wife, legal battles, family illnesses, or receiving a lengthy prison sentence. For example, "Check this out, homie; stop hard timing and focus on doing your time. Don't worry about the time they just gave you; it will fly by fast."

Has The Keys: This means a person was the "Shot Caller" for their "Faction." For example, "Who is running this yard?" The answer is, "Buzzard has the keys."

Have Coming: Something the "Title 15" says an inmate has coming to them every day. These things are nonnegotiable; if an inmate doesn't get them, they will demand them immediately. For example, "Yo CO, I didn't get my 'Worker Shower' today. I want it now! I want what I have coming!"

HDSP: High Desert State Prison.

He Has To Go: This means a person needs to be "Removed" from the prison yard. For example, "Sniper messed up; he has to go."

He Took It Right To The Butt: This describes someone who gets emotional about a situation. For example, "I told the homie I didn't want to move in the cell with him, and he took it right to the butt."

He Wants Problems: When someone doesn't like someone else, they will push an issue to provoke a physical altercation. For example, "Cavemen wants problems because he is always 'Mad Dogging.'"

He's Busting My Ear: This expression is used to describe a situation in which one person becomes irritated or angry due to something another person says. For example, "He's busting my ear, blood.

He keeps saying cuz whenever he talks around me."

He's Got An Issue Coming: This means an inmate has done something that his "Faction" believes warrants a "DP." For example, "Redwood played with the wrong person. He's got an issue coming."

Head Up: When a person treats an adversary respectfully and gives them a fair fight. For example, "I will give you a head up, homie. What you wanna do?"

Heading For A Wreck: When a person's bad behavior is going to land them in serious trouble. For example, an inmate is late for lockup, so you tell him, "You're heading for a wreck, Sleepy."

Headquarters: The prison, yard, or building where the "Shot Callers" live. For example, "Pelican Bay used to be the headquarters for the 'Big Homies.'"

Heart Check: To test a person to verify if they will fight when confronted or back down like a "Punk." Many people can put up a good "Front," but very few will stand their ground without showing fear when confronted with a violent beating by numerous gangsters. A heart check separates the men from the boys and silences somebody who constantly "Sells Wolf Tickets."

Heart Pumps Kool-Aid: A "Lame" who consistently avoids confrontation when tensions escalate. For example, "Don't trip off that punk. His heart pumps Kool-Aid."

Heat: An inmate-manufactured weapon made of metal, melted plastic, or any other hard material that can be sharpened to a point.

Heat Meds: There are certain medications that inmates take in prison with heat warnings. When the temperature reaches a certain limit at the prison, an announcement is made over the intercom warning inmates about those conditions. For example, when the temperature gets above 90 degrees, the officer will say over the intercom, "90-degree heat warning is in effect." Heat meds are officially referred to as "Triple-CMS."

Heat To The Pad: When an inmate brings attention to himself by disrespectful behavior, which compels an officer to do a cell search. For example, "Check this out, homie, you need to stop being a 'Rebel' and bringing heat to the pad."

Heat To Your House: When an inmate brings attention to himself by disrespectful behavior, which compels an officer to do a cell search. For example, "You need to talk to your 'Cellie' because he keeps bringing heat to your house."

Heat Warning: There are certain medications that inmates take in prison with heat warnings. When the temperature reaches a certain limit at the prison, an announcement is made over the intercom warning inmates about those conditions. For example, when the temperature gets above 90 degrees, the officer will say over the intercom, "90-degree heat warning is in effect." Heat meds are officially referred to as "Triple-CMS."

Heat Wave: When officers at a prison are doing too much and annoying the inmates. For example, "You know after an officer gets assaulted, there will be a heat wave for a few days."

Heavies: A well-respected convict who is known for "Pushing A Hardline," and he isn't afraid to get his knife and make fools "Pay In Blood" for being "Out Of Pocket."

Heavy Hitter: A well-respected convict who is known for "Pushing A Hardline," and he isn't afraid to get his knife and make fools "Pay In Blood" for being "Out Of Pocket."

Heavy Hitter: This refers to the leader of a prison gang or "Car" who wields significant influence over his comrades. If an officer has a persistent problem with a convict, they usually talk to the heavy hitter to resolve it. Heavy hitters in prison help keep things in order, and I have asked them numerous times to put their homies in check before they got into a "Wreck." The following is an example of me talking to a heavy hitter to resolve an issue on a level III "Mainline" yard. I was searching an inmate's cell and found a bag of "Pruno" cooking, so I placed it outside the cell while I finished what I was doing. When I exited the cell a few minutes later, I noticed the pruno was gone. I immediately talked to the "Crip," heavy hitter nicknamed Ant. I told him, "If that bag of pruno isn't at the 'Officer's Podium' in 10 minutes, I'm going to 'Hit Your House.'" Ant calmly strolled away from me and motioned for another Crip to come to him. Ant talked to him, and the other Crip walked to a 55-gallon trash can, got the bag of pruno from the bottom, and handed it over to me with a smile on his face.

Heavyweight: The leader of a prison gang or "Car" who wields significant influence over his comrades. If an officer has a persistent problem with a convict, they will usually talk to the heavyweight to resolve it. Heavyweights in prison help keep things in order, and I have asked them numerous times to put their homies in check before they get into a "Wreck."

Held Over: When a correctional officer is ordered to stay for another shift because no other officers will voluntarily work a vacant post. There is no choice in the matter; they will be severely punished if they refuse to work after being held over. Sometimes, after our shift, the prison gates would be locked until an officer was assigned to work a vacant position. They decide who will be held over by our seniority number in reverse order, so the "Fish" cops were always "Ordered Over."

Held The Line: When an inmate doesn't bow down to any pressure and earns the respect of his comrades. For example, "Shadow was rushed by eight 'Peckerwoods,' and he held the line."

Hermano: The name for a member of the "Nuestra Raza."

Hiding Behind The Bible: This is said to an inmate whose peers believe he is hiding behind the Bible. Maybe an inmate suddenly wants to be a Christian in prison, and other people think they joined the Christian "Car" because they feared "Prison Politics." The skeptical observers will scrutinize every move of the professed Christian, and if they see him gamble or drink "Pruno," they will say, "See, you're hiding behind the Bible. You aren't a Christian; you are just scared."

Hiding Behind The Feather: This is said about an inmate whose peers believe he is hiding in the Native American "Car." For example, an inmate who is only part Native American suddenly wants to run with them when previously they didn't associate with them.

High Drama State Prison: A common nickname for High Desert State Prison.

High Power: A high-level security area of the Los Angeles County Jail.

High Power: An inmate always acting hardcore and ready to fight over situations where they think somebody disrespected them. For example, "Malo thinks he is all high power with his bad attitude."

High Power: The leaders of a prison gang or "Car" who wield significant influence over their "Faction." For example, "Bruiser came to my door and told me, 'I need you to pass this 'Filter' to the homies. It's coming from Corcoran; it's coming from the high power."

High Power Hour: An inmate always acting hardcore and ready to fight over situations where they think somebody disrespected them. For example, "High-Top thinks he is all high power hour with his bad attitude."

High Power Module: A "Pod" in L.A. County Jail that houses the "Heavyweight" convicts from various gangs.

High Side: To disrespect another inmate. For example, "Did you see Stretch high side Shorty? He took it like a punk."

His Hand Stays Raised: A convict who is always "On Deck" to go on a "Mission" because they lust for blood and power. For example, "Hatchet is pushing a 'Hardline,' his hand stays raised."

His Voice Is Heard: This describes a convict who honors his word and handles himself respectfully. He will handle his business when it's time to kick things off. For example, "Yeah, I have heard of Mouth. He is well-respected, and his voice is heard."

Hit: To arrive at a prison after being assigned there. For example, "If you have 'Bad Paperwork' anywhere you hit, you are 'No Good.'"

Hit: When a convict gets drugs regularly from a visitor, "Free Staff," package, mail, or corrections officer. For example, "Slugger is going to hit this weekend during his visit."

Hit A Couple Laps: You say this to someone in prison when you want to talk with them privately as you walk around the cement track. For example, "Greyhound, let's hit a couple of laps, homie."

Hit A Lap with Me: An inmate will say this to another person when he wants to talk privately. For example, "Bats, hit a lap with me, big dog."

Hit A Lick: When a person is going to do something, usually of an illegal nature, to gain money or material items. For example, "Homie, do you want to hit a lick with me during yard tonight?"

Hit A Lick: When an inmate masturbates in his cell, usually with his "Fifi." For example, "I need some 'Cell Time' homie, I'm gonna hit a lick."

Hit & Miss: A hidden message exchanged among prisoners involves using urine to write on paper, which becomes visible only when a flame is held behind the paper.

Hit Drill: Some "Factions" in prison conduct drills among their members whereby they practice attacking another person. For example, gang members will post up in their assigned areas on the yard or "Building," and the "Bombers" will make their move and simulate an attack on their victim. Most of the time, the victim in this drill will be one of their members who knows it's just training. However, sometimes, during these drills, they will test one of their homies to see if he is aware and able to detect the attack on him before it happens.

Hit Him With The Razor: An order in prison that means to slice someone in their neck or face with a "Tomahawk." For example, "Bandit stole from the 'Kitty,' you need to hit him with the razor."

Hit List: Every prison gang has a ledger of "No Good" former members who will be "Poked" whenever the opportunity becomes available. Every prison will have a copy of this list, and it is usually kept in the "Hole." These lists are very extensive and can have hundreds of names on them. The hit list is usually "Hooped" for safekeeping.

Hit My Pad: When officers search an inmate's cell. For example, "The cops hit my pad, and they found my 'Banger' in my shoe."

Hit The Yard: To "Drive Up" to a prison after being assigned there. For example, "Dopey just hit the yard, and the 'Lame' already is in debt with a needle hanging out of his arm."

Hit The Wall: This means to talk through a hole in your cell wall to your neighbor. In the "SHU" at Corcoran Prison, there is a small hole in the wall for the television cables used to communicate with your neighbor in the adjacent cell. For example, "I hit the wall and got at my neighbor. It was Sleepy from Orange County."

Hit That Button: This refers to an inmate who has succumbed to pressure or intimidation and "Checks-In" to "Protective Custody." For example, "Rooster hit that button when he found out he was going to get 'Checked' by the homies."

Hit Your House: This is when an officer does a "Cell" search. For example, "Check this out, Coco, if you are late for 'Lockup' again, I'm going to hit your house."

Hitter: A convict sent on a "Mission" to "Remove" or "Discipline" other people. For example, "Bam Bam is the hitter for the 'Woods.'"

Hitter: The convict bringing drugs or other "Contraband" into prison.

Hitting: When a convict gets drugs regularly from a visitor, "Free Staff," package, mail, or corrections officer. For example, "Boxer has been hitting the last two weeks during visits."

Hitting Up: To aggressively question another person about their gang affiliation. For example, "Who do you 'Run With' homie?"

Hitting Up: To confront another person verbally or physically.

Hobby: Hobby refers to distinctive creations made by inmates. Essentially, they are arts and crafts items that inmates create. Currently, in California prisons with hobby access, inmates order items from a catalog such as cardstock, canvas, paint, beads, acrylics, watercolors, and many other supplies.

Hobby Craft: Many years ago, in California prisons, this was the particular craft that an inmate engaged in. These crafts encompassed activities like leatherwork, woodwork, jewelry making, silk screening, ceramics, and creating stained glass windows. Inmates would then sell the items they crafted in prison gift shops. Currently, in California prisons with hobby access, inmates order items from a catalog such as cardstock, canvas, paint, beads, acrylics, watercolors, and many other supplies.

Hobby Draw: This is the amount of money allowed for the inmates to purchase for their "Hobby Craft."

Hobby Shop: In the past, some prisons offered hobby shops with distinct sections dedicated to various creative pursuits such as leatherworking, woodworking, jewelry crafting, silk screening, ceramics, and the creation of stained glass windows. Inmates were tasked with procuring their materials for these endeavors. Upon completing their projects, they could showcase them in the prison's external gift shop and retain the proceeds. Some inmates generated several thousand dollars by selling their handcrafted items under the banner of "Hobby" within the prison environment. Currently, in California prisons with hobby access, inmates order items from a catalog such as cardstock, canvas, paint, beads, acrylics, watercolors, and many other supplies.

Hobby Store: In the past, incarcerated individuals could vend their crafted "Hobby" items at the hobby store within the prison. Remarkably, certain inmates managed to generate thousands of dollars annually by selling their hobby creations.

Hoe Stroll: This refers to the streets of a less reputable area where prostitutes stroll to engage in their solicitation activities.

Hogs, Frogs, & Pollywogs: This refers to the three types of people in prison. The hogs are the "Shot Callers," the frogs are the soldiers, and the pollywogs are the "Riff Raff."

Hold Your Mud: The act of refraining from providing information or cooperating during an investigation, even when faced with significant pressure and the threat of severe punishment. This entails not divulging information to law enforcement, even if it results in extended prison time due to not revealing information about a "Crimey." This term can also apply to officers who refuse to inform on their fellow officers, even when faced with the prospect of "Adverse Action," which could potentially lead to job loss.

Holding Cage: A confined space resembling a phone booth where inmates are placed temporarily. These cages resemble traditional phone booths but feature mesh wire walls. Essentially, they function as individual holding cells designed for short-term use.

Holding Court: The situation where "Shot Callers" gather to discuss "Prison Politics." This refers to instances when a shot caller convenes with fellow gang members to talk shop.

Hole: This is where inmates are sent for breaking the rules in prison. Basically, the hole is a jail within a prison. The inmates are in their cells for 23 hours a day. They have limited personal items due to security reasons. The inmates are allowed a shower once every three days. They can exercise on a small yard behind the "Housing Unit" with "Gun Coverage."

Hole Birthday Card: Gang members have a tradition of crafting personalized birthday cards for fellow members whose birthdays occur while in the "Hole." All the members sign these cards and include lighthearted comments to lighten the mood.

Holiday Relief: A position usually held by a "Fish" officer where they work different posts to cover other officers on holidays. I learned a lot doing this, but building a good "Rapport" with convicts was impossible when I only supervised them for a day at a time.

Holiday Spread: A unique community meal on holidays that everyone in the "Car" contributes to. When the food is finished cooking, everyone eats together, like a park barbecue. These holidays include Christmas, Thanksgiving, Super Bowl, Cinco De Mayo, Mexican Independence Day, and New Year's Day.

Home Turf: A gangster's hometown.

Homeboy: This term refers to a gangster from the same hood as another person.

Homeboy Favoritism: This term refers to showing preferential treatment to specific individuals, often at the expense of equally deserving peers. For instance, homeboy favoritism may manifest when someone receives special treatment due to belonging to the same area, being a relative, or making money for the "Big Homies." Homeboy favoritism can lead to resentment within the "Faction."

Homeboy Love: When gang members look out for one another. For example, "Pretty Boy showed me some homeboy love and gave me the 'Hook Up' for his sister."

Homeland: Thousands of CDCR inmates were once forced to do their time in out-of-state prisons in the "COCF." When they talked about the California prisons, they called it the homeland. For example, "Dang homie, these prisons are way better than the ones in the homeland."

Hometown: This term refers to a person from the same city. I am from Long Beach; if I were in prison, I would refer to dudes from Long Beach as Hometown.

Homie: A "Comrade" who has remained true through thick and thin, whether on the streets or in prison.

Homie Hook-Ups: When homeboys do favors for their homies. As officers, we would use this phrase whenever we saw an undeserving officer get a good job. We would say he got a homie hook-up from the sergeant or lieutenant.

Homies: This is another term for "Southerners." For example, "The homies run the 'CDCR.'"

Honor Building: This is a building where the convicts agree to a strict policy of not participating in any illegal activities. They agree to attend self-help groups and other programs and maintain a clean disciplinary record. If they break their agreement, they will be removed from the building. One Honor Building, which I was told about in the California Department of Corrections and Rehabilitation, features couches and gaming consoles in the dayroom for inmates to use.

Honor Yard: This is a yard where the convicts agree to a strict policy of not participating in any illegal activities. They agree to attend self-help groups and other programs and maintain a clean disciplinary record. If they break their agreement, they will be removed from the yard. The Honor Yard is also known as the "Progressive Programming Facility."

Hooch: A fermented alcoholic beverage that can be produced by blending various ingredients, including apples, oranges, fruit cocktails, ketchup, and sugar. The mixture is then cooked in a plastic garbage bag for three days to facilitate fermentation. Hooch possesses a disgusting taste and odor, and its color varies depending on the type of fruit used, ranging from red to orange. In correctional facilities, a single cup of hooch is typically sold for $8.00, while a cup of the more potent "White Lightening" commands a price of $20.00.

Hook-Up: The hook-up is the information needed to contact another person. For example, "Hey homie, give me your sister's hook-up so I can get some letters."

Hook-Up: The act of giving advice or material items to a comrade in need.

Hooked-Up: Inmates who belong to prison gangs. For example, "Monk hooked-up with the 'Black Guerilla Family' at San Quentin."

Hook-Up On Game: When an older convict gives advice to a young "First Termer" to help him navigate the treacherous waters of the penal system. This process helps the youngster stay away from trouble and getting into a "Wreck." It also includes how to make a knife. The "Big Homie" will tell the "Fish" to make a knife, and then he will grade it. If the knife isn't good enough, he will have him make it again. He will also teach him how to make a "Bomb" to melt plastic for a knife if he has no metal. He will instruct him on how to defend himself and on various exercises.

Hoop: When a convict places items of "Contraband" in his rectum to avoid discovery by officers. Some convicts become very proficient at this and can do it in seconds. When a "Banger" is placed inside of the "Prison Safe," it will have a protective layer of cellophane to prevent his insides from being perforated.

Hooped: When a convict places items of "Contraband" in his rectum to avoid discovery by officers. Some convicts become very proficient at this and can do it in seconds. When a "Banger" is placed inside of the "Prison Safe," it will have a protective layer of cellophane to prevent his insides from being perforated.

Hooping: When a convict places items of "Contraband" in his rectum to avoid discovery by officers. Some convicts become very proficient at this and can do it in seconds. When a "Banger" is placed inside of the "Prison Safe," it will have a protective layer of cellophane to prevent his insides from being perforated.

HooSane: This term refers to the alliance between the Hoover Criminal Gang and the Insane Crip Gang. This collaboration originated in prison during the 1990s.

Hoover Car: The Hoover "Car" within the prison system consists of inmates affiliated with the Hoover Criminal Gang based in Los Angeles.

Hop On Him: When an individual physically attacks another person with extreme violence. For example, "Krazy Boy came at me 'Sideways,' so I had to hop on him."

Hop On His Head: When a person physically assaults someone else violently. For example, "Wildman came at me 'Sideways,' so I had to hop on his head."

Hop On His Helmet: When an individual physically attacks another person with extreme violence. For example, "Big Nasty stole my honeybuns, so I had to hop on his helmet."

Horn: This is the term used for a phone in prison. For example, "I need to get on the horn and get at my old lady. The homie told me he saw her with Sancho."

Hospital Security Coverage: When an inmate is at a hospital for any length, an officer will be stationed outside their door to secure the area.

Hot Kite: A "Kite" about gang business or one that contains "Contraband."

Hot Message: A "Kite" about gang business or one that contains "Contraband."

Hot Money: This refers to drug debts owed to the "Mexican Mafia." It is crucial to repay these debts promptly and in full. The money owed will be doubled every two weeks. Once the drug debt reaches

$1,000, they will be "Removed."

Hot One: This refers to a murder. For example, "They got me locked up for a hot one."

Hot Pot: A device inmates use to boil water for cooking food.

Hot Shot: When a correctional officer sprays an inmate with pepper spray.

Hot Shot: When gang members wish to eliminate an associate discreetly, they administer a lethal dose of drugs, causing an overdose. This method serves as an effective cover for murder and occurs more frequently than many might realize.

Hotter Than A Popcorn Fart: Describes an inmate who is very upset. For example, "Toro was hotter than a popcorn fart when his old lady didn't show up to visit him today."

House: A convict's "Cell."

House Mouse: This inmate is in everyone's business and knows all the drama. For example, "Snoopy is a house mouse; watch what you say around him."

Household: The people you associate with or the people from your county.

Household Policies: The rules and regulations that govern a particular "Car" in California prisons. Each gang has policies that they adhere to and enforce to varying degrees.

Household Procedures: The policies and procedures that govern a particular "Car" in California prisons. Each gang has policies that they adhere to and enforce to varying degrees.

Household Rules: The rules and regulations that govern a particular "Car" in California prisons. Each gang has different rules they adhere to and enforce to varying degrees.

Housing Codes: The prison administration uses codes to designate if an inmate needs special accommodations for a physical disability or other reasons. They include S: Single Cell Status. R: Sex Offenders. M: Mobility. V: Vision. H: Hearing. W: Wheelchair. DPO: Intermittent wheelchair needs.

Housing Interview: This term refers to when a prison official asks a newly arrived inmate to their facility if they have any enemies and who they run with.

Housing Score: When an inmate goes to a "Reception Center," he is eventually given a housing score, determining his "Security

Level." These security levels range from Level I to Level IV. The inmate's housing score is based on various factors such as their crimes, length of sentence, escape risk, age, and other factors. The housing score that determines the housing security level is: 0-18 Level I, 19-35 Level II, 36-59 Level III, 60+ Level IV.

Housing Security Level: When an inmate goes to a "Reception Center," he is eventually given "Points" determining his housing security level. These security levels range from Level I to Level IV. The inmate's housing security level is based on various factors such as their crimes, length of sentence, escape risk, age, and other factors. The points that determines the housing security level is: 0-18 Level I, 19-35 Level II, 36-59 Level III, 60+ Level IV.

Housing Unit: A prison facility constructed from concrete and steel, featuring a total of 100 cells, each designed to accommodate two inmates, located at Centinela Prison. Each housing unit has four phones, twelve benches, eighteen metal tables, one clothes iron, two sinks, two water fountains, two televisions, and eight showers. Two "Floor Officers" supervise all 200 convicts in the housing unit, and they ensure that all inmates receive their "State Issue" i.e., showers, phone calls, yard, "Dayroom," mail, medical appointments, visits, and meals.

How Long Have You Been Down: The number of years a prisoner has spent incarcerated in prison. For example, "How long have you been down, homie?"

Hoyo: A word that translates to "Hole." This is where inmates are sent for breaking the rules in prison. Basically, the hole is a jail within a prison. The inmates are in their cells for 23 hours a day. They have limited personal items due to security reasons. The inmates are allowed a shower once every three days. They can exercise on a small yard behind the "Housing Unit" with "Gun Coverage." For example, "I took off on that officer after he felt the 'Fierro' in my pocket, and they gave me eighteen months in the hoyo."

Hub & The Dub: In prison, the "Crips" from Compton and Watts are in the same "Car" and ride together. This means they back the play of one another. The Hub refers to Compton, and the Dub stands for Watts.

Huelga: The Huelga is an Aztec design of an eagle and a symbol used by "Nortenos." The Huelga is also a tattoo that some Nortenos get on their bodies for "Putting In Work."

Huffing & Puffing: When a person is highly agitated and speaks rashly or irrationally. For example, "That fool was huffing and puffing about what he would do to me. When I caught him alone, he 'Peed On Himself.'"

Hug & Squeeze: When a "Shot Caller" delivers this encoded "Carnival Talk" message, it means to kill the person. For example, "Hug and squeeze Gumby for me."

Hug-A-Thug: This term describes a situation where lenient or overly accommodating prison administration goes to great lengths to appease inmates without a legitimate need.

Hujambo: This word means hello in Swahili, and some Black inmates use Swahili words in prison to get back to their cultural heritage.

Humble On My Rumble: When a convict has to tone down his actions because he doesn't have a lot of comrades on the prison yard. For example, "I had to be humble on my rumble at Folsom because we were outnumbered 10 to 1."

Hung Up His Gloves: This phrase describes a gang member retiring from their involvement in gang activities, regardless of the reason. For example, "I heard Boxer hung up his gloves."

Hunger Strike: When inmates get together and refuse to eat until the administration addresses their grievances. The Pelican Bay "SHU" inmates had a hunger strike, protesting their being locked down indefinitely. This brought attention to their situation, and they recently had a favorable court decision regarding that issue.

Hustle: This refers to any scheme to obtain money or drugs in prison or on the streets.

Hustling Backwards: Doing something that isn't productive and hurts you at the end of the day. For example, "My take on the gang life is it's watered down, polluted, and hustling backwards. There is no future in it."

Hygiene: The deodorant, toothpaste, mouthwash, lotion, etc., that inmates have. For example, "Comrade, I have lots of hygiene in my locker. What do you need?"

Hype Kit: A hypodermic needle and other supplies used to "Mainline" drugs while in prison.

Hyping Up: To instigate a fight by challenging another homie's manhood. For example, "Playboy, ain't that the cat who disrespected your old lady? Are you going to let him get away with that?"

I

I Don't Want Any Problems: This means you don't want a confrontation, so you choose to avoid conflict. For example, "My bad homie, I will turn my music down. I don't want any problems."

I Fell Down: This phrase refers to being arrested and caught up in the system. For example, "When I fell down and landed on my first Level IV yard, I learned the hardest lessons about prison life."

I Got You: This means you will "Hook Up" whoever you are talking to with something they want or need. For example, "Hey, youngster, you are going to be good. We are all in this together. Just ride through this, and I got you when we get out of the 'Hole.'"

I Need That: This is said when something is important to a gangster. For example, "If I catch you on the streets, you're done! I need that."

Ice Pick: A deadly inmate-manufactured weapon that resembles an ice pick.

IE: This is how the "Peckerwoods" in prison from the Inland Empire abbreviate their city in the tattoos that they get. The IE car is the biggest White "Car" in California prisons.

IE Car: IE stands for Inland Empire, and in prison, the "Crips" from Riverside and San Bernardino are in the same "Car" and ride together.

If It's 50/50, It's 100% All Bad: This is a saying by "Mainline" convicts that means a "50/50 Yard" is a "No Landing Zone."

If The Judge Could See Me Now: A common thing said by convicts when they are living comfortably in prison. If several convicts are in a group smoking weed and drinking "Wine," one of them will most likely say, "If the judge could see me now."

If You Don't Have Life Then Don't Act Like You Do: This means the big homies doing "All Day" run the show in prison. They are never getting out, so they have nothing to lose. If you have a "Date," do your time and try to get home to your family. This also applies to officers; we had a saying in my day that relates to this, "They live here, I'm just here for 8 hours."

If You're In The Mix, You're Going To Get Stirred: This means if you involve yourself in "Prison Politics," there is a price to pay.

If You're Word Is No Good You're No Good: All a man has in prison is his word. Believe it or not, many convicts honor their word at all costs. As an officer, I often looked a convict in his eyes and asked him, "Do I have your word you will do it?" Every time they replied yes, they honored it.

I.G.I.: These are the Institution Gang Investigators who investigate gangs and their particular members.

ILTAGS: Inmate Leisure Time Activity Groups are 12-step recovery programs that assist inmates in living a sober life.

In-House: I always kept things in-house in my housing unit and never "Put Paperwork" on the men there. Whenever I found "Pruno" in their cells, I would display it on the floor next to the "Officer's Podium," and at the end of the evening "Dayroom," I would have my "Porter" empty it down the sink. The convicts would always get a good laugh from this, and one time, the pruno cooking in the large trash bag was about to explode, and a Crip named T-Baby told me, "Superman, you got to 'Burp The Baby.'" Convicts respected that I didn't write them up for stuff like that because it could add time to their sentences. I felt that we should handle things like men between ourselves and move on after we resolve our differences.

In The Hat: This old-school term originates from when gang members in prison would draw pieces of paper out of a hat to determine which would go on the "Mission" to kill their victim.

In The Mix: Someone who is involved in many things on the prison yard and knows who to talk to to resolve things. The poster boy of being in the mix in prison would be the "MAC Rep."

In The Pocket: A term used by convicts for an officer who is a "Mule" bringing "Contraband" into prison. The officer won't enforce the rules because they fear the gang will "Pull Their Covers."

In The Pocket: When a person is close to another person. For example, "Solo and I were in the pocket real tough for a while."

In The Wood: A term used by "Peckerwoods" meaning that another White inmate is in their "Car" and in "Good Standing."

In Violation: This means an inmate has done something that his "Faction" believes warrants a "DP." For example, "Stomper is in violation. He's got an issue coming."

Incident Report: Most "Factions" in prison require their members to write an incident report to the upper management when involved in an altercation or other serious situation.

Incremental Release: When there is "Tension" between "Factions," the administration will gradually release them to see if things will "Kick Off" between the two groups.

Independent Riders: A violent group on the "SNY" prison yards.

Indeterminate Sentence: A prison sentence without a set time. For example, life with the possibility of parole.

Indeterminate SHU Sentence: This was an old policy of the California Department of Corrections and Rehabilitation where once a convict was "Validated" as a prison gang member, they were placed in the "SHU" indefinitely. Some convicts under this policy were in the SHU for decades. In 2011, convicts banded together regardless of race and went on a "Hunger Strike" to protest this policy. Their efforts paid off, and as a result, this CDCR policy has ended.

Indigent: This term refers to an incarcerated individual who has maintained a balance of less than $25 on their "Books" for 30 days. In such cases, the prison authorities typically provide indigent inmates with complimentary stamps and envelopes. These complimentary envelopes are commonly known among inmates as "Welfare Envelopes."

Infiltrators: Another name "Mainline" inmates use to refer to "SNY" inmates.

Infirmary: The prison hospital where sick or injured inmates are housed in "Cells." One officer is assigned to the Infirmary at Centinela Prison. They are in charge of giving showers, "Cell Feeding," doing "Security Checks," and ensuring the safety of the doctors and nurses treating the inmates.

Informal Count: This type of "Count" in prison is when an officer positively identifies inmates under their direct supervision.

Informant: A person who has collaborated or is currently cooperating with the police to provide information about their homies' criminal activities.

Ink Slinger: A convict who is a tattoo artist and his peers will often pay him "Canteen" for his services. There is usually an ink slinger in each "Housing Unit" who always has a "Rig" and ink in his possession.

Inland Empire: The gangs from the Inland Empire are comprised of two different "Cars" in prison: the Riverside car and the San Bernardino car. The Inland Empire car goes by "IE," and the San Bernardino car goes by "Berdoo."

Inmate: An inmate is not a convict, but they are both prisoners. A convict honors their word and runs a clean "Program." An inmate isn't known for doing those things.

Inmate Advisory Council: The Inmate Advisory Council (IAC) is made up of a group of convicts from each race who act as representatives for their constituents. They are the mediators between themselves and the prison administration, intending to ease tensions among the convicts by voicing their concerns to upper management on the yard, such as captains, lieutenants, and sergeants. IAC members are authorized to travel the yard and visit other "Housing Units" as part of their official duties. They carry a blue identification card that gives them access to otherwise off-limits areas. During "Lockdown" periods, IAC members are regularly released from their cells and visit each housing unit to talk to their people and help alleviate the stresses of being confined to their cells for extended periods.

Inmate Lap Dogs: A derogatory term used by convicts to describe other inmates who try to keep the peace between them and correctional officers. They will get special treatment from the officers for the work they do for them, and this can cause tension with other convicts.

Inmate Lover: What officers call another officer who they think does special favors for inmates. For example, "Officer Smith is an inmate lover; he gives them extra phone time whenever they ask."

Inmate Pay Rates: Inmates can make between .08 to .37 cents an hour at prison jobs. The inmate's salary at these pay rates ranges from

$12 to $56 a month. There has been talk of paying inmates in California minimum wage for their jobs in prison.

Inmate Trust Account: This is where an inmate keeps his money to buy things in prison or from approved vendors. Family members can deposit money into an inmate's account, and any money earned from his prison job goes there.

Inner Council: The Inner Council is comprised of four senior members who advise the "NF Generals" and provide a system of checks and balances to them.

Insight: Insight is a comprehensive evaluation of an inmate's childhood traumas, character flaws, unmet needs, behaviors, actions, and thought patterns. Gaining insight is challenging, as it requires overcoming significant defensiveness, resistance, and resentment. Understanding their past is essential for comprehending the reasons behind their actions. Each inmate does insights, which are a crucial document that they hand over to the parole board to show that they are ready to be granted parole.

Institutional Classification Committee: This is the highest level of committee at a prison, and it must have a minimum of three members and is chaired by the Warden or Chief Deputy Warden. Inmates go to this type of committee for various reasons, including bad behavior, eligibility for placement in minimum facilities, and "SHU" term assessment.

Institutional Gang Investigators: These are the gang investigators who document gangs and their particular members at a prison.

Institutionalized: A convict who has been locked down for a long time and accepted prison as a comfortable way of life. Some convicts fear getting out of prison because they are institutionalized and used to being told what to do and taken care of.

Intake: The building or yard where all incoming and outgoing convicts pass through in the prison for processing.

Integrated Yard: These yards started in 2018 and are supposed to be half "General Population" and half "Sensitive Needs Yard."

Integrated Yard Policy: This is the official CDCR policy on how inmates of warring "Factions" in the "SHU" would "Program" on the yard. Before the "Gladiator Fights" at Corcoran State Prison from 1989-1994, the official CDCR policy was to place enemies together on the SHU yard. This idiotic policy, of course, led to untold and unwarranted violence on many levels.

Investigative Employee: This staff member assists an inmate during the investigative process during an "RVR" hearing.

Investigative Services Unit: The Investigative Services Unit is similar to the detectives of the prison. They investigate inmates and officers alike for alleged nefarious activities. They are called the "Goon Squad" or "Black Patches" by officers and inmates.

Iron Pile: The weightlifting area on the prison yard. The weights were removed in 1997 from the "Mainline" (They have weight machines in "Fire Camps") in California prisons. I have heard two reasons why they were removed. The first reason I heard was because the inmates were getting too big and strong, so the administration took them away out of fear. The second reason for removing the weights was that inmates were seriously injured when attacked with dumbbells and bars. As an officer who walked the mainline level III and IV yards for several years, I believe they took them away because officers and administration were getting intimidated by the massive size of the "Swole" convicts. The administration used reason two to justify their fear of the muscle-bound convicts who spent all their free time driving iron on the weight pile. When the weights were removed, the "Yard Crew" loaded the weights onto the back of the trucks. Numerous convicts have stated they were angry at the inmates for helping them remove the weights. I don't know if they were attacked for helping, but it caused tension.

Iron Pit: Weightlifting area on the prison yard.

Ironwierd: A nickname for Ironwood State Prison.

Islander Car: The Islander "Car" is under the umbrella of the "Other" car in prison.

ISP: Ironwood State Prison.

Isolation Units: These are the areas of a prison where inmates are placed for disciplinary, safety, and security issues. These Isolation Units are generally referred to as the "Hole."

Isolation Wing: These are the areas of a prison where inmates are placed for disciplinary, safety, and security issues. These Isolation Wings are generally referred to as the "Hole."

Issue: What the "Title 15" states a convict shall have every day, for instance, a shower, two hot meals, yard, clothes, etc. For example, "I didn't get my 'Worker Shower.' I want my issue!"

It's A Wrap: When someone or something is finished. For example, "Homie, if you don't pay your drug debts in prison, it's a wrap. You better talk to your people and have them handle that."

It's All About The Numbers: This means that power in prison is based on how many members a "Faction" has. Whatever faction has the most soldiers on a yard usually means they will run the "Program."

It's Better To Be Caught With It Than Without It: This means the yard is so violent or things are about to "Go Up" with another "Faction" that you need to have a "Banger" on you for protection. If your enemy catches you without your banger, that could be the end of your life, so you had better be "Strapped."

It's On: This means the next time you encounter someone, you will attack them "On Sight." For example, "It's on with Switch. The next time I see him, I'm going to 'Put Hands' on him."

It's Your Story You Tell It: When you know another inmate is not telling you the truth, that is your response to them. For example, if someone tried to run some "Drag" on you, your answer would be, "It's your story. You tell it, homeboy."

J

J Cat: A slang term referring to an inmate who is mentally ill. During my time as an officer, there was a notable crisis within the California Department of Corrections, with mentally ill inmates being placed in the general inmate population. Unfortunately, there weren't sufficient resources to adequately house these inmates in medical facilities like Vacaville Prison due to space constraints.

Jack Artist: An inmate who likes to masturbate while watching female correctional officers or "Free Staff."

Jacket: The reputation a person has in prison. People can have a "False Jacket" put on them by their peers who are "Politicking" against them.

Jacket: This is an old-school term that refers to a convict's "C-File." This folder has all the information regarding a convict's history, behavior, disciplinary actions, etc., while in prison.

Jailhouse Lawyer: A troublesome inmate who likes to argue with officers and file frivolous "602s" against them. A jailhouse lawyer also assists other inmates with their court cases and complaints against officers or the administration. A jailhouse lawyer is usually paid in "Canteen" for his services.

Jailhouse Liar: An inmate who has a "Jacket" for telling lies about how much "Dirt" they did on the streets or how much money they had before getting "Cracked."

Jailing: To do time in County Jail. For example, "It was my first time jailing, so I had a lot to learn."

Jailing: This term refers to how a convict does their time. For example, "I have been jailing for a long time. I know the 'Get Down.'"

Jale: A word that translates to job, meaning going on a "Mission" in prison.

Jam Up: To aggressively question another person about their gang affiliation. For example, "Who do you 'Run With' homie?"

Jammer: An inmate-manufactured device used to inject intravenous drugs. The Jammer is made of an eye dropper, a sharpened guitar string, and a shaft of a plastic ink pen that has been cut down to size.

Jap Flaps: The thin and cheap slippers that inmates were issued in the California Department of Corrections and Rehabilitation.

Jim Jones: This is the name for the Kool-Aid packets the inmates get in their "Sack Lunch."

Jingles: This term refers to the Folger Adams brass keys the officers use to open doors in prison. For example, "The jingles make a distinctive sound when the officers are walking."

Joint: A term inmates use to refer to prison. For example, "I first went to the joint when I was 23."

Jolt: A prison sentence. For example, "I did a ten-year jolt for bank robbery."

Juice: The level of influence wielded by a person to accomplish tasks or achieve certain privileges within the prison system. For example, "Lemon used his juice to get that job as the 'Visiting Room Porter.'"

Juice Card: The level of influence wielded by a person to accomplish tasks or achieve certain privileges within the prison system. For example, "How did Snail get moved from Housing Unit Alpha-1 to Alpha-3?" The answer is, "He used his juice card with the Captain."

Juiced Up: When a convict gets the green light from the "Big Homies" to run a prison yard. For example, "Whiskey is juiced up, so you better fall in line, homeboy."

Jump: The very beginning of something. For example, "Porky, right from jump, you know I got love for you. But you need to stop eating my honeybuns."

Jump: To attack or take swift action against someone. For example, "Tiger thought I wouldn't jump when he came at me 'Sideways,' but I 'Fired On Him' and broke his jaw."

Jump Off: When numerous convicts are involved in a fight amongst themselves. For example, "Things are about to jump off between the 'Crips' and 'Woods.'"

Jump Street: The very beginning of something. For example, "Dirty D, right from jump street, you know I respected you. But your feet are stinking up the cell."

Junta: A word that translates to meeting. For example, "The homies are having a junta in the chapel."

Jura: A term used to refer to law enforcement or the police.

Just Gay For The Stay: This means precisely what the phrase implies.

Jute Ball: A Jute Ball is the "Reduced Food Rations" that an inmate got in the Los Angeles County Jail. It is described as a disgusting mix of dry, tasteless food.

K

K-9: A term used by some convicts for correctional officers.

K Wing: This is the "Administration Segregation" at "Tracy" prison.

Kamikaze Hit: A term referring to a situation in which a convict violently assaults someone while being closely observed by correctional officers and fellow inmates. The assailant typically carries out the attack despite the risk of facing gunfire from the "Observation Tower" officer's "Mini-14" rifle or potential retaliation from the intended victim's homies.

Kamikaze Mission: A term referring to a situation in which a convict violently assaults someone while being closely observed by correctional officers and fellow inmates. The assailant typically carries out the attack despite the risk of facing gunfire from the "Observation Tower" officer's "Mini-14" rifle or potential retaliation from the intended victim's homies.

KANO: This acronym stands for Kumi African Nation Organization. This is a militant and highly organized prison gang comprised of Black convicts.

Kanpol: A "Nahuatl" word that means "Southerner."

Keep Away: An inmate who is kept away from other inmates for various reasons.

Keep It G: When people are down for theirs and they won't let anyone disrespect them. They won't back down from a fight or yield to any pressure.

Keep It Gangsta: When people are down for theirs and they won't let anyone disrespect them. They won't back down from a fight or yield to any pressure.

Keep It Moving: When a convict is doing his own "Program" and not tripping off other people. For example, "I don't get involved in that. I keep it moving."

Keep It Official: When a person tells it like it is with no filter, they don't play any games and "Keep It Gangsta."

Keep It Pushing: When a convict is doing his own "Program" and not tripping off other people. For example, "I keep it pushing, homie. I'm trying to get home to my family."

Keep It Solid: A person who "Holds Their Mud" and is quick to "Put in Work" for "The Cause." For example, "You must be down for your crown, homie. You have to keep it solid. There is no other way to go about it in the penitentiary."

Keep Telling Yourself That: This is what you tell someone when they are "Talking Out The Side Of Their Neck." For example, If someone tells you they can do more "Burpees" than you, simply reply, "Keep telling yourself that."

Keep Your Eyes & Ears Open & Your Mouth Shut: This basic prison advice will keep you from getting in a "Wreck."

Keeping Point: When a gang member looks out for others while his homies conduct illegal activities.

Keeway: This word means "Crip" in Swahili, and some Black inmates use Swahili words in prison to return to their cultural heritage.

Keister: When a convict places items of "Contraband" in his rectum to avoid discovery by officers. Some convicts become very proficient at this and can do it in seconds. When a "Banger" is placed inside of the "Prison Safe" it will have a protective layer of cellophane to prevent their intestines from being perforated.

Kept It Solid: A person who "Holds Their Mud" and is quick to "Put in Work" for "The Cause." For example, "My boy Rock kept it solid in the penitentiary. He pushed a 'Hard Line.'"

Key Board: A space on the wall in secure areas in the prison where keys and key rings that officers use are kept. Officers "Chit Out" these keys, and they are responsible for returning them after their shift is over.

Key Holder: The leader of a prison gang or "Car" who wields great influence over his comrades. If an officer has a persistent problem with a convict, they will usually talk to the key holders to resolve the issue. Key holders in prison help keep things in order, and I had asked them numerous times to put their homies in check before they got into a "Wreck." For example, "Who is running this yard?" The answer is, "Rhino is the key holder."

Key The Door: In some older prisons, officers use keys to lock and unlock cell doors. For example, "Hey, CO, key the door so I can get my prison identification card."

Keying The Gates: When an officer is opening the doors in a "Section" or "Tier." For example, "Gomez is keying the gates. Get ready to ride."

Keyed In: In some older prisons, officers use keys to lock and unlock cell doors. For example, "I tried to open my door to get out of my cell, but I was keyed in."

Keys: This refers to who is running the yard for a particular "Car." For example, "Who has the keys for the 'Woods' in this 'Unit?'"

Keys To The House: The leader of a prison gang or "Car" who wields great influence over his comrades. If an officer has a persistent problem with a convict, they will usually talk to the key holders to resolve the issue. Key holders in prison help keep things in order, and I had asked them numerous times to put their homies in check before they got into a "Wreck." For example, "Whose running this yard?" The answer is, "Tio has the keys to the house."

Keys To The Pod: The leader of a prison gang or "Car" who wields great influence over his comrades. If an officer has a persistent problem with a convict, they will usually talk to the key holders to resolve the issue. Key holders in prison help keep things in order, and I had asked them numerous times to put their homies in check before they got into a "Wreck." For example, "Whose running this pod?" The answer is, "Fox has the keys to the pod."

Keys To The Unit: The leader of a prison gang or "Car" who wields great influence over his comrades. If an officer has a persistent problem with a convict, they will usually talk to the key holders to resolve the issue. Key holders in prison help keep things in order, and I had asked them numerous times to put their homies in check before they got into a "Wreck." For example, "Whose running this unit?" The answer is, "Active has the keys to the unit."

Kick Back: This means to chill out and stop with the drama. For example, "Kick back homie, you need to stop 'Hard Timing.'"

Kick Down: When an inmate is "Hitting," he needs to give a portion of the drugs to the "Fellas." If he doesn't kick down, he will eventually get a "Green Light" put on him. For example, "They need to give 'Respectos' to the 'Senores.' They need to kick down, or else."

Kick Off: When numerous convicts are involved in a fight amongst themselves. For example, "It's about to kick off between the

'Bloods' and 'Woods.'"

Kick Out Yard: This is a yard that inmates get released to after doing time in the "SHU."

Kick Outs: A more advanced variation of a "Burpee."

Kick Rocks: An expression that conveys the desire for someone to leave and stop bothering you. For example, "Kick rocks punk!"

Kick Us Down: To share one's belongings. For example, "Dude just 'Hit' some weed, and he didn't kick us down."

Kicked Him Off The Table: When a "Camarada" with "Status" is removed from his position on the "Mesa." Getting kicked off the table can happen for various reasons in prison.

Kicked Out: When an inmate is released from the "SHU," it's called being kicked out. For example, "After my three years in the SHU, I got kicked out to A Yard."

Kicker: When convicts make "Pruno," the kicker is the ingredients that turn the juice into alcohol. Kickers are made from various substances such as yeast, bread, or fruit.

Kicking: When a person is going through heroin withdrawals. For example, "When I first 'Landed' in 'County,' I was in my cell curled up on my bunk because I was kicking."

Kicking Up: When profits from illegal activities go to a particular gang's "Big Homies." Usually, 1/3 of profits is paid in "Taxes" in this manner. For example, "Looney got 'Poked' because he wasn't kicking up to the 'Big Homies.'"

Kicking Up Dust: When an inmate makes a name for himself by "Putting in Work." For example, "Bronco is kicking up dust!"

Kicks: This refers to an inmate's shoes.

Killapat: A nickname for Calipatria State Prison.

Kill Kite: A kite with an order to kill somebody in prison.

Kill Game: What you say to a homie when they are telling stories that you know aren't true. For example, "Kill game Buzzard, I know what happened. Stop 'Fronting.'"

Kisu: This word means knife in Swahili, and some Black inmates use Swahili words in prison to return to their cultural heritage. For example, "Grab that kisu, homie. I'm about to blast some holes in those fools."

Kite: A written letter from one convict to another. According to some "Household Policies," kites are to be shared between "Cellies," who are gang members. Trouble usually starts if cellies refuse to share their kites because suspicion instantly arises.

Kite Name: Gang members will use false names on "Kites" to confuse enemies and prison administration. For example, Wild Bill and Blazer are communicating via kites. Instead of using their real "Street Names," they will address each other as Cowboy and Bronco.

Kitty: 1/3 of all drugs brought into prison for the "Peckerwoods" goes to the Kitty, and from there, it gets distributed to the "Big Homies."

Kitty: A community supply of hygiene items that some "Factions" have for members of their groups who don't have any.

Kitty Box: An emergency supply of food that some inmates have and store in their cell in case their race goes on an extended "Lockdown." A sample of what they might have in their Kitty Box: 20 bags of beans, 100 soups, and 5 jars of coffee.

Knee Knocker: The nickname for the 40mm launcher that the officers use to stop fights and riots.

Knife Beef: The sentence a convict receives after getting caught with a knife. For example, "I caught a nine-month knife beef."

Knifer: An old-school term for a convict known for being good in knife fights. For example, "Buck is a knifer. I don't play around with him."

Knock Him Down: To take someone out with your hands or a weapon. For example, "Look at that fool. I can't wait for things to 'Kick Off' because I'm going to knock him down."

Knocked Down: To take someone out with your hands or a weapon. For example, "Big Joe got knocked down for going against the 'Program.'"

Knuckle Check: After a fight in prison, inmates near the combatants will have their knuckles checked to see if they were involved in the melee.

Kumi African Nation Organization: This is a militant and highly organized prison gang comprised of Black convicts.

Kumi 415: A well-organized California prison gang consisting of Black inmates.

Kuncke Up: To fight with another person.

KVSP: Kern Valley State Prison.

L

La Clica: This term is used for "La Eme." For example, "The taxes from their drug sales were going to La Clica."

LA County Jail: Numerous convicts claim that LA County Jail is more violent, political, and dangerous than any state prison in California. I have heard many accounts from respected convicts of how treacherous LA County Jail is and the officers' alleged misconduct. In short, LA County Jail has a long and storied reputation of being a hellhole. As bad as LA County Jail is, it is even worse for the White inmates since there are so few of them, and they usually end up getting in a "Wreck."

La Eme: The "Mexican Mafia" is a prison gang that exercises authority over virtually every Hispanic street gang in Southern California.

La Máquina: The group exercises performed by "Norteños" in a militaristic fashion in prison.

La Mesa: In the context of the "Nuestra Familia" prison gang's history, "La Mesa" denotes the trio of "Shot Callers" who formerly held authoritative positions within the gang. This term is also commonly known as "The Table."

La Vida Loca: This translates to "The Crazy Life," and it encapsulates the tumultuous existence of a gangster, marked by both extreme highs and lows. A distinctive symbol representing la vida loca is a three dot tattoo often placed near the eye or on the hand.

LAC: California State Prison, Los Angeles County, or Lancaster Prison.

Laced Tight: A convict who is "With The Business" and they are familiar with "Prison Politics." For example, "Knots is laced tight; don't play with him."

Laced Up: When an older convict kicks down game to a young "First Termer" to help him navigate the treacherous waters of the penal system. This process helps the youngster stay away from trouble and getting himself into a "Wreck." This schooling also includes how to make a knife. The "Big Homie" will tell the "Fish" to make a knife, and then he will grade it. If the knife isn't good enough, he will have him make it again. He will also teach him how to make a "Bomb" to melt plastic for a knife if he has no metal. He will instruct him on how to defend himself and on various exercises. For example, "The homies that 'Schooled' me were disappointed in me, so my punishment was more severe than if I would have been just an average homie. But for me, someone who was laced up and in a leadership position, my discipline was excessive because they felt let down."

Laid Down & Licked His Nuts: When an inmate doesn't fight back and becomes a pushover. It means acting like a "Punk." For example, "Did you hear about Bulldog? Those dudes stole his 'Canteen,' and he just laid down and licked his nuts. He didn't even do anything. He just watched them do it."

Lame: A person who gets no respect from their peers. A worthless, goodfor-nothing person who does not stand up for themselves.

Lame Status: When people in a "Car" ignore a person because of their bad behavior. Their fellow gang members will not associate with them until they redeem themselves. This is usually accomplished by "Putting in Work" by going on a "Mission" and doing a "Clean Up."

Land: To "Drive Up" to a prison after being assigned there. For example, "Homies don't want to land at Centinela Prison because the 'Big Homie' there is vicious and he will send you on a 'Hot One' even if you are 'Short To The House.'"

Landed: To "Drive Up" to a prison after being assigned there. For example, "Vulture landed at Folsom, and I had a little 'Care Package' waiting for him."

Laudatory Chrono: This is the CDCR form "128-B" given to an inmate who completes a program or does something worthy of recognition. A Laudatory Chrono goes into the inmate's "C-File." A Laudatory Chrono is also called a "Good Guy Chrono."

Laugh Now, Cry Later: This common gang member philosophy means to live life to the fullest today and worry about the consequences later. The tattoo associated with this mindset is two theatrical masks: one is laughing, and one is crying.

Law Library: An office on the prison yard filled with law books and other materials that convicts have access to. Convicts will research case law and try to fight their convictions using these materials. Some inmates hire a "Jailhouse Lawyer" to help them with their cases and file paperwork. Inmates also used the law library to meet up and discuss various gang business. Inmates used the Law Library to settle a beef with each other by fighting when they couldn't otherwise get at each other in person. For example, if the convicts were on different yards, they would arrange a meeting in the Law Library to settle their differences.

Lay Down: When an inmate succumbs to fear and pressure and doesn't fight back in a given situation.

Lay Down My Flag: When a gang member retires from the gang. For example, "After my 'Road Dog' got 'Backdoored' by the homies,

I had to lay down my flag."

Lay It Down: When a gang member retires from gang life. For example, "Some cats land on a 'No Good' yard and just lay it down and stay."

Lay The Yard Down: In prison, an officer activates their alarm when a fight or emergency occurs. W hen an alarm is sounded, all inmates in the yard must lie on the ground immediately. The tower officer will broadcast commands over the microphone, instructing inmates to "Get down! Get down! Get down!" All inmates need to obey this order, and this process is commonly referred to as laying the yard down.

Lay The Yard Down: Inmates use this term when they are going to "Check" one of their homies for breaking their rules. When they plan to do this, they will warn other "Factions" out of respect. For example, "We are going to lay the yard down tonight because we are 'Cleaning House.'"

Layover: When inmates "Catch A Chain" to another prison on the "Grey Goose," usually they will stay at another prison for a short period.

Leaking: To bleed after being "Poked," slashed, or "Smashed." For example, "Scarface got 'Booked' in the neck, and he was leaking all over the yard as he fought for his life."

Legal Mail: This is mail inmates get from their legal representatives and other official entities, and officers are not allowed to read it. All regular mail inmates send or receive is inspected and read by prison staff.

Legend: This term refers to a high-ranking prison gang member with a lot of "Status." For example, "That dude right there is a legend.

You see the 'Entourage' around him? They are all 'Strapped.'"

Lemac: This term is Camel spelled backwards, and it was used for a cigarette.

Let Him Know The Business: When a convict gives someone their "Issue" because they "Had It Coming." For example, "Cricket, did you hear what that 'Lame' said? You better let him know the business."

Let It Burp: When making "Pruno" in prison, one must release the gasses from the plastic trash bag, or it will burst. This process is called "Burping The Baby." For example, "Popeye, you need to let it burp because your bag is about to burst."

Let It Slide: This phrase describes a situation where something occurs, and rather than responding with aggression or vocal confrontation, a person chooses not to make a fuss about it. For instance, "Bouncer bumped into me on the way to chow, but I let it slide because I'm 'Short To The House.'"

Let Me Get An Issue: When a convict wants a piece of something, someone else has, he might say this. For example, "Let me get an issue of that 'Black' homie."

Let These Hands Go: To physically attack someone. For example, "If that 'Lame' comes anywhere near me, I'm going to let these hands go."

Let's Get Mobile: This phrase is used when one inmate wishes to walk and have a private conversation with another. For example, "Wheels, let's get mobile, homeboy."

Let's Walk: This is said to another inmate when you want to talk privately with them. For example, "Chopper, let's walk homeboy."

Leva: A term for a "Lame." For example, "Don't mess with that vato. He is a leva."

Leva Status: When a prison gang member is placed under investigation by his comrades for wrongdoing. He will be kept to the side, and no gang business or "Politics" will be shared with him until he is cleared of any violations. For example, "Reaper is on Leva status. Stop going to his door."

Level I Killer: When inmates on low-level soft yards act too hardcore for the situation. Convicts from hardcore yards laugh at these inmates when they come across them after their "Points" drop and go to lower-level yards. For example, "These level I killers on this yard crack me up."

Level II Killer: When inmates on low-level soft yards act too hardcore for the situation. Convicts from hardcore yards laugh at these inmates when they come across them after their "Points" drop and go to lower-level yards. For example, "Sinbad is way out of line with his level II killer attitude."

Level IV Killer: When inmates on low-level soft yards act too hardcore for the situation. Convicts from hardcore yards laugh at these inmates when they come across them after their "Points" drop and go to lower-level yards. For example, "Krazy thinks he is a level IV killer with that attitude of his."

Life Flight: When an inmate gets assaulted so severely, they are flown on a helicopter to an emergency room at a local hospital.

Life On The Installment Plan: When an inmate keeps going to prison after getting released. Basically, this means they are doing a life sentence on several different prison terms. For example, "Badger is doing life on the installment plan. This is his fourth term."

Life Without: This refers to an inmate serving a life sentence with no chance of parole.

Lifer: An inmate doing a life sentence.

Lifer Graveyard: A Level II prison primarily housing inmates with life sentences. Inmates serving life sentences are ineligible for placement in Level I prison yards, even if their "Points" decrease. Consequently, after many years of incarceration and reductions in their points, lifers often find themselves relocated to a Level II lifer graveyard prison.

Lifted My Hand: When a convict is ready and willing to go on a "Mission" and "Put In Work" for the "Cause." For example, "In prison, I lifted my hand because I was trying to make a name for myself."

Line: This is short for "Mainline." For example, "When I first hit the line, I shot my 'Paperwork' to the 'Camarada.'"

Line Staff: This term refers to correctional officers.

Linea: A word that translates to "Line," and it refers to the "Mainline." For example, "I know Midget from the linea at Centinela."

Lined Out: This term describes a situation when a convict dresses meticulously for a visit, ensuring that their clothing is neatly ironed, with creases in his shirt and pants.

Linked Up: When two people or "Factions" form an alliance. For example, "The 'Southerners' are linked up with the 'Northerners' in the penitentiary."

Lip Singing: To tell stories that aren't true or to speak aggressively to someone without intending to back it up with violence. For example, "That fool is just lip singing, he won't 'Bust A Grape.'"

List: When the "Shot Callers" give a "Green Light" to their "Soldiers" to assault or kill somebody. These inmates "In The Hat" are usually put on a list that is "Hooped" and then transported from prison to prison.

Listed: The act of being placed on a "Bad News List," "In The Hat," or "Green Lighted." For example, "Sancho got listed because he was messing with the old lady of the 'Big Homie.'"

Listen Twice As Much As You Speak: In prison any idle word you speak can come back and bite you. You must be very careful with what you say about people and what you volunteer for.

Live Comfortable: Every convict's goal is to live as comfortably as possible while in prison. This means having plenty of "Canteen," getting "Packages" regularly, having access to a cell phone, having money on their "Books," and having a woman who will ride out that time with him. For example, "You know how it is homeboy. I'm trying to live as comfortable as possible in here."

Llavero: This word means "Key Holder," referring to the "Shot Caller" in a prison setting.

Llaves: The word translates to keys, and in prison, it refers to the convict who is the "Key Holder" for his "Car."

Loaded: When a person is high on drugs. For example, "That 'Tecato' is always loaded with a needle hanging out of his arms."

Loaf: A Loaf is the "Reduced Food Rations" that an inmate got in the Los Angeles County Jail. It is a disgusting mix of tasteless, dry food.

Loc: A term that "Crips" call each other. For example, "What's up, Loc? When did you 'Pull Up?'"

Lock In A Sock: A primitive weapon consisting of a lock, batteries, tuna can, or other heavy item placed in a sock, then swung like a medieval flail.

Lock It Up: An inmate who has succumbed to pressure or intimidation and no longer feels safe on the "General Population" and "Checks In" to "Protective Custody."

Lock It Up: This command instructs a convict to enter their cell and close their door. For example, "Conejo, lock it up!"

Lockdown: This is when inmates are confined to their cells for an extended period of time. They get a shower every three days and two hot meals delivered to their cells. Lockdown usually occurs on the "Line" when inmates assault officers or riot amongst themselves. Lockdown can also refer to inmates in the "SHU," "Hole," or "Adjustment Center."

Lockdown Bag: An emergency supply of food that some inmates have in their cells in case their "People" go on an extended "Lockdown." A sample of what they might have in their lockdown bag: 20 bags of beans, 100 soups, and 5 jars of coffee.

Locked Down: When inmates are confined to their cells for extended periods of time. They get a shower every three days and two hot meals delivered to their cells. Being Locked Down usually occurs on the "Line" when inmates assault officers or riot amongst themselves. Locked Down can also refer to inmates in the "SHU," "Hole," or "Adjustment Center."

Locked It Up: When an inmate succumbs to pressure or intimidation and no longer feels safe in the "General Population" and "Checks In" to "Protective Custody." For example, "Hawk locked it up because a little bird told him that he was going to get 'Moved On.'"

Locked Up: When an inmate is secured in his "Cell." For example, "Where's Smiley?" The answer is, "He's locked up for the night."

Locker: In "Dorm" settings, inmates will each have a locker to store their belongings. These lockers will have a combination lock to secure their possessions. In cell living, each inmate has a shelf that some refer to as a locker.

Lockup: When inmates are required to be in their cells in prison.

Locs: The infamous black sunglasses that were popularized in prison.

For example, "Check out Slim. He's rocking those locs."

LOI: This term describes the Letter Of Instruction issued to officers who violate official policy.

Lollipop: Some inmates make homemade lollipops and sell them. They will use a Q-tip for the handle after removing the cotton. They will mix Kool-Aid, coffee creamer, and crushed Jolly Ranchers to make the candy. A tootsie roll will be placed in the center of the lollipop. They will roll up the mixture and put it on the Q-tip to make a lollipop. These lollipops sell for .50 each in prison.

Lone Wolf: To go against the "Program" in prison. To be a "Rebel" and put one's life in danger by choosing to walk alone and "Do Your Own Time."

Long Beach Crip Car: The Long Beach Crip "Car" in prison is composed of Crips from Long Beach, California. The two biggest "Factions" in this alliance are the East Side Insane Crips and the Rolling 20 Crips.

Long Termer: This is an inmate who has been down for a long time. Generally, an inmate who has been down over twenty years is a long termer. For example, "That old G is a long termer, he has been down for 25 years."

Loose Program: When a person or "Car" in prison does things sloppy or lackadaisically. A loose program is the opposite of a "Tight Program." For example, "The leadership ran a loose program when I was on C yard at Calipat."

Lop: This term is used to describe an individual who lacks respect and credibility among their peers. It characterizes someone as a worthless and ineffectual person who fails to assert themselves or gain the respect of others. For example, "Smith is a lop! He doesn't know what the word 'no' means. He lets the inmates do whatever they want."

LOP: This stands for loss of privileges, and inmates can lose privileges such as "Canteen" after being found guilty during a "Rules Violation Hearing."

Lops, Lames, & Part-Time Games: This saying describes dealing with shady dudes in prison. For example, "Prison is nothing but 'Lops,' 'Lames,' and part-time games."

Loss Of Privileges: Inmates may experience the forfeiture of privileges like access to the "Canteen" following a determination of guilt in a "Rules Violation Hearing."

Lost Their Date: When inmates do something serious that causes their "Release Date" to be extended. For example, "Many people lost their date and caught more time behind what Shady did on the yard to the Blacks."

Love Cup: This means to get a cup of "Pruno" or "White Lightning" from someone even if you didn't pay for it or help with the ingredients.

Love Shack: The name for the building where inmates' wives stay the night with them on prison grounds during a "Conjugal" visit.

Love Shack: A little building in older prisons where inmates would go to have sexual relations with "Punks."

Lowriding: When an inmate is being flashy and showing off. For example, "Solo was lowriding on the yard. He was acting a fool out there."

Lumped Up: Someone who gets beat up badly and their face is full of lumps. For example, "Did you see Scarecrow after they were done with him? He got lumped up."

Lunch Box Assessors: A box or metal bin at the "Staff Entrance" that an officer's lunch box must fit in, or it will not be allowed inside.

LWOP: Life without the possibility of parole.

M

MAC Rep: The Men's Advisory Council (MAC) is made up of a group of convicts from each race who act as representatives for their constituents. They are the mediators between themselves and the prison administration, intending to ease tensions among the convicts by voicing their concerns to upper management on the yard, such as captains, lieutenants, and sergeants. MAC Reps are authorized to travel the yard and visit other "Housing Units" as part of their official duties. They carry a blue identification card that gives them access to otherwise off-limits areas. During "Lockdown" periods, MAC Reps are regularly released from their cells and visit each housing unit to talk to their people and help alleviate the stresses of being confined to their cells for extended periods.

Macuahuitl: A "Nahuatl" word some "Southerners" use when referring to a "Banger." For example, "Slide me your macuahuitl. I'm going to 'Poke' that fool."

Mad Doggers: The dark sunglasses that gangsters wear. For example, "Homie, have you seen my mad doggers? I left them right here on my bunk."

Mad Dogging: To stare at another person with a mean look on your face.

Made A Name For Myself: When a gang member "Put In Work" for his gang and gained a good reputation among his peers. For example, "I made a name for myself in prison because my hand was always raised, and I never hesitated to put in work."

Made The Call: When a "Shot Caller" makes a decision about a certain situation, and all members under him must enforce it. For example, "A White Blood 'Drove Up' so 'Kites' started flying and we waited on P-Nut for a verdict. He made the call to stab him off the yard."

Maestro: A designated "Norteño" who hands out weekly assignments on Norteño culture and philosophy that gang members must complete.

Mafioso: This term refers to a member of the "Mexican Mafia." For example, "Bugsy is a mafioso, so watch what you do around him."

Mail Call: This is the procedure for distributing mail to inmates in prison. In my "Housing Unit," we would get the mail around 1500 hours, and I would have it handed out before the evening meal.

Mail Out: When an inmate sends money to a P.O. Box or other address to buy some form of "Contraband" in prison. For example, "I bought three $100 dollar bills from Chino for a $500 mailout."

Main Hitters: This is the core group of a "Faction" who are known for getting blood on their hands whenever duty calls. For example, "We had a small group of main hitters on the yard, and we gave those 'Africanos' the blues."

Main Street: The "General Population" of convicts who have minimal restrictions placed on their activities and privileges as opposed to inmates in the "SHU" or "Hole."

Mainline: The "General Population" of convicts who have minimal restrictions placed on their activities and privileges as opposed to inmates in the "SHU" or "Hole."

Mainline Status: This is a convict who is assigned to the "General

Population" or the "Mainline." Being on the mainline has certain privileges that inmates assigned to other groups cannot enjoy fully.

Make A Homie, Don't Break A Homie: This means to build your gang members up. It's a mindset of not victimizing your people but making them better so your "Car" will get stronger due to their growth.

Make A Name For Myself: When a gang member "Put In Work" for his gang and gained a good reputation among his peers. For example, "I had to make a name for myself in prison. I was just a youngster with a lot to prove to the homies."

Make Fresh Blood: The term used when prison gangs "Open The Books" and recruit new members into their organization. For example, "Danger said it's time to make fresh blood."

Make My Rounds: This means a convict does some "Dirt" for the "Big Homies" and gets sent to the "SHU" and meets the "Brass." For example, "I got sent to the 'Back' and met the big homies. I made my rounds and 'Made A Name For Myself.'"

Make Paper: When an inmate makes parole.

Make Sheet: This administrative form was kept in "O Wing" at Correctional Training Facility, Soledad, from the 1960s through the 1980s. Each inmate had a Make Sheet that described certain behavioral characteristics. Staff would use the Make Sheets as a quick reference guide on the background of the inmates in the "Adjustment Center."

Make The Call: When a "Shot Caller" makes a decision about a certain situation and all members must enforce it. For example, "A White Crip 'Drove Up' so 'Kites' started flying. We waited on

Bash to make the call if we were going to 'Blast' him."

Make Them, Don't Break Them: This means to build your homies up instead of breaking them. It's a mindset of not victimizing your people but making them better so your "Car" will get stronger due to their growth.

Making Money: When a convict makes money in prison from illicit activities. For example, "If you are making money, you need to pay 1/3 to the 'Big Homie' in the 'Back.'"

Making Your Bones: "Putting in Work" for your gang and gaining respect from other members. It can also be the "Mission" a gang associate is given to gain membership into the prison gang.

Malias: When a "Dope Fiend" goes through withdrawal because they can't get any dope. For example, "That 'Tecato' has the malias. He is sleeping all day and dripping sweat all over the cell."

Mama Mini: This is the nickname for the "Mini-14" that some convicts use when referring to it. For example, "Listen up, little homie, you know the police have Mama Mini in the tower. Watch yourself on that 'Mission' because you know they are just looking for a reason to take one of us out."

Management Cell: Inmates who cause problems in "Administrative Segregation" are placed in these cells for a period not to exceed 10 days. Inmates placed in Management Cells lose privileges such as yard and some of their property.

Mandatory: Something in prison where a response to it is expected and mandatory. For example, if someone has "Funny Charges," they will be "Removed."

Mandatory Blast: This means if a person with a "Green Light" on them ever crosses your path in prison, you must "Blast" them. If you have the opportunity and fail to "Poke" them, you will be in "Violation" with your "Car." For example, "Any 'Chomo' is a mandatory blast, homeboy."

Mandatory Hit: This means if a person with a "Green Light" on them ever crosses your path in prison, you must "Blast" them. If you have the opportunity and fail to "Poke" them, you will be in "Violation" with your "Car." For example, "Any 'Snitch' is a mandatory hit, homeboy."

Mandatory Hole Appearance: There were some prison gangs like the "Nazi Low Riders" who required their members to report to the "Hole" and "Tap In" with the "Big Homies" when they returned to prison. In order to do this, they would have to physically attack someone so they would get sent to the hole.

Mandatory Movement: In prison, being a gang member means you can't spend all your time in your cell. Your gang requires you to come out to designated areas like the "Dayroom" and the yard daily to socialize with other gang members. This is mandatory because prison gangs need to maintain their numbers in case rival gangs attack them.

Mandatory Override: These overrides require prison staff to place inmates in a higher "Housing Security Level" than their actual "Points" dictate. There are five mandatory overrides: history of escape, history of a sex offense, history of violence, sentenced to death, and sentenced to life without possibility of parole.

Mandatory Yard: When a "Faction" orders all members to go to yard under threat of violence if they refuse. There are many reasons for a "Collective" to order a mandatory yard. Some of these reasons are preparation for a riot, discussion of important matters, and someone in their faction is going to get "Whacked," and this is the only way to get at them because they have been hiding out.

Mando: Something in prison where a response to it is expected and mandatory. For example, if a person calls you a "Punk," it's mando that you "Take Off" on him.

Mano: This word translates to "hand," and it refers to the "Mano Negra" or "Black Hand" tattoo the "Mexican Mafia" members get. Some old-school Mexican Mafia members got the "Mariposa" tattoo instead of the Mano Negra.

Mano Negra: This translates to "Black Hand," referring to the black hand tattoo that "Mexican Mafia" members get. The black hand signifies "death to our enemies."

Manwich: When inmates partially cook ramen noodles and place them between two pieces of bread.

Mariposa: This word translates to butterfly, and some "OG" gangsters claim this was the original name of "La Eme." Some "Mexican Mafia" members used a butterfly tattoo many years ago.

Mark: A lazy, sloppy, and good-for-nothing person nobody respects in prison.

Mark Out: When a person doesn't fight back and acts like a "Punk."

Marked Out: When a person doesn't fight back and acts like a "Punk." For example, "Did you hear about Sleepy? Pirate stole his honeybun, and he didn't even do anything. He just watched him do it."

Marriage Chrono: A marriage "Chrono" is an official document that inmates sign stating they will get along and there is no threat of violence between them.

Married: When an inmate is a member of a prison gang. For example, "Chato is married; be careful what you say around him."

Marrying Nancy Flores: When a convict becomes a member of the "Nuestra Familia" prison gang.

Mashed: When a person is violently attacked.

Mat: This is what inmates call their mattress in prison. For example, "Kilroy, you need to use your 'Juice Card' and get me a new mat. Mine is 'Shot Out.'"

Mattresses Rolled Up: Some "Factions" require a mattress to be rolled up on the bunk during "Program" hours. This shows that a convict is "Programming" and ready for duty. An inmate will get a "DP" if they fail to do this with their mattress.

Max Row Yard: This was the narrow exercise yard at Soledad Prison for inmates who were "Slammed Down" in "Max Row" in the "Adjustment Center." The dimensions of this yard were 40' x 150'. The yard had a basketball hoop, two shower heads, a speed bag, exercise bars, a handball court, and a punching bag.

Maxed Out: When a person is violently attacked. For example, "Pharaoh owed money to the wrong vatos, and he got maxed out."

Maxed Out: When an inmate serves his full sentence because of disciplinary issues. In other words, they are not getting "Day for Day" due to their bad behavior.

Mean Mugging: To stare at another person with a mean look on your face.

Meat Gazer: An inmate who stares at naked men while they are in the shower.

Mechanical Restraints: There are several types of mechanical restraints used by the California Department of Corrections and Rehabilitation. These types of restraint equipment include handcuffs, waist chains, leg irons, flex cuffs, and safety chains.

Med-Line: This is where inmates on the yard receive their medication. They are observed swallowing it to prevent them from selling it to other inmates.

Medical Parole: This program is available to terminally ill inmates with six months or less to live. The inmates who qualify for this medical parole must also be deemed no longer a threat to society and have a place to go when they are released.

Melt Down: The process of melting plastic in prison and making a "Banger" out of the hardened plastic after it cools off. For example, "The homies are going to melt down those food trays and make some 'Fierros.'"

Mental Health Program: The Mental Health Program ensures inmates in the California Department of Corrections and Rehabilitation have access to adequate mental health services.

MEPD: This is the minimum eligible parole date of an inmate. By statute, inmates serving life sentences are eligible for parole hearings one year before their MEPD.

Mesa: The mesa is a governing body for "Southerners" on a prison yard comprised of "Bloqueros" who work directly under the "Yardero." The mesa maintains order and discipline on the yard for their "Faction."

Mesa: The governing body of the "Nuestra Familia" prison gang. There is a Mesa for the state and federal prison systems of the Nuestra Familia.

Mesero: This is a "Bloquero" who is on the "Mesa." The mesa is a governing body for "Southerners" on a prison yard comprised of bloqueros who work directly under the "Yardero." The mesa maintains order and discipline on the yard for their "Faction."

Mess Around: When asked this in prison, it means if you do drugs. For example, "Do you mess around, homie? I got some 'Black' if you do."

Messed Up His Date: When a convict does something in prison that results in him getting more prison time and losing his original parole "Date." For example, "Blanco caught three years for that 'Removal' and messed up his date."

Mexican Mafia: The "Mexican Mafia" is a prison gang that exercises authority over virtually every Hispanic street gang in Southern California.

MHP: This acronym stands for Mental Health Program. It ensures that inmates in California's correctional facilities have access to adequate mental health services.

Mi Vida Loca: This saying translates to My Crazy Life. Mi Vida Loca refers to a gangster's life of highs and lows. A three dot tattoo near the eye or on the hand represents Mi Vida Loca.

Mind Frame: A common word on the streets and in prison that describes a person's state of mind. For example, "I do self-help in my cell. I read. I work out; I try to stay in a positive mind frame."

Mind Your Manners: In prison, a person will mind their manners or be dealt with accordingly. For example, "Check this out, youngster, never talk to Brains like that again. You need to mind your manners."

Mini Writing: This refers to the very small writing on "Kites."

Mini-14: This is the rifle that was in the "Control Booth" and "Tower" of every yard and "Housing Unit" at Centinela State Prison. The Mini-14 is chambered in the .223 round.

Miss Me With That: This is what you say to a person who is lying to you or causing unnecessary drama. For example, "Miss me with that. I'm not trying to hear that."

Mission: When a gang member is given orders by a "Shot Caller" to attack someone.

Mission Boy: A "Crash Dummy" is a person who is used to carry

out tasks or activities that others don't want to do themselves. For example, "Diablo told me never to let anyone put a knife in my hand and never to be another man's mission boy."

Mixed Yard: These yards started in 2018, and they are supposed to be half "General Population" and half "Sensitive Needs Yard."

Mixer: A derogatory term for a person who is too friendly with other races in the penitentiary.

MK-9: This is the "OC Spray" that is carried by officers in the California Department of Corrections and Rehabilitation.

Modified Program: When the normal "Program" in a prison is changed in any way, this is called a modified program. Often, this occurs after a riot between different "Factions." It can also happen in cases like prisons dealing with Covid-19.

Molotov Cocktails: In old-school prisons with bars on the prison cell doors, throwing homemade Molotov Cocktails into the cells of enemies was not unusual. It was fairly common at prisons like San Quentin in the 60s-80s.

Mongolian: This is a style of haircut that some prison gang members get. The Mongolian haircut is a shaved head with a patch of long hair that hangs down the back of the head.

Moonshine: A potent form of alcohol that sells for $20.00 a cup or

$40.00 a quart. To check the quality of the white lighting, they light it with a flame.

Mota: A slang term for marijuana.

Motor Boats: This is an old-school term for an inmate with 20-inch arms. For example, "Big Tookie had them motor boats."

Mount Up: When a convict prepares to go on a "Mission." For example, "It's time to mount up homeboy. Get your 'Banger.'"

Mouthpiece: This person has the authority to speak for a "Big Homie." For example, "Lips is the mouthpiece for the 'Brass,' his words carry weight."

Move On: When a person or group attacks others. For example, "We are about to move on those 'Nazis.'"

Moved On: When a person or group gets attacked. For example, "Those punks just got moved on. They had it coming."

Movement Sheet: Every week, there is a list of officers who change jobs in the prison, and this list is called the Movement Sheet.

Movida: This word translates to move. For example, "Two homies pulled a scandalous movida that got their 'Varrio' 'Greenlighted.'"

Mr. All That: An inmate always acting hardcore and ready to fight over any situation they think they were disrespected. For example, "Rooster thinks he is Mr. All That with his bad attitude."

MRD: The Max Release Date is the latest day an inmate will be released if he doesn't "Program" while in prison.

Mud: This is an old-school term used for coffee.

Mule: A person that smuggles "Contraband" into prison for a gang.

Mule: An inmate who holds "Contraband" in their cell, area, or on their person for someone else. For example, "They just let that fool kick it with them because he is their mule."

Murder Medals: The symbolic medals a gang member has for doing murders for his gang. For example, "My murder medals have no expiration date. Everything I did lives on in my legend as a rider."

Murder Mouthing: To talk aggressively and make threats to another person. For example, "I tried to warn that murder mouthing fool. Now look at him."

Murder Ones: The infamous black sunglasses that were popularized in prison. Some convicts even stenciled 187 onto the sides of the frames of their sunglasses. For example, "Check out Sparks. He's rocking those murder ones."

Mutual Combat: When two inmates fight in CDCR, this is the official term for it that is placed on the incident reports.

My Bad: This is the way most convicts apologize in prison. You will never hear "I'm sorry" because that would be weak for a convict to say. You will often hear "My bad" and "Spensa" as a form of making amends.

My Happy Life, My Sad Life: This common gang member philosophy means to live life to the fullest today and worry about the consequences later. The tattoo associated with this mindset is two theatrical masks: one is laughing, and one is crying.

My Issue: Something the "Title 15" says a convict shall get daily.

These things include food, a phone call, yard, "Dayroom," etc. For example, an inmate not given his daily shower will tell the officers, "I want my issue. Give me my shower!"

My People: The members of your race or "Car" in prison.

Mzungu: This word means White person in Swahili. Some Black inmates use Swahili words to return to their cultural heritage.

N

NAC: This acronym denotes a non-affiliated convict, referring to an inmate who is not a gang member. The term NAC is often used in a derogatory manner by the "Peckerwoods" when referring to "New Booty."

Nahuatl: Some "Southerners" utilize the Aztec language to reconnect with their cultural heritage.

Nailed: This term refers to stabbing someone in prison with a "Banger." For example, "Woody got nailed for burning the 'Big Homie.'"

Name Dropping: An inmate will claim to know certain high-ranking and well-known gang members to gain credibility on the yard. For example, some dude "Drives Up" and says he worked under a particular "Mexican Mafia" member on the streets.

Navy SEALs: A push-up when you bring one knee towards your chest each time you go up.

Nazi Low Riders: A prison gang who used to do the bidding of the "Aryan Brotherhood" on the "Mainline" when the "Brand" was locked down in the "Security Housing Unit."

Nazis: A term used by some "Factions" to describe the White convicts who are pushing a "Hard Line" on "Prison Politics." For example, "Word on the street is those Nazis are going to 'Move On' the White Crip."

NCC: The Northern Cali Crip "Car" in prison is composed of "Crips" from Northern California.

NDPF: This acronym stands for "Non-Designated Program Facility." In the last few years, due to the expansion of "SNY" yards and new prison reform laws across California, the leadership of California Department of Corrections and Rehabilitation in Sacramento began to merge numerous SNY and "General Population" facilities, rebranding them as Non-Designated Programming Facilities (NDPF). Historically, residents from these two population groups would refuse to be housed in the same yards, often resulting in violent confrontations. However, after some years of these new merging implementations, individuals have come to coexist in these yards with minor incidents across the California prison system. Nevertheless, a few higher security level "GP" yards remain intact; CDCR is actively working to phase them out and integrate them into the Non-Designated Programming Facilities in the hopes of eradicating gang activities and pursuing the rehabilitation of the inmate population.

Ndugu: This word means brother in Swahili, and some Black inmates use Swahili words in prison to return to their cultural heritage.

Negative Count: The type of "Count" is when an officer records the number of empty beds in their "Housing Unit" or "Dorm."

Neighborhood Car: The Neighborhood "Car" in prison comprises "Crips" from the Neighborhood Gang.

Neighbors: The convicts in the cells next to one another. For example, "Trigger, ask our neighbors if they have a 'Shot Of Coffee.'"

Neutral: A term used to describe "Non-Affiliated" inmates.

Neutral Area: A place where fights among convicts are strictly prohibited. The "Visiting Room" is a prime example of a neutral area. If an inmate starts a fight in a neutral area, he will get a "DP" from his "Car."

Neutrons: A term used to describe "Non-Affiliated" inmates.

Never Trust A Dope Fiend: This tenet of prison life will save you many problems. A "Dope Fiend" can never be trusted; they will break their word and betray you to get another fix because they have no honor or integrity. Numerous people have been seriously hurt and killed in prison because some drug addict didn't pay what he owed.

New Arrival Application: Within each "Housing Unit" the "Norteños" have assigned an inmate as the designated "Tier Security" for each tier. The Tier Security personnel are responsible for screening new arrivals and providing them with the new arrival application, which includes questions about their personal information such as their name, "CDC Number," age, previous prison history, and "Street Name." This information is processed through their established "Channels" to determine if the new arrival is in "Good Standing."

New Arrival Process: This means checking the background of a new arrival in prison. This information is processed through their established "Channels" to determine if the new arrival is in "Good Standing."

New Arrival Status: This means a new arrival in a prison setting is still having his information cleared by his "Car." While on new arrival status, convicts will be treated as if they were on "Freeze" until their background information clears.

New Booty: A person new to prison or jail who has no clue about "Prison Politics" or the "Convict Code."

New Corcoran: This is the common name for the California

Substance Abuse Treatment Facility and State Prison, Corcoran.

New Delano Prison: This is a common nickname for Kern Valley State Prison.

New Flowers: This is an "SNY" prison gang. They were started in the early 90s in High Desert State Prison. Word on the street says a small faction of New Flowers is still on the "Mainline" who don't associate with the New Flowers in SNY.

New Folsom Prison: This is the common nickname for California State Prison, Sacramento.

New Heads: New convicts who just "Landed" on the prison yard. For example, "After a long 'Lockdown,' there was a lot of new heads on the yard, so we had to 'Clean House' and get rid of the 'Trash.'"

New Life K9 Program: In this program, incarcerated individuals train service dogs meant to aid first responders with various disabilities.

Next In Line: The inmate next in line to do a "Mission" for his gang. For example, "Ajax, you have a 'Clean Up.' That means you are next in line."

NF: This is the acronym for the "Nuestra Familia," which is a prison gang from the northern part of California. Nuestra Familia means "our family." The Nuestra Familia controls the actions of all "Northerners" in California.

NF Generals: The three leaders of the "Nuestra Familia."

NGN: This acronym stands for No Good Norteño, and it is a list of "No Good" former members who are to be "Poked" whenever the opportunity becomes available. Every prison will have a copy of this list, and it is usually kept in the "Hole." These lists are very extensive and can have hundreds of names on them. The NGN list is usually "Hooped" for safekeeping.

Nickle: A five-year prison sentence.

NIK Drug Test Kit: The NIK test is the presumptive drug test utilized by the California Department of Corrections and Rehabilitation. If a questionable substance is detected within the prison, this test will be administered to ascertain whether or not it is a drug.

NLR: This acronym represents the Nazi Low Riders. This prison gang formerly carried out tasks for the "Aryan Brotherhood" on the "Mainline" during the period when the "Brand" was confined to the "Security Housing Unit."

No Cell Phone Policy: The "Mexican Mafia" and "Nuestra Familia" leadership have an edict whereby no "Southerner" or "Northerner" can have a "Contraband" cell phone unless they are making money for the organization. If the inmate with the cell phone isn't making money, they have to relinquish it to the leadership of their "Faction." The "Brass" of these two "Structures" want the members of their governing bodies to be the only ones with these cellphones on the prison yards. If a member of one of these factions has a cell phone without permission, they will face a "DP" from their collective.

No Good: This signifies that a gang member has violated their organization's "Household Policies" and has been deemed unworthy. For example, "Big Red is no good. There is a 'Green Light' on him, so get your 'Banger' and 'Blast' him."

No Good List: Every prison gang has a ledger of "No Good" former members targeted for attack whenever the opportunity becomes available. These lists are very extensive and can have hundreds of names on them. The no good list is usually "Hooped" for safekeeping.

No Hands Policy: On Level IV prison yards, it is common for gangs to enforce a no hands policy, prohibiting members from engaging in physical altercations using their fists. If a dispute cannot be resolved peacefully, gang members are permitted to retrieve a "Banger" and engage in a knife fight within a designated cell. This policy is implemented to ensure that gangs maintain their full complement of soldiers. "Factions" on Level IV yards cannot afford to lose members over petty disputes because that would render them vulnerable to attacks from rival factions.

No Homie On The Floor: This was a "Southerner" policy that meant no homie was allowed to sleep on the floor in L.A. County Jail. Years ago, due to overcrowding, some inmates in "Pods" had to sleep on the floor. The "Southsiders" would make someone of another race, usually a "Wood," relinquish their bed under threat of violence.

No Hostage Policy: According to Title 15 section 3304, hostages held within the California Department of Corrections and Rehabilitation will not be considered eligible for recognition in bargaining.

No Hustle Russell: An inmate who doesn't have any skills to "Come Up." An inmate who never has any "Canteen" or people putting money on his "Books." For example, "That 'NAC' is a straight up no hustle Russell. He is always begging for coffee and soups."

No Landing Zone: A prison yard that "Mainline" convicts are not allowed to "Program" on by their "Faction." If they are transferred to a no landing zone, they must attack someone so they get taken off of the yard. If a convict programs on a no landing zone, their gang members will "Remove" them when it is discovered. For example, "In 2021, when I was locked up, Donovan Prison was a no landing zone for 'Peckerwoods.'"

No Man's Land: The empty space located between the buildings and the surrounding fence of a correctional facility.

No No: Something that will get you into a "Wreck" in prison. For example, "Hey 'Wood,' did you just smoke after that Black dude? That's a no no."

No No List: Every prison gang has a ledger of "No Good" former members who are targeted for attack whenever the opportunity becomes available. These lists are very extensive and can have hundreds of names on them. The no no list is usually "Hooped" for safekeeping.

No Warning Shots: The concrete walls of state prisons in California feature prominent signs that serve as a warning. They indicate that if a physical altercation between inmates results in serious injury, the officers stationed in the towers will use a Mini-14 rifle to neutralize the aggressor.

No-Fly Zone: A place in prison where fights among convicts is strictly prohibited. The "Visiting Room" is a prime example of a no-fly zone. If an inmate starts a fight in a no-fly zone, he will get a "DP" by his "Car."

No-Go: A prison yard that "Mainline" convicts are not allowed to "Program" on by their "Faction." If they are transferred to a no-go yard, they must attack someone so they get taken off of the yard. If a convict programs on a no-go yard, their own gang members will "Remove" them if it is ever discovered. For example, "In 2019, when I was locked up, Donovan Prison was a no-go for 'Peckerwoods.'"

Non Active Verses Active: Active inmates adopt a stringent stance on "Prison Politics," while inactive prisoners, primarily those on Level I and II yards, are endeavoring to serve their sentences peacefully. Notably, an active inmate cannot visit an inactive yard and "Program" with inactive inmates without jeopardizing their active status among their peers. Essentially, active inmates perceive themselves as "Mainline," while they view inactive inmates as "SNY."

Non Affiliated: An inmate who does not belong to a gang. In other words, they are just a "Civilian" doing their time.

Non Designated Program Facility: These yards started in 2018 and are supposed to be half "General Population" and half "SNY."

Non Program Yard: This yard is the new "Mainline," according to the California Department of Corrections and Rehabilitation. The convicts on these yards refuse to "Program" with "SNY" inmates.

Norco: This is a correctional institution officially known as the California Rehabilitation Center. It was previously referred to as the Norconian Club but was abandoned in 1940 and repurposed as a prison in 1962.

Norte: This word translates to north, and "Northerners" use it in graffiti and tattoos.

Norteño: The term "Norteño" denotes an individual hailing from the northern region, and a significant proportion of Hispanic gang members originating from Northern California identify as such. The prison gang "Nuestra Familia" exercises authority over Norteños both within correctional facilities and in the streets.

Norteño Administrator: The head authority of the "Norteño" education department in prison. This would be the person who is above the "Maestro" or "Norteño Teacher" in their prison chain of command.

Norteno Soldado: This is a "Norteno" who desires a closer commitment to the struggle of the Norteno cause.

Norteño Teacher: A designated "Norteño" who hands out weekly essays on Norteño culture and philosophy that the gang members must complete.

Northern Raza: The majority of Hispanic gang members hailing from Northern California are affiliated with the Norteños. The prison gang known as "Nuestra Familia" exercises control over the Norteños both within correctional facilities and in the streets.

Northern Riders: A "Norteño" movement started around the year 1999. The Northern Riders originally were Norteños who rebelled against their gang's politics that they disagreed with. They eventually became a well-respected and violent group on the "SNY" yards.

Northern Star: This is a tattoo of a star that a "Norteno" earns by "Putting In Work." If the star is colored in, it means they took a life.

Northern Structure: On January 22, 1984, the "Nuestra Familia" prison gang created a subgroup to offer protection and training to its members before they advance within the organization. This "Faction" can be compared to a minor league team, serving as a preparatory stage for the major leagues.

Northerner: Most Hispanic gang members from Northern California are northerners. The "Nuestra Familia" prison gang controls the northerners in prison and the streets.

Not A Good Look: Something that makes an inmate look bad. For example, "Spider, it's not a good look how you are always talking to those guards."

Not Coming Through: When someone agreed to do something for you, and they didn't.

Note: A written note from one convict to another.

Nothing Changes In Here But The Faces: This means things in prison remain the same, day after day. The only thing in prison that changes is the people who come and go.

Nothing Coming: When an inmate disrespects an officer, and the officer refuses to give him things as a result. For example, a "Problem Child" asks an officer for a favor, and the officer replies, "You got nothing coming."

Now What: After verbally confronting someone, this statement is a challenge to physical combat, especially if the previous words were harsh. Any person with self-respect would feel obligated to retaliate. For example, "Yeah, I just called you a punk! Now what?"

NSOL: This term refers to a member of the "Northern Structure." For example, "Get at Termite because he is an NSOL."

Nuestra Familia: Literally means "Our Family," and they are a prison gang that was formed by Hispanics from northern California to protect themselves from "La Eme."

Nuestra Raza: On January 22, 1984, the "Nuestra Familia" prison gang created a subgroup to offer protection and training to its members before they advance within the organization. This "Faction" can be compared to a minor league team, serving as a preparatory stage for the major leagues.

Nueva Flores: This is an "SNY" prison gang, and Nueva Flores translates to "New Flowers." They were started in the early 90s in High Desert State Prison. Word on the street says there is a small "Faction" of New Flowers still on the "Mainline" who don't associate with the New Flowers in SNY.

Number: The five-digit number assigned to all California Department of Corrections and Rehabilitation convicts.

Nut Check: To test a person to verify if they will fight when confronted or back down like a "Punk." Many people can put up a good "Front," but very few will stand their ground without showing fear when confronted with a violent beating by numerous gangsters. A nut check separates the men from the boys and silences somebody who constantly "Sells Wolf Tickets."

Nutter: A "J Cat" inmate, someone who is crazy. For example, "Why does Loko always stand by the phone and talk to himself? Is he a nutter?"

O

O Wing: The infamous "Adjustment Center" at Soledad State Prison.

O Wing Exercise Yard: This was the narrow exercise yard at Soledad Prison for inmates who were "Slammed Down" in "Max Row" in the "Adjustment Center." The dimensions of this yard were 40 x 150 feet. The yard had a basketball hoop, two shower heads, a speed bag, a handball court, exercise bars, and a punching bag.

OA: The acronym OA denotes the position of "Overall Authority," which is held by the "Norteño" responsible for supervising a specific "Housing Unit" or "Pod" within a correctional facility.

Observation Tower: In each yard, a designated "Tower" houses an officer who oversees inmates when they are outside their respective "Housing Units." This officer uses the public address system to summon inmates to the yard or for appointments as necessary. In the event of an emergency, the tower officer will instruct inmates to take cover by shouting "Get Down." Additionally, a "Mini-14" rifle is present in the tower, intended for use solely to protect lives during instances of violent assault.

OC Spray: The acronym OC stands for Oleoresin Capsicum, which is the technical term for pepper spray.

OCS: The Office of Correctional Safety plays a vital role in fulfilling the mission of the California Department of Corrections and Rehabilitation. Its primary objective is to safeguard the welfare of the general public while collaborating with the investigative tasks of the California Department of Corrections and Rehabilitation.

Off Program: When a prison gang member is investigated by his comrades for wrongdoing. He will be kept to the side, and no gang business or "Politics" will be shared with him until he is cleared of any violations. For example, "Mack is off program, so don't discuss any of our business with him."

Off The Chain: An inmate who is acting way too rambunctious and drawing too much attention to himself and his "Car." For example, "Krazy Boy, you are off the chain! You need to 'Pump Your Brakes' homie."

Off The Dribble: It means to state the obvious in a situation. For example, "Off the dribble, you know I will handle my business if things get 'Cracking.'"

Off The Hook: An inmate acting way too rambunctious and drawing too much attention to himself and his "Car." For example, "Crazy Ray, you are off the hook! You need to 'Slow Your Roll,' homie."

Off The Reservation: When a gang member is in "Bad Standing" with his "Faction" and the "Big Homie" puts a "Green Light" on him. For example, "Cowboy is off the reservation. Handle that."

Off The Top: It means to state the obvious in a situation. For example, "Off the top homie, you know I will handle my business if things 'Kick Off.'"

Off Tier Report: Whenever "Norteños" exit their designated tier or "Housing Unit" for medical appointments or other reasons, they must submit a written report detailing their whereabouts and any individuals they encountered during their absence. This report is subsequently submitted to "Tier Security" upon their return to their respective cells.

Office Of Correctional Safety: The Office of Correctional Safety plays a vital role in fulfilling the mission of the California

Department of Corrections and Rehabilitation. Its primary objective is to safeguard the welfare of the general public while collaborating with the investigative tasks of the California Department of Corrections and Rehabilitation.

Officer's Podium: The desk utilized by the "Floor Officers" in a "Housing Unit" or "Dorm" setting.

OG: A well-respected original gangster who has spent a lifetime "Putting In Work" and earning his stripes.

Okey Doke: To fall victim to deception or manipulation by an individual. For example, "I feel like such a 'Fish,' Clever made me fall for the old okey doke yesterday."

Old Corcoran: The common name for California State Prison, Corcoran.

Old Delano Prison: This is the common nickname for North Kern State Prison.

Old Folsom: The nickname for Folsom State Prison, which opened in July 26, 1880.

Old Man Date: When an old inmate gets a release date due to his advanced age. For example, "Grey Beard just got an old man date because of his age."

Old Timer: An older inmate who has been locked up for decades.

Old-G: This is a nickname for an older inmate.

On: A verbal warning used by convicts to alert fellow gang members what tier an officer is on. For example, "Cops on one" or "Cops on two."

On A Campaign: This means a person in prison is "Politicking" against someone and "Smutting Up" their name. For example,

"Casper is on a campaign against Felix. He won't let it go. It's personal."

On & Cracking: This indicates that a significant event is imminent. For example, when a person known for making money in prison arrives on the yard, his homies might say, "That's Indio; it's on and cracking now." If a war between "Factions" is about to "Jump Off," someone might say, "It's on and cracking with the Blacks."

On Blood: A serious declaration made by a "Blood" gang member, confirming the truthfulness of their statement. For example, "This is on Blood homie, Bam Bam snitched to the 'Po Po.'"

On Crip: A serious declaration made by a "Crip" gang member, confirming the truthfulness of their statement. For example, "This is on Crip homie, Ace snitched to the 'One Time.'"

On Deck: The next inmate in line to do the following "Mission" for his gang. For example, "Bash, you are on deck."

On Freeze: When a gangster with authority is stripped of his power by other high-ranking members. Being put on freeze can happen for a number of reasons in prison, and it is not uncommon.

On His Bumper: When a person aggressively confronts someone else about an issue they feel strongly about. For example, "The homies were on his bumper for what he yelled out of his cell."

On His Head: When a person violently assaults someone. For example, "They jumped on his head for what he was yelling on the tier last night."

On His Helmet: When a person violently assaults someone. For example, "The homies jumped on his helmet for not paying what he owed."

On His Neck: When a person violently assaults someone. For example, "That officer came at the homie foul, so he jumped on his neck."

On His: When an inmate is known for a specific type of behavior.

For example, "It's straight knocking fools out on his homeboy."

On Hold: When a prison gang member is investigated by his comrades for wrongdoing. He will be kept to the side, and no gang business or "Politics" will be shared with him until he is cleared of any violations. For example, "Wicked is on hold, so don't discuss any of our business with him."

On Ice: When a gangster with authority is stripped of his power by other high-ranking members. Being put on ice can happen for several reasons in prison, and it is not uncommon.

On My Bumper: When someone keeps harassing you and they won't leave you alone. For example, "Mustang is on my bumper, and he won't stop asking me to move into his cell."

On My Set: A solemn declaration made by a gang member, confirming the truthfulness of their statement. For example, "This is on my set, homie. Weasel is a snitch."

On Paper: Indisputable evidence against a person of violations that they have committed. For example, "We have it on paper that China snitched on Puppet."

On Paper: When a person is still on parole. For example, "I'm still on paper, homeboy. I have to watch what I do."

On Point: When convicts are on point, they are watching for anything or anyone that may be out to harm them or their homies.

On Sight: This means the next time you see someone, you will hurt or kill them without asking questions. For example, "It's on sight with the 'Peckerwoords.'"

On Sight With Weapons: This means the next time you see someone, you will attack them with weapons. For example, "Pincushion is a snitch! It's on sight with weapons."

On Swole: A very muscular or "Yoked" person. For example, "Hulk was on swole."

On That Kind Of Time: This describes the manner in which a convict does his prison time. For example, "I ain't on that kind of time, homie. I'm 'Doing My Own Number.'"

On The Beach: When an officer is suspended for 30 or 60 days without pay. For example, "I got 60 days on the beach for 'Holding My Mud' during that investigation."

On The Dead Homies: A serious declaration made by a gang member, confirming the truthfulness of their statement. For example, "On the dead homies, I didn't take your weed."

On The Hang: This refers to the size of a person's arms just hanging down without flexing them. For example, "That's a big dude. He has 20s on the hang."

On The Leg: An individual who persistently seeks validation and approval from others. For example, "Why is Officer Buck always following the sergeant around?" The answer is, "He's on the leg trying to get that 'Homie Hook Up' for '2nd Watch.'"

On The Leva: When people in your "Car" ignore you because of your bad behavior. Your fellow gang members will not associate with you until you redeem yourself, and that is usually accomplished by "Putting in Work" by doing a "Clean Up."

On The Next Thing Smoking: The inmate "On Deck" to do the next "Mission" for his gang. For example, "Maniac, you are on the next thing smoking."

On The Row: Convicts housed in "Death Row" at San Quentin State Prison. They have their own section, and in the past, they were given meals of better quality than the "General Population."

On The Shelf: When people in a "Car" ignore a person because of their bad behavior. Their fellow gang members will not associate with them until they redeem themselves. This is usually accomplished by "Putting In Work" by going on a "Mission" and doing a "Clean Up."

On The Shine: When people in your "Car" ignore you because of your bad behavior. Your fellow gang members will not associate with you until you redeem yourself, and that is usually accomplished by "Putting in Work" by doing a "Clean Up." For example, "Blackie is on the shine for not paying his debts."

On The Strength: Something that is given for free out of respect. For example, "Mousie, you can have these soups on the strength."

On The Wall: Whenever an inmate was causing problems, he would be told to "get on the wall." When the inmate placed both hands on the wall and spread his feet, he would be searched for "Contraband." Inmates were aware that keeping their hands on the wall during these searches was crucial, as any deviation from this procedure would indicate to officers that additional measures may be necessary to guarantee their safety.

On Their Square: An area in prison that another gang has control of.

For example, "The 'Bloods' were on their square by the basketball court."

One Brother: A common saying among the "Aryan Brotherhood" is that all it takes is one Aryan Brotherhood member to take over a prison. This is possible because one brother will have the backing of the entire organization.

One Debt Policy: Some "Factions" allow their members to have at most one drug debt at a time. If a member gets two drug debts, he will be "Violated" or "Removed." The one debt policy or "Zero Debt Policy" depends on who your current "Shot Caller" is.

One Hitta Quitta: A person who frequently knocks people out. For example, "Killa Twan has a one hitta quitta. He stays knocking fools out."

One Hitta Quitta: The phrase refers to an inmate-manufactured weapon that is only good for one stabbing because it is made of weak material. For example, "I have a one hitta quitta, and I'm going to 'Poke' Thumper."

One In The Hole: When the officer in the tower chambers a round in the Mini-14 rifle, sometimes officers on the yard near the inmate trying to kill someone else might yell, "One in the hole." While yelling this, they step back so they don't get hit with the bullet. After seeing how bad most correctional officers did during range qualification, I used to joke that I feared being shot by them during a riot.

One Time: A "Kite" that has an important message on it and should be destroyed after reading.

One Time: A slang term for a correctional officer.

One Up One Down: When inmates need to watch out for various reasons, one homie will stay awake while the other sleeps. After a few hours, they will switch so the other homie can rest.

One Way: A "Kite" that has an important message on it and should be destroyed after reading.

One-For-One: When inmates want to pass the time, they tell stories to each other. They take turns recounting a story, and their homie tells one after they finish. They do this for hours, and it helps them pass the time. For example, "Let's do a one-for-one, homeboy."

Open Line: When "Canteen" opens on the yard and anyone can buy items as long as they haven't maxed their "Draw" for the month. Open line usually occurs on Saturday.

Open Locker Policy: When "Bunkys" agree to share their "Canteen" with each other. They can take food from each other's "Locker" without asking.

Open Shelf Policy: When "Bunkys" agree to share their "Canteen" with each other. They can take food from each other's shelves without asking.

Open The Books: When a prison gang recruits "Fresh Blood" into their organization after the "Books Were Closed." For example, "A little bird told me that 'La Eme' is going to open the books and 'Make Fresh Blood.'"

Open The Tier: In the "Hole," the "Shot Caller" will yell out of his cell and say good morning to each of his comrades in their cells, and they will reply good morning. Once the tier is open, they can "Fish" and talk to people in other cells.

Opening The Books: When a prison gang recruits "Fresh Blood" into their organization after the "Books Were Closed." For example, "I heard the 'Brand' are opening the books."

Opening The Tier: In the "Hole," the "Shot Caller" will yell out of his cell and say good morning to each of his comrades in their cells, and they will reply good morning. Once the tier is open, they can "Fish" and talk to people in other cells.

Opening Up A Yard: When this happens, a bunch of new inmates are shipped to a prison yard, and all of the "Factions" start to fight over who gets what bench, bleacher, area to hang out at, good jobs, etc. Every "Car" wants the most advantageous location to call its own and the best inmate jobs, so wars will be waged over who gets what. A new yard is notorious for violence as these crucial issues get settled.

Ops: This word is short for opposition and refers to a person's enemies.

Oranges: The orange jumpsuits worn by "Fish" inmates before they are assigned to a prison or yard.

Ordered Over: When a correctional officer is ordered to stay for another shift because no other officers will voluntarily work a vacant post. There is no choice in the matter; they will be severely punished if they refuse to work after being "Held Over." Sometimes, after our shift, the prison gates would be locked until an officer was assigned to work a vacant position. They decide who will be held over by our seniority number in reverse order, so the "Fish" cops were always ordered over.

Oriental Toilet: A "Strip Cell" from many years ago had a hole in the floor used as a toilet.

Orientation Building: The "Housing Unit" on the prison yard where the "Fish" inmates are housed for approximately two weeks until their paperwork is caught up. These inmates must wear orange jumpsuits, and when they walk to the "Dining Hall," their hands must be behind their backs.

OTC: This acronym stands for Out To Court. This refers to when an inmate is away from prison and at a county jail fighting their case.

Other: This term refers to convicts with an Oriental, Islander, or Native American heritage. Other convict's closest allies in prison are the Black convicts. The four racial breakdowns in prison are White, Black, Hispanic, and Other.

Other Side: In prison, there are two groups of inmates, "Mainline" and "SNY." When they talk about the other group, this is how they describe it. For example, "The other side is full of 'Chomos,' snitches, and dope fiends."

Other Side Of The Fence: In prison, there are two groups of inmates, "Mainline" and "SNY." When they talk about the other group, this is how they describe it. For example, "The other side of the fence is full of crash dummies who are controlled by the 'Big Homies.'"

Out Bad: When an inmate can't take the pressure on a prison yard and tells the officers they need "Protective Custody." For example, "I am never going out bad. They are going to have to take me off of this yard feet first before that ever happens, homeboy."

Out Count: A record of all inmates authorized to be away from the cells during "Count."

Out Date: The specific day that an inmate is supposed to be released from prison.

Out Of Bounds: An area in prison where convicts are not allowed. For example, "Get away from that cell door! You are out of bounds!"

Out Of Bounds: When a gang member gets caught slipping by his enemies on their turf. For example, "My homie Risky was killed a few days after he was paroled. He was caught out of bounds on Whittier Boulevard."

Out Of Bounds: When a person is doing something disrespectful. For example, "Don't ask me that question, homie. You are out of bounds!"

Out Of Line: When a person acts disrespectfully, or against the organization's rules, continued behavior will result in disciplinary action. For example, "Rojo, I heard what you said to your old lady at your visit. We don't get down like that. It was out of line. We, as 'Norteños,' are supposed to be professional at all times."

Out Of Pocket: To express or engage in behavior significantly beyond acceptable norms or boundaries. For example, "8-Ball, you were out of pocket. Don't ever do that again."

Out Of State Prisons: Many inmates under the jurisdiction of the California Department of Corrections and Rehabilitation were compelled to serve their sentences in correctional facilities outside California, specifically in Arizona and Oklahoma. These facilities afforded the inmates certain privileges that were not permitted in California prisons, including access to video game consoles.

Outfit: A prison-made device used to inject intravenous drugs. The outfit is made of an eye dropper, a sharpened guitar string, and a shaft of a plastic ink pen that has been cut down to size.

Over-Familiarity: When prison staff members become excessively familiar with inmates, it is known as over-familiarity. Correctional officers receive training to prevent this from happening to ensure they do not form intimate connections with inmates, as these relationships can compromise their personal and professional ethics. As a result, various protocols have been established, such as avoiding using inmates' first names, refraining from bringing outside items to inmates, abstaining from sharing food, avoiding physical contact like hugs or taps on the shoulder, and not making phone calls on behalf of inmates.

Overall Authority: This is the "Norteño" who oversees an individual "Housing Unit" or "Pod" in a prison or jail setting.

Override: When an inmate gains admittance to a program or prison he doesn't normally qualify for.

Owe The House: Profits from illegal activities that go to the "Big Homies" of a gang. Usually, 1/3 of profits are owed to the House.

Owes The House: This means a homie messed up, and he owes 113 to 1,300 "Burpees," depending on the severity of his infraction.

Own The House: A prison or prison yard where a particular gang has a tight grip on running the "Program." For example, "The 'Homies' own the house at Calipat."

P

P Code: When an inmate can't be placed below a level II prison yard. This is also called a "Hard 19," the 19 refers to the inmate's "Points," and to go to a level 1 prison yard, he can't have more than 18 points.

P-38: This is a tiny and flat can opener that inmates use to open cans of food in prison. The P-38 can opener was included in the field rations of U.S. service members from World War II into the 1980s.

Pack Out: When a group of inmates violently attack another person, get them on the ground, and then kick and stomp them.

Pack Them Out: When a group of inmates violently attack another person, get them on the ground, and then kick and stomp them.

Package: In the old days, an inmate was allowed a "Quarterly Package" from family and friends weighing up to thirty pounds every four months. These packages include food, snacks, "Hygiene," clothes, and other items. The packages would first go through "Receiving and Release" to be x-rayed for "Contraband" before being given to the inmate. Families can no longer personally send packages to their loved ones in prison. They order these items from a CDCR-approved vendor, and then the vendor will ship them to the inmates in prison.

Packed Out: When a group of inmates violently attack another person, get them on the ground, and then kick and stomp them. For example, "Joker didn't pay his gambling debts so that's why he got packed out."

Packing Out: When an inmate packs his property before he is transferred to a different location. For example, "Homie, I'm packing out this morning. I got my ticket to Pleasant Valley Prison."

Packing Wounds: When inmates get "Poked" in prison, they sometimes pack their wounds to stop the bleeding. The following is a true story about a convict who packed his wounds. Two inmates got the "Green Light" to move on the "Shot Caller" for not kicking 1/3 of the drug sales up to the "Big Homies." They "Booked" him quickly, and no officers saw the assault. The victim entered his cell and packed his wounds with Folgers instant coffee. The victim waited for evening yard, brought his "Banger," and started "Blasting" the dude who stabbed him earlier.

Pad: Another name for a prison cell. For example, "I got those soups I owe you, comrade. They are in my pad."

PAD: This acronym stands for Personal Alarm Device, and some officers assigned to specific posts must always have it on them. If there is an emergency, the officer will press their PAD, and a loud alarm will sound on the outside of the building accompanied by a flashing light, and other officers will sprint to its location.

Padrino: The "Mexican Mafia" member who sponsors a recruit or membership into "La Eme."

Paid In Blood: To get revenge on another person or group by spilling their blood. For example, "Yeah, those vatos got us last week, but today they paid in blood."

Paint Job: This means a person has a lot of tattoos. For example, "Diamond is a 'Punk,' he is just 'A Lame With A Paint Job.' His homies don't even respect him."

Painting The Yard Red: When a prison yard is so violent, blood is always spilled. For example, "Calipat C-Yard was 'Rocking,' we painted the yard red with blood."

Paisa: The name for someone from a country south of the border that isn't Mexico.

Paisano: This is the name for a Mexican National in prison.

Palabra: A word that translates to word. For example, "Duke broke his palabra to the 'Big Homie,' he has to go."

Paño: An intricate picture that is drawn on a prison handkerchief. These works of art are usually sent home to loved ones for special occasions.

Paper For Paper: This is when a convict pays back a drug debt with drugs instead of money. A "Paper" in prison is commonly $50 worth of drugs. For example, "Nah, homie, I don't want paper for paper. You need to pay me what we agreed on."

Papered Up: When convicts place drugs into little pieces of paper in preparation for distribution in the penitentiary. These "Papers" usually sell for $50.

Papers: A little square piece of folded paper that has $50 worth of heroin in it. This is the standard amount of heroin that is sold in prison.

Paperwork: This paperwork shows what crime a convict was incarcerated for and all relevant court documents. Every convict in a "Car" has their "Black & Whites" checked by other gang members to verify they don't have any "Bad Charges."

Paradise: An old-school nickname for California Men's Colony State Prison in San Luis Obispo.

Parking Lot Therapy: Back in the day, officers would physically assault other officers in the parking lot over severe issues like snitching, sleeping with their old lady, heated disagreements, etc. Sometimes, officers would throw a slice of cheese on the car windshield of an officer who snitched on their partners.

Parole Hold: The law that allows a parole agent to place a parolee in custody if they violate their conditions of parole.

Parole Period: The time a parolee is on parole.

Parole, Snitch, or Die: This phrase refers to the only options available for release from the "Security Housing Unit" before the Ashker court case against the State of California.

Party: To drink and do drugs in prison. For example, "Back at Folsom, me and my comrades would party all of the time."

Party Line: When three or more convicts are involved in a conversation via vents or plumbing pipes within their cells. The water from the toilet can be emptied, and they can talk via the plumbing pipes to other convicts in different cells. For example, "Scooby, get on the party line, homie."

Pass: A "Kite" from the "Shot Caller" sent with prison gang members when they go to the "Hole" to verify that they had permission to attack their victims. If an inmate "Whacks" another inmate without permission, some prison gangs will discipline them when they get to "Administrative Segregation."

Patterns: The process of tattooing in prison. For example, "Puppet 'Blasted' these patterns on me, homeboy."

Pay In Blood: In gang life, there are always repercussions for reckless behavior. Most of the time, your enemies will slide through and make you pay in blood for what they perceive as disrespect.

Pay Number: A job in the prison that will pay an hourly wage. Inmates can make between .08 to .37 cents an hour at prison jobs. The inmate's salary at these pay rates is $12 to $56 monthly.

Pay The House: Profits from illegal activities that go to the "Big Homies" of a particular gang. Usually, 1/3 of profits has to be paid to the house.

Pay Your Debts: This is one of the most crucial rules of prison life for those incarcerated. So many people have been seriously hurt and killed in prison because some drug addict didn't pay what he owed. Countless riots have been started over some "Dope Fiend" not paying his debts. Gambling is another area where inmates can cause severe problems by not paying what they owe.

Paying Rent: Profits from illegal activities that go to the "Big Homies" of a particular gang. Usually, 1/3 of profits is paid in rent in this manner.

Paying Rent: When an inmate must pay another person or group of people "Canteen" for him to safely live among them.

Paying Taxes: Profits from illegal activities that go to the "Big Homies" of a particular gang. Usually, 1/3 of profits is paid in taxes in this manner.

PBSP: Pelican Bay State Prison.

PC: This acronym stands for Protective Custody. Protective custody prison yards are the majority of yards in CDCR now. These yards are considered "No Good" by the "General Population" convicts. The inmates on protective custody yards are the natural enemies of the general population convicts because many of them are former members of the gangs on the "Line." Most inmates in protective custody are there for drug or gambling debts and "Bad

Paperwork." Protective custody yards tend to be more chaotic and violent than the "Mainline" because the gang structure is less rigid than the general population gangs.

PC Move: When an inmate feels pressure from his homies or another person and does something right in front of the police to get thrown in the "Hole." For example, some dude "Short To The House" is told he is "On Deck" for the next "Mission." He doesn't want to catch any more time, so he leaves his "Banger" out in the open so the police see it, and they send him to the hole until he is paroled.

Peace Treaty: This ended the war between "Northerners" and "Southerners." This bloody prison and street war lasted from approximately 1968 to 2012.

Peckerwood: A solid White "Convict," and they usually go by "Wood" for short.

Peckerwood Flats: An area at Soledad Prison where the "Woods" would hang out.

Peckerwood Pie: Some "Peckerwoods" refer to their "Spread" as a Peckerwood Pie.

Pedazo: A word that translates to "piece" and can be used to describe a "Banger" or "Tomahawk" in prison. For example, "Grumpy, slide me that pedazo, homie."

Peed On Himself: When an inmate shows fear or cowardice and fails to do what is expected. For example, "I told Trey if he ever got at me like that again that I would put hands on him. He peed on himself and apologized."

Peel Out: This means to remove your clothing for a "Strip Search" or to show off a muscular physique. For example, "You think you're bigger than me, youngster? Peel out! Let's see what you are working with."

Peeling Caps: When a convict gets violently hit in the head with a prison-made weapon such as a "Lock In A Sock." For example, "During the riot at Tracy, they were peeling caps."

Peels: These are the paper-like jumpsuits inmates wear when transported on the "Grey Goose."

Peep This Out: This means to pay attention. For example, "Peep this out homie, you need to 'Slow Your Roll' because you are 'Heading For A Wreck.'"

Peeped The Move: When a convict is aware of other inmates subtly sliding up on him to confront him about an issue. Once he recognizes their play, he either goes on the offensive or, if possible, plays it cool to survive until he has his homies with him. For example, "Kilo peeped the move when those cats posted up on his flank and asked him if he wanted any problems, and he said no."

Pegada: This is when an inmate has violated the "Reglas" of his gang, and for punishment, his homies will "Poke" him with a "Banger."

Pen: This is short for the word penitentiary. For example, "Listen up, little homie, the pen ain't no place to be. When you get out this time, stay out. You need to do right by your family and change your life. There is nothing here for you, brother."

Pencil Whip: This means to fill out paperwork to report an incident in prison. An officer can pencil whip paperwork on an inmate, or an inmate can pencil whip paperwork on an officer via a "602" Inmate Appeal Form.

PENI: Stands for Public Enemy Number 1, and they are a vicious and ruthless White gang who has direct ties to the "Aryan Brotherhood." PENI pushes a "Hardline" of "Prison Politics."

PENI Death Squad: These members of Public Enemy Number One are even more violent and bloodthirsty than regular members. The PENI Death Squad is similar to the special forces of PENI because they are a cut above the rest in perpetrating violence.

Penitentiary Chances: This means living a reckless life and taking chances on getting busted and doing a lengthy prison sentence.

Penitentiary Reputation: The "Status" a convict has among his peers. The respect a convict is given by the other members of his "Car." Many times in prison, all a man has left is his reputation, so he will go to great lengths to preserve it.

People: The people in prison who belong to your race and "Car." For example, "Listen up youngster, you have to back the play of your people in prison, or it will be you getting 'Poked.'"

Pepsi Generation EME: The younger generation of "Mexican Mafia" members. This is how the old-school EME members referred to the new "Carnals " that came to power in the 80s and 90s.

Perro: A word that translates to dog, and in gang life, it means a close homie. For example, "Huero is my perro, we go way back to 'YA.'"

Personal Hard Candy: This is a "Green Light" put on a specific person versus a Green Light put on an entire "Barrio." For example, "Popeye from Lomas has a personal hard candy on him."

Peseta: A derogatory term for the "25" "SNY" group.

Peter Gazer: An inmate who stares at naked men while they are in the shower.

PFL: A tattoo that White inmates get that means "Peckerwood" for life.

Phone: In the "Security Housing Unit" or the "Hole," the toilet can be emptied of water and used to talk to other convicts. For example, "Flaco, get on the phone, homie."

Phone Time: Things have changed regarding phone times in California prisons. When inmates get to a yard, they are all given a tablet. This tablet lets them text, call, and video chat with people. The first few calls are free to the inmates.

Physical Treatment: Getting physically assaulted in a violent manner. For example, "Lowdown didn't pay his debt to Bruiser, so he got the physical treatment."

PIA: Acronym for the Prison Industry Authority, run by the state of California, employs inmates for a meager wage to make merchandise for sale at a significant profit. The inmates make anywhere between .30 to .95 cents an hour before deductions.

Pick: A weapon made in prison similar to an ice pick. For example, "The homie pulled out a pick and walked up to the dude and ran it through his neck."

Pick & Poke: A tattoo done in prison with a sharpened staple dipped in ink. The homie doing this primitive tattoo will repeatedly poke the staple into the skin to get the ink into the dermis layer.

Picked Up Cases: When convicts put in serious work in prison and pick up charges from the local district attorney. For example, "The homies all picked up cases for that hit on Pelon."

Picture Count: This type of "Count" in prison uses the inmate's picture identification to verify who they are.

Picture Day: This is the day that "IGI" goes around the prison and takes updated pictures of gang members in the prison.

Piece: A prison knife made out of metal, melted plastic, or any other hard material that can be sharpened to a point.

Piece For Piece: When two convicts agree to a knife fight. This usually takes place in a prison cell. For example, "Big James and Bronco went piece for piece in the cell."

Piece Of St:** This is one of the most common terms that "Active" convicts use to describe inmates who are "SNY." The inmates in SNY will say this term doesn't apply to them. They claim "Chomo's" and "Snitches" are the actual pieces of s**t, not them. For example, "Looney went to the other side of the fence. He is a piece of s**t."

Piece Of Trash: This is one of the most common terms that "Active" convicts use to describe inmates who are "SNY." The inmates in SNY will say this term doesn't apply to them. They claim "Chomo's" and "Snitches" are the actual pieces of trash, not them. For example, "Savage went to the other side of the fence. He is a piece of trash."

Piece Of Work: A person who can sometimes be challenging to get along with. For example, "It's like that? You are a piece of work, homeboy."

Pig: A slang term for a correctional officer. For example, "I filed a '602' on that pig for harassment."

Pig Iron: Back in the day in CDC, when they still had the "Weight Pile," this term was used for the weights.

Pill Call: This is the designated time that inmates who receive medication on the prison yard line up at the "Pill Line" to receive it.

Pill Line: This is where inmates on the yard who get medication line up to get their pills. The inmate must be observed swallowing their pill after receiving it so they can't go and sell it to other inmates.

Pilli: A "Nahuatl" word some "Southerners" use when referring to a "Mexican Mafia" member. For example, "That 'Carnal' had a lot of 'Reach.' That pilli had anything he wanted."

Pinching: This term refers to an inmate who takes drugs that don't belong to them.

Pincushion Smith: An infamous White inmate who was sliced and stabbed dozens of times by the orders of the "Brand," yet kept surviving. One inmate described him as "A big cockroach and you couldn't kill him."

Pinochle: A very popular card game in prison.

Pinta: A word that translates to prison.

PIP: The Psychiatric Inpatient Program provides intense treatment for inmates in the California Department of Corrections and Rehabilitation mental health program.

PIP Inmates: These are inmates in the Psychiatric Inpatient Program in the California Department of Corrections and Rehabilitation.

Pipeline: The person and the way drugs and other "Contraband" enter the prison.

Piru: Piru's are part of the "Bloods" family, originating on Piru Street in Compton, California. Piru's are Bloods, but all Bloods aren't

Piru's. Pirus primarily wear the color burgundy.

Pisas: These are Mexican nationals in the California Department of Corrections and Rehabilitation.

Pissed On Himself: When an inmate shows fear or cowardice and fails to do what is expected. For example, "I caught Smurf in the 'Blind' and he pissed on himself after I slapped him."

Pisser: The name inmates use for the urinals in prison.

Pisto: A word that some inmates use for "Pruno."

Pistol: A prison knife made out of metal, melted plastic, or any other hard material that can be sharpened to a point.

PK: The staff cafeteria has greasy and horrible-tasting food with outrageous prices. If I ever ate at the PK, I would get yogurt, orange juice, and some hard-boiled eggs. This was the healthiest food available, and I wanted my body fat to be very low.

Placa: A word used in prison that translates to the "Street Name" of a gang member. For example, Flaco, Creeper, Silent, Termite, Sleepy, Tiny, Oso, Thumper, Primo, Pelon, Stranger, Smiley, Toro, Spanky, and Tio are all placas.

Placa: A slang word for a tattoo. For example, "Homie, who did that placa on your neck?"

Placa: A slang word for police. For example, "Lefty has been talking to the placa. He is 'No Good.'"

Placement Score: When an inmate goes to a "Reception Center," he is eventually given a placement score, determining his "Security Level." These security levels range from Level I to Level IV. The inmate's placement score is based on various factors such as their crimes, sentence length, escape risk, age, etc. The placement score determining the housing security level is 0-18 Level I, 19-35 Level II, 36-59 Level III, and 60+ Level IV.

Plain As Jane: When something is very obvious to people. For example, "It's plain as Jane that Trooper is the one 'Dropping Kites' to the police. Every time a homie starts to come up and threaten his position, they get 'Rolled Up.'"

Plantation: Some Black inmates refer to prisons as plantations and a continuation of slavery. They believe the prison system is racist, cruel, inhumane, and focused on the oppression of Black men.

Plantation System: Some Black inmates feel the prison system is a continuation of slavery. They believe the system is racist, cruel, inhumane, and focused on the oppression of Black men.

Plastico: This is an insult directed at a fake homie who folds under pressure. This term can also mean a homie has disregarded his Mexican roots.

Play For Keeps: This means a person or group of people push a "Hardline" regarding their business. If you play around with them, you will "Pay In Blood." For example, "You better watch out, homie, those vatos play for keeps."

Play Now, Pay Later: This common gang member philosophy means to live life to the fullest today and worry about the consequences later. The tattoo associated with this mindset is two theatrical masks: one is laughing, and one is crying.

Play Out Of Pocket: The process of disarming a person so that you can easily take advantage of them in some fashion. When a person is being played for a fool, they have no idea they are being set up.

Play The Dummy: When you know someone is trying to get over on you, but you play along to expose them later. For example,

"Sometimes you have to play the dummy to catch the dummy."

Play With Weapons: This means a person or group is known for using weapons when they fight other people or "Factions." For example, "Those dudes play with weapons. They have 'Priors.'"

Play Your Part: When an inmate puts in the work for his gang. Every prison gang member will play their part by doing things that need to be done for their "People."

Playa: This word translates to beach, but in prison, this means to take a shower. For example, "Who has next in the playa?"

Playboys: Another name for the "Northern Riders," aka "Certified Riders."

Played Him Out Of The Box: The process of disarming a target for assault or robbery by making them believe that you are friends. Playing them out of the box makes them easier to kill or rob because they aren't expecting it. For example, "How did you ever 'Poke' Big Mike?" The answer, "I played him out of the box, homie. He thought we were going to 'Mainline' some 'Black', but I just played him to get close and make my move."

Playing With Feelings: When a person is easily offended. For example, "I didn't know you were playing with feelings homeboy. If you wanted to work with feelings, homie, you should have been a dentist."

Playing With My Nose: This means a person is snorting drugs. For example, "When we went on 'Lockdown,' I started playing with my nose."

Plug: The convict bringing drugs or other "Contraband" into prison.

For example, "Pirate is the plug for the 'Southsiders.'"

Plugged: When someone gets "Blasted" in prison. For example, "Blizzard got plugged today on the yard. They poked ten holes in him."

Plugged Him: When someone gets "Blasted" in prison. For example, "Biggum got plugged today on the yard. They poked 15 holes in him."

Plugged In: When an inmate is a member of a prison gang. For example, "Venom is plugged in. Be careful what you say around him, homie."

Plugged In: When a convict communicates with the "Brass" of a prison gang. For example, "Bulldog is plugged in, so he has the ear of the 'Big Homie.'"

Plumbing Crew: A group of inmates who help fix plumbing issues on prison grounds. They have access to every yard, so they can easily pass "Contraband" anywhere in the prison.

Plushed Out: When a person "Comes Up" materially or financially in prison, they live very "Comfortable."

Po Po: A slang term for a correctional officer.

Pod: A small-sized housing unit in some California prisons, such as Pelican Bay State Prison. Also, in most county jails in California, the housing units are called pods. For example, "That fool Joker 'Drove Up' to our pod and started 'Stepping On Toes.'"

Podium: The area in a "Housing Unit" or "Dorm" with a desk or podium where the Corrections Officer sits or stands.

Pods: In most county jails and some prisons in California, the housing units inmates live in are called pods. For example, "What pod were you in back in county?"

Point Blank Period: This statement is used for emphasis to finish a sentence. For example, "That punk has to go. Point, blank, period!"

Point Man: The convict responsible for keeping watch during the illegal activities of his homies. The point man will give an alarm signal agreed upon previously or create a diversion to give his homies time to escape.

Points: When an inmate goes to a "Reception Center," he is eventually given points determining his "Security Level." These security levels range from Level I to Level IV. The inmate's points are based on various factors such as their crimes, length of sentence, escape risk, age, and other factors. The points determining the housing security level are 0-18 Level I, 19-35 Level II, 36-59 Level III, and 60+ Level IV.

Poison: When an inmate mixes his feces, urine, insect guts, and blood and lets it ferment in a cup until mold forms on top. The inmate then coats his "Shank," "Spear," or "Tomahawk" with the putrid concoction and then attacks his victim, more than likely giving him a severe infection. Poison is especially devastating when the inmate making it has H.I.V. or hepatitis.

Poison: When someone is pushing an idea or movement that goes against the gang's philosophy. For example, many times in prison, when a gang member becomes a Christian and starts talking to others about Jesus and the Bible, they are branded as poisoning people by the "Shot Callers." They will warn them to stop talking about it; if they don't, they will be "Removed."

Poisoning People: When someone is pushing an idea or movement that goes against the gang's philosophy. For example, many times in prison, when a gang member becomes a Christian and starts talking to others about Jesus and the Bible, they are branded as poisoning people by the "Shot Callers." They will warn them to stop talking about it; if they don't, they will be "Removed."

Poke: When an inmate stabs another person with a "Banger." For example, "Dude came at me sideways, so I had to poke him."

Poked: The act of stabbing someone in prison with a "Banger."

Poked Up: When an inmate gets stabbed numerous times in prison. For example, "That fool got poked up real good. They had to airlift him."

Poking: To stab someone with an inmate-manufactured weapon. For example, "Calipat was scandalous. They were poking fools on the regular."

Police: A slang term for a correctional officer.

Police Lover: A derogatory term convicts use for an inmate who is too friendly with correctional officers. For example, "We warned the homie about being a police lover. He is talking to the police too much and joking with them. If he doesn't stop playing like that, we are going to 'Smash' him."

Polishing The Rock: This means a person is "Putting In Work" for the "Aryan Brotherhood" on the streets or in prison. For example, "Viking hit the streets and hasn't stopped polishing the rock."

Polite Killers: Believe it or not, in California prisons, most convicts are very polite. Throughout the day, you will hear hundreds of "My Bad," "Spensa," and "Good Looking Out." Don't let this fool you. Once you disrespect a convict in prison, he will aggressively confront you without hesitation.

Political Ink: These are tattoos that can only be earned in prison.

These types of tattoos, for the most part, are for shedding the blood of your rivals. These tattoos are taken very seriously, and if an inmate gets one without having earned it, his gang members will discipline them and make him remove them, cover it up, or earn it.

Politician: A convict who is very good at "Politicking" in prison. For example, "Straight up, I was a politician in the penitentiary."

Politicking: To use your influence in your "Car" to try and get another member "Removed," "Disciplined," or just to "Smut Up" his name because you don't like him. Politicking means pushing a "Hardline" against any group or person in prison.

Politicking With Emotions: This behavior is frowned upon when homies engage in "Prison Politics" based on emotions. An example of politicking with emotions would be a "Big Homie" showing "Homeboy Favoritism."

Politics: The rules that govern convict behavior within their gangs and prison in general. For example, "So why did Ghost get shanked?" The answer is, "Politics, homie."

Politics Is A Lifer's Game: This prison saying means you don't have to get involved in "Prison Politics" if you don't have a life sentence. Try to stay away from the politics and "Do Your Own Time."

Pony Express: This refers to the regular mail inmates get via the postal service.

Pookie: A slang term for methamphetamines.

Popcorn Balls: Inmates cook pancake syrup and peanut butter to make the caramel. They put the caramel in a bowl and make little balls with the popcorn. Homemade popcorn balls sell for $1 in prison.

Popoca: This word is used for tobacco in prison. It is a "Nahautl" word that means to smoke.

Popped: When a person gets arrested. For example, "I got popped because that punk snitched on me."

Popped: When a convict's cell door is opened so they can exit. For example, "That crooked officer popped my door when the enemy was on the tier."

Popped Off: When many convicts are involved in a fight amongst themselves. For example, "It popped off between the 'Southerners' and 'Northerners' during 'Yard Recall.'"

Popped Out: When a convict's cell door is opened so they can exit. For example, "I popped out Big Tony so he can go to his visit."

Popping Doors: When officers in the "Control Booth" open cell doors in the "Housing Unit." For example, "In the Pelican Bay SHU, those officers were popping doors and setting the homies up."

Popping Off: When many convicts are involved in a fight amongst themselves. For example, "It was popping off between the 'Peckerwoods' and the 'Kumis.'"

Popping Sockets: When inmates stick prison-made devices into electrical sockets to light their cigarettes and joints. Due to this dangerous process, the electrical socket will have burn marks around it from the electricity arcing. For example, "The homies are over there popping sockets."

Pops: This is a nickname for an older inmate.

Porch: The cement area near a convict's cell or bunk.

Porter: A convict whose job is to clean up a specific area in prison, and he usually gets paid for this job by the state. The average pay for a porter is about .25 an hour. A porter is also referred to as a "Tier Tender" or "Trustee."

Positive Count: This type of "Count" in prison is the inmates the officers see living and breathing.

Post And Bid: Every two years, correctional officers get to bid on positions (posts) based on seniority. Because of this, the veteran officers get the "good" jobs with excellent days off, and the rookies will get the Level III and IV "3rd Watch" jobs with Wednesdays and Thursdays or similar strange days off.

Post Orders: For each post in prison, there is a binder with all of the officer's responsibilities and duties listed line by line. A "Fish" officer should become very familiar with their post orders so they will have a clue on what they are supposed to do for the eight hours during their shift.

Posted Up: Being a "Soldier" for your gang when others are around. Standing defiantly in the face of your enemies while protecting your turf.

Potty Watch: When an inmate is suspected of ingesting drugs, he is placed in a cell in the "Infirmary" with no running water, and his feces is checked for "Contraband."

Power Move: It's relatively common in prison for gangs to fight within their own ranks over who will be the one calling the shots on a particular yard or prison. More often than not, once the dust settles, the soldiers who supported the losing side will be "Removed" by the ones who won the battle. Ultimately, most of these power moves are over who will control the drug trade on a particular yard or prison. Countless loyal homies have ended their careers by being on the losing side of these civil wars.

Power Struggle: It's relatively common in prison for gangs to fight within their own ranks over who will be the one calling the shots on a particular yard or prison. More often than not, once the dust settles, the soldiers who supported the losing side will be "Removed" by the ones who won the battle. Ultimately, most of these power struggles are over who will control the drug trade on a particular yard or prison. Countless loyal homies have ended their "Careers" by being on the losing side of these civil wars.

PREA: This acronym stands for the Federal Rape Elimination Act. In 2021, there were 215 reported cases of nonconsensual sexual acts in the California Department of Corrections and Rehabilitation, according to the PREA annual report.

Press: To test a person to verify if they will fight when confronted or back down like a "Punk." Many people can put up a good "Front," but very few will stand their ground without showing fear when confronted with a violent beating by numerous gangsters. To press someone is used to separate the soldiers from those who are "Selling Wolf Tickets."

Press Him: To try and intimidate another inmate to do something you want or to give you something he has. For example, "Wild Bill was on the phone, and I tried to press him about his phone time, and he 'Took Off' on me."

Pressed: When a person is confronted about their gang affiliation. For example, "As soon as I 'Landed' in county jail, I was pressed on where I was from."

Pressure Case: An inmate who has succumbed to the pressure of "Prison Politics" or other issues on a prison yard.

Pressure Groups: This is an old-school term used by the California Department of Corrections to describe a "Disruptive Group" of inmates.

Primo: A word that translates to cousin.

Primo: This is a "Camarada" who has a lot of "Status" among his peers, and their name is well known in the prison system and the streets. A primo works under a "Carnal" and will likely be "Pulled" in the future.

Priors: Used to describe a person who is notorious for doing certain things. For example, "T-Dog will kill a cat just for looking at him sideways. He has priors, homie."

Prison Dad: A convict who has been down for a long time, and they take a youngster under his wings to "School" him. He looks after the youngster like a son and cares for his well-being.

Prison Father: A convict who has been down for a long time, and they take a youngster under his wings in order to "School" him. He looks after the youngster like a son and cares for his well-being.

Prison Is A Numbers Game: This means that power in prison is based on how many members a "Faction" has on the yard. Whatever gang has the most soldiers on a yard means they will run the "Program" on that yard.

Prison Line: The prison rumor mill and line of communication that follows every convict and keeps tabs on everyone. There are no secrets in prison.

Prison Pocket: When a convict places items of "Contraband" in his rectum to avoid discovery by officers. Some convicts become very proficient at this and can do it in seconds. When a "Banger" is placed inside of the prison pocket, it will have a protective layer of cellophane to prevent their insides from being perforated.

Prison Politician: A convict who enjoys "Prison Politics" and being involved in the political drama on the prison yard. For example, "Stalker is a prison politician."

Prison Politics: The rules governing convict behavior within their own gangs and prison. For example, "So why did Creeper get shanked?" The answer is, "Prison politics, homie."

Prison Roll: A thinly rolled cigarette or joint.

Prison Safe: When a convict places items of "Contraband" in his rectum to avoid discovery by officers. Some convicts become very proficient at this and can do it in seconds. When a "Banger" is placed inside of the prison safe, it will have a protective layer of cellophane to prevent their insides from being perforated. For example, "I stashed the 'Clavo' in the prison safe, homie."

Prison Tip: A prison gang in the California Department of Corrections and Rehabilitation.

Privilege Group: There are four privilege groups of inmates, and each group has different benefits to help promote a desire in the inmates to "Program."

Problem Child: An "Inmate" who does not have any respect for other people and they are constantly complaining and causing problems with your "Program."

Problems: When a person is having confrontations or drama with other people. For example, "That punk doesn't want any problems. He's not going to push the issue."

Program: This word means the routine for a person or administration in prison. For example, "Why are you messing with my program?"

Program Failure: An inmate can be designated a program failure for various reasons, including refusing to work and other rules violations.

Program Office: On each prison yard, there is a Program Office where the "Yard Officers," "Search and Escort Officers," Sergeant, and lieutenant have their offices. The Program Office is the command center of each prison yard for the correctional facility.

Program Sergeant: The program sergeant is in charge of each yard (under the lieutenant), and if you have an excellent program sergeant on a yard, things run smoothly. If you have a terrible program sergeant, the officers are in for one long and highly stressful shift.

Program Yard: This yard is a "50/50 Yard," according to the California Department of Corrections and Rehabilitation. The inmates on this yard who were once considered "Mainline" will "Program" with "SNY" inmates on their yard.

Programmer: A convict who follows the rules and does not give the officers any problems. Don't confuse being a programmer with being a "Punk" because they are entirely different. Frequently, programmers are the coldest killers in the entire prison. They don't like to bring unnecessary heat from the officers, so they keep a low profile.

Progressive Programming Facility (PPF): This is a yard where the convicts agree to a strict policy of not participating in any illegal activities. They agree to attend self-help groups and other programs and maintain a clean disciplinary record. If they break their agreement, they will be removed from the yard. The Progressive Programming Facility is also known as the "Honor Yard."

Property Card: A form held in "Receiving and Release" lists every electronic device (and other items) an inmate is authorized to have. If a television or radio were not on a convict's property card, he was not allowed to have them because they were not officially his.

Protect Your Neck: This means to watch yourself because your enemies are around and be ready to "Get Down." For example, "Check this out, youngster, this is a Level IV yard. You need to protect your neck at all times. They 'Play For Keeps' around here."

Protective Custody: Protective Custody prison yards are the majority of yards in CDCR now. These yards are considered "No Good" by the "General Population" convicts. The inmates on Protective Custody yards are the natural enemies of the general population convicts because many are former gang members on the "Line." Most inmates in Protective Custody are there for drug or gambling debts and "Bad Paperwork." Protective Custody yards tend to be more chaotic and violent than the "Mainline" because the gang structure is less rigid than the general population gangs.

Protective Housing Unit (PHU): This is a small special unit for 2030 high-profile inmates. People like Charles Manson and Sirhan Sirhan are housed there. They have a garden for those confined there to grow things and other amenities. They are kept away from other inmates due to their notoriety and the likelihood of being attacked by other inmates looking to make a name for themselves.

Protocol: The rules and regulations of a prison gang that all of its members must follow. The protocol is also referred to as "Household Policies," "Household Rules," "Bible," or "Code Of Conduct."

Prove Your Status: When a convict pushes a "Hardline" to gain "Status" from his "Car." For example, "If you're never going home, the best thing you can do is prove your status among your peers so people fear and respect you."

Pruno: An alcoholic beverage made from the following ingredients: apples, oranges, fruit cocktails, ketchup, and sugar. It is cooked for three days in a plastic trash bag until it ferments and produces an alcoholic beverage. Pruno has a putrid taste and smell; depending on what fruit is used, it can be red or orange. The going rate for a cup of pruno in prison is $8.00, and for a cup of the more potent "White Lightening," $20.

PSU: This acronym is Psychiatric Services Unit, a "Housing Unit" for inmates with mental health concerns.

Psychiatric Services Unit: This a "Housing Unit" for inmates with mental health concerns.

Public Pretender: The nickname convicts have for public defenders in court cases.

Pull: The influence that a convict or officer has to get things done in prison. For example, "Crook has a lot of pull. He has good 'Clecha.'"

Pull His Wig: To kill another person. For example, "There is a target on C yard. I need you to remove him once you hit that yard. You need to hit him and hit him good. You are doing 'All Day,' so you have nothing to lose, homie. If you can pull his wig, that's even better."

Pull Up: When a convict arrives at a new prison. For example, "What's up, homie? When did you pull up?"

Pull Your Card: Call someone's bluff or reveal secrets about them that they try to cover up.

Pull Your Covers: To call someone's bluff or to reveal damaging information about them. For example, "I am going to pull your covers about getting with that 'Punk' at Soledad."

Pull Your Card: To take out of circulation, to kill another person.

Pull Your Covers: Call someone's bluff or reveal damaging secrets about them. For example, "If you continue to mess with my program, I'm going to pull your covers about 'Dropping A Kite.'"

Pulled: When an inmate becomes a member of a prison gang. For example, "Comrade, did you hear that Peanuts got pulled?"

Pulled A Mission: When a convict is directed by his "Big Homies" to go and assault someone who is "No Good." For example, "I pulled a mission and ended up at San Quentin 'Ad-Seg' overflow."

Pulled Away: When a gang member retires from gang life for whatever reason. For example, "After my mom died, I pulled away from the streets."

Pulled His Status: When a gangster with authority is stripped of his power by other high-ranking members. A convict getting his status pulled can happen for several reasons in prison, which is not uncommon.

Pulled Me Out: When officers remove an inmate from a cell for several reasons. For example, "They pulled me out for a medical appointment," or "They pulled me out for my visit."

Pulled Over: Taking an inmate aside and performing a "Clothed Body Search" followed by questions concerning his suspicious or disrespectful behavior. For example, "I was pulled over on the way to chow."

Pulled Up: When a convict arrives at a new prison. For example, "Hey Spanky, guess who just pulled up?"

Pulling Heat: To pull out your "Banger" on another convict and either "Poke" him or threaten to poke him. For example, "If any of our people go around pulling heat on our homies over minor stuff, they got to go."

Pulling Paperwork: When the "Shot Callers" on the yard check the "Paperwork" of members in their "Faction." Paperwork is checked to verify nobody in their "Car" has any "Bad Charges." If a member is discovered to have "Funny Charges," their homies will violently remove them from the yard.

Pump Your Brakes: A warning to stop what you are doing before you get into a "Wreck." For example, "You need to pump your brakes, homie, before Sick Rick smashes you."

Pump-Up Case: When an inmate allows others to "Pump Him Up" and make him do things he usually wouldn't do. For example, "Don't be a pump-up case comrade. There's nothing worse in prison than to let someone pump you up. You let those cats create a problem by pumping you up."

Pumping Heart Into Him: To instigate a fight by challenging your homie's manhood. For example, "Venom, that cat owes you three books of stamps. Are you just going to let him punk you like that?"

Pumping You Up: To instigate a fight by challenging your homie's manhood. For example, "Diamond, ain't that the cat who disrespected your old lady? Well, are you going to let him get away with that?"

Pumpkin Head: This term refers to a person beaten so severely that their head swells to the size of a pumpkin. One incident at Centinela Prison is forever ingrained in my mind. I had just entered the prison for my shift, and the entire facility was on "Lockdown" after a riot on the Level IV yard. I was directed to go to the "Infirmary" to help since my yard was on lockdown, and they needed my assistance. As soon as I entered the infirmary, I observed a Black inmate lying on the bed, staring into my eyes. His head was so big after the beating from other inmates that I still cannot believe it. His eyes had so much fear and pain as he looked deeply into my eyes, frantically searching for my reaction regarding the damage to his head and face.

Punch Some Holes in Him: When an inmate stabs another inmate with a "Banger." For example, "I caught that 'Chomo' in a blind spot and punched some holes in him."

Punk: If you are labeled a punk in prison, you get no respect, and the other convicts see your life as worthless.

Punk City: Protective Custody prison yards are the majority of yards in CDCR now. These yards are considered "No Good" by the "General Population" convicts. The inmates on Protective Custody yards are the natural enemies of the general population convicts because many are former gang members on the "Line." Most inmates in Protective Custody are there for drug or gambling debts and "Bad Paperwork." Protective Custody yards tend to be more chaotic and violent than the "Mainline" because the gang structure is less rigid than the general population gangs.

Punked: When an inmate gets bullied out of something that is his or something he "Has Coming" to him. For example, an inmate cuts in front of another person in line, and they don't say anything because they are afraid.

Punked Out: When an inmate gets bullied out of something that is his or something he "Has Coming" to him. For example, some cat takes his phone time or dessert, and the victim gives it up without a fight.

Punta: A prison-made device used to inject intravenous drugs. The Punta is made of an eye dropper, a sharpened guitar string, and a shaft of a plastic ink pen that has been cut down to size.

Purple Passion: An infamous "Booty Bandit" in the California Department of Corrections and Rehabilitation. Purple Passion is described as a "Crip" who is tall and "Yoked."

Pushback: A gang member who has been "Removed" for breaking their "Code Of Conduct." Becoming a pushback involves extreme violence, ranging from a severe beating to getting "Poked" numerous times. For example, "Big Worm is a pushback. He is no longer welcomed in the 'Movement.'"

Pushed Back: When gang members remove a member for breaking their "Code Of Conduct." Being pushed back involves extreme violence, ranging from a severe beating to getting "Poked" numerous times. For example, "The homie got pushed back at Corcoran, he is 'No Good.'"

Pushes A Hardline: When a gang member goes to the extreme in gang banging or other issues. For example, "Big Lou pushes a hardline, so watch what you say around him, homie."

Pushing The Issue: When an inmate won't let an issue with someone else go away. They will keep bringing it up and stirring the pot. For example, "Shotgun broke my headphones, and I kept pushing the issue until his people put some money on my 'Books.'"

Put A Demo Down: When an inmate needs to let people know not to mess with him by "Catching A Fade," so they will see he isn't the one to play with. For example, "I walked into the 'Housing Unit' and put a demo down on the first punk to come at me 'Sideways.'"

Put Boots On You: When someone kicks you when you are on the ground. For example, "When those officers come in this cell, they are going to put boots on you. So go for what you know, comrade."

Put Hands: To physically attack another person. For example, "Sinbad came at me 'Sideways,' so I put hands on him."

Put Hands & Feet On Him: When a person gets "Smashed" without weapons. The victim is beaten with punches and kicks only. For example, "Ruthless put hands and feet on Snail after he came at him 'Sideways.'"

Put In Check: To talk to a person and let them know that their bad behavior cannot continue or that there will be severe consequences. For example, "Check this out, youngster, you need to put in check anyone who comes at you 'Sideways.'"

Put In The Hat: This old-school term originates from when gang members in prison would draw pieces of paper out of a hat to determine which one would go on the "Mission" to kill their victim.

Put In Work: When a gang member enhances his gang's reputation by doing acts of violence or criminal activity to gain money.

Put It On Paper: To have a person put whatever they are telling you in writing on a "Kite." This is sometimes done in prison to cover your bases if that person asks you to pass a verbal message to them and then denies it when the receiving party gets angry. People in prison get "Crossed Up" all the time by their homies, so having things on paper will get you out of trouble when they try to double-cross you.

Put Mitts On Him: To physically attack another person. For example, "Kermit came at me 'Sideways,' so I put mitts on him."

Put On: When a gang member is initiated into a gang by a beating from several other members. For example, "I was put on the 'Set' by three 'Reputable' homeboys."

Put On Blast: To verbally berate a person.

Put On Burn: When people talk badly about you.

Put On Game: When an older convict kicks down game to a young "First Termer" to help him navigate the treacherous waters of the penal system. This process allows the youngster to stay away from trouble and get himself into a "Wreck." It also includes how to make a knife. The "Big Homie" will tell the "Fish" to make a knife, and then he will grade it. If the knife isn't good enough, he will have him make it again. He will also teach him how to make a "Bomb" to melt plastic for a knife if he doesn't have any metal. He will instruct him on how to defend himself and various exercises.

Put On Ice: When a prison gang member is investigated by his comrades for wrongdoing. He will be kept to the side, and no gang business or "Politics" will be shared with him until he is cleared of any violations.

Put On Pause: This means to delay something until a later date. For example, "Check this out, homeboy, your drug debt issue will be put on pause until we deal with the 'Southsiders' and the war that's brewing with them."

Put On Shine: When people in your "Car" ignore you because of your bad behavior. Your fellow gang members will not associate with you until you redeem yourself, and that is usually accomplished by "Putting in Work" by doing a "Clean Up."

Put On The Shelf: When a prison gang member is investigated by his comrades for wrongdoing. He will be kept to the side, and no gang business or "Politics" will be shared with him until he is cleared of any violations.

Put Paperwork: The act of writing a "CDC 115" or "RVR" detailing an inmate's misconduct. Writing paperwork on inmates can result in time being added to their sentence or their parole date being extended. This term can also refer to an inmate writing a "602" on an officer for alleged mistreatment or misconduct.

Put Some Water On It: To flush your toilet because of the foul odor. For example, "Homie, you are foul. Put some water on it before I 'Fall Out.'"

Put That On His Ears: To say something knowing it will cause a reaction. For example, "You put that on his ears and pumped him up. You are a 'Cold Piece.'"

Put That On Pause: It means to stop whatever you are doing. For example, "Hey, homie, you need to put that on pause. Your issue with Cisco can wait until we deal with those 'Peckerwoods.'"

Put Tips On: To punch another person in the face. For example, "Malo came at me 'Sideways,' so I put tips on him."

Put Up On Game: This is when a person gives "Schooling" to another person to help them function at a higher level. For example, "I was put up on game by the homies as soon as I 'Landed' at Corcoran."

Put Up To Bat: The next inmate in line to do the following "Mission" for his gang. For example, "Psycho was put up to bat by the 'Big Homie.'"

Puto Mark: The scar on an inmate's face caused by a severe slash from a "Tomahawk." This puto mark usually starts by the ear or corner of the lips and typically spans the length of the face. The puto mark is usually for snitches, drop-outs, or other "No Good" inmates, and the large and very noticeable scar will forever brand them.

Putting In Work: When a gang member enhances his gang's reputation by doing acts of violence or criminal activity to gain money.

Putting Iron In His Diet: Stabbing someone in prison with a "Banger."

Putting It Out There: This is what you say when you want to tell some secret information. For example, "I'm just putting this out there, but Pretty Boy is going to 'Hit' this weekend at his visit. His old lady will be bringing him some 'Black.'"

PVRTC: Parole violator returned to custody.

PVSP: Pleasant Valley State Prison.

PVWNT: Parole violator returned with a new term.

PW: This is the paperwork that shows what crime a convict was incarcerated for and all relevant court documents. Every convict in a "Car" has their "Black & Whites" checked by other gang members to verify they don't have any "Bad Charges."

Q

Quarterly Package: Many years ago, an inmate was allowed a "Package" from family and friends weighing up to thirty pounds every four months. These packages include food, snacks, "Hygiene," clothes, and other items. The boxes would first go through "Receiving and Release" to be x-rayed for "Contraband" before being given to the inmate. Families are no longer allowed to send packages to their loved ones in prison personally. Currently, they order these items from a CDCR-approved vendor and they ship them directly to the inmates in prison.

Queen: To be used as a "Punk" by another inmate.

Quiet Cell: Many years ago, these types of cells were in places like Folsom, San Quentin, and Soledad Prisons. A quiet cell was in the "Isolation Wing" of the prison with a regular cell door, then a tiny vestibule and another solid steel door to isolate the inmate in that cell.

Quiet Time: In "Dorm" living, the different "Cars" usually agree to times when their people will be quiet in consideration of others who might be trying to sleep or relax. Quiet time is generally between the hours of 2200 hours to 1000 hours.

R

R&R: The building where all incoming and outgoing convicts pass through in the prison for processing.

Rabbit: An inmate who is likely going to try and escape. For example, "Conejo is planning a 'Fence Parole' tonight. He is a runner; he has some rabbit in him."

Race Is For Survival, But Business Is Supreme: In the penitentiary, race plays a prominent role but takes a backseat to making money.

Race Traitor: This is a person in prison accused by his "People" of going against their race. A "Skinhead" was in my "Housing Unit" with large swastikas tattooed all over his body. One night during "Dayroom," he approached the "Officer's Podium," asking me for an extra phone call because a phone was open. I told him no, and he got mad and angrily stated, "You aren't White." I looked at him, "Sideways," and replied, "It isn't about color. What matters is being a man who takes care of his loved ones. How are you doing that in here?"

Racial Integration: A CDCR policy forcing races to cell and bunk together. The races in the past would not cell or bunk with another race because it was strictly prohibited by their own "People."

Rack: This is the name for a bed in prison, and most of the time, a rack will be double stacked like a bunk bed. If a rack isn't double-stacked, it's called a "Cadillac Rack" because it's more desirable than a regular double-stacked rack.

Rack: To have a cell door opened. For example, "I'm going to rack your door so you can go to your visit."

Rack Of Bread: A loaf of bread in prison. For example, "The homie from the kitchen just gave us a rack of bread."

Rack Status: When convicts in a "Dorm" setting are confined to their racks and cannot move without permission. This is the dormitory version of a "Lockdown." Gang members also discipline some of their members in the same way. For example, "Check this out, Sleepy, you will be on rack status for three days because of what you did."

Racked: To have a cell door opened. For example, "I'm going to have your door racked so you can go to the 'Program Office' because the sergeant needs to talk to you."

Rake: A word used for a comb. For example, "Run a rake through what's left of your hair, homeboy."

Raise His Hand For Me: This means a person with "Status" in the gang world will speak on your behalf to recommend you for something or defend your name against "Politicking." For example, "Turtle told me when the time is right, he will raise his hand for me."

Raise My Hand To Bless You: This is sometimes said to a "Camarada" who is being used by a "Big Homie" to manipulate him to do his dirty work. This promise means that he plans to speak up for him to become a big homie, too. He has no intention of raising his hand for him and recommending that he become a big homie because he is just using him as a "Crash Dummy." For example, "Pee Wee, if you take care of that problem I have, I will raise my hand to bless you."

Raised My Hand: When an inmate volunteers to go on a "Mission" and "Book" someone. For example, "I found out my cellie was a

'Chomo' after seeing his 'Paperwork,' so I raised my hand to give him what he has coming."

Ran Me Down: When an older convict kicks down game to a young "First Termer" to help him navigate the treacherous waters of the penal system. This process allows the youngster to stay away from trouble and get himself into a "Wreck." It also includes how to make a knife. The "Big Homie" will tell the "Fish" to make a knife, and then he will grade it. If the knife isn't good enough, he will have him make it again. He will also teach him how to make a "Bomb" to melt plastic for a knife if he has no metal. He will instruct him on how to defend himself and on various exercises. For example, "I was new to the yard, and my cellie had been there for a year, so he ran me down on the 'Program.'"

Ran Through: To be taken advantage of in prison. For example, "That fool got ran through in county. He was giving his 'Canteen' away because he was scared."

Ranfla: A word that translates to "Car." For example, "Is Primo in your ranfla?"

Rank Out: A person who acts gangster but will deny their gang affiliation when they are "Pressed" by a "Rival."

Ranker: A person who acts gangster but will deny their gang affiliation when they are "Pressed" by a "Rival."

Rapo: A term for an inmate who was convicted of raping someone. In most "Cars" in prison, they will attack the rapist and remove them from the yard when they find out about this.

Rapport: This frequently misspelled word is often used in prison, and it means having a good working relationship with another person or group. For example, "I have a good rapport with Deadeye. I will 'Get At Him On Paper' to resolve this issue."

Rat: To "Snitch" on your gang members and cooperate with an investigation.

Rat Pack: When a group of inmates violently attack another person, get them on the ground, and then kick and stomp them.

Rat Tail: This is the string attached to the handle of a "Banger" that is "Hooped." The rat tail's purpose is to make pulling the knife out of the rectum easier.

Rattle Your Program: This is when something serious happens in prison that impacts you and how you live. For example, a "Big Homie" puts a "Banger" in your hand and tells you to go "Blast" your "Cellie."

Raza: A word that means "race." Hispanic gangs use the term Raza to promote solidarity among gang members from different areas. For example, "The raza shouldn't be killing each other on the streets."

RD: This is short for a "Restrictive Diet." Many years ago, some inmates could be placed on a restrictive food diet in the "Adjustment Center." In San Quentin, Soledad, Tracy, Chino, and Folsom Prisons, the food on this diet was called a "Dog Biscuit." The Dog Biscuit was made by compressing leftover food into a cube and drying it out. This dehydrated mass of slop was then given to the inmates on reduced food rations. The inmates got two Dog Biscuits a day served with a slice of bread.

Reach: The ability of a gangster to get things done and their influence with their peers. For example, "Bouncer has a long reach. He has a lot of 'Camaradas' underneath him."

Reading The Yard: When a convict can see the body language and vibe of people on the yard to determine if something is about to "Jump Off."

Ready To Ride: When a convict has his "Hand Raised" for the next "Mission." They are ready and willing to "Put In Work" for the "Cause."

Real In The Field: This means prison and the streets are a cold game, and you can't trust anyone, not even your comrades. For example, "It's real in the field, homeboy! You better watch yourself on that yard."

Real One: A "Solid" gang member who will fight without hesitation.

Real Tough: This means to associate with someone or do something with full effort. For example, "I used to hang with Frog real tough back in the day."

Reasonable Force: The force that an objective, trained, and competent correctional employee, faced with similar facts and circumstances, would consider necessary and reasonable to subdue an attacker, overcome resistance, effect custody, or gain compliance with a lawful order.

Rebel: To go against the "Program" in prison. For example, "Homie, you need to stop being a rebel and bringing 'Heat To The Pad.'"

Rec Recall: When Rec Recall is announced by the "Tower Officer," the inmates must return the recreational items they checked out. Inmates can check out basketballs, handballs, etc.

Recall: When a prison gang member is told to report to the "Hole" or "SHU" by the "Fellas." In order for the recalled member to get to the "Back," he would have to attack someone. A recall is usually a serious issue that needs to be cleared up quickly.

Receipts: This is proof of accusations being made about someone. A prime example of this is court documents. For example, "Blood Hound is a snitch. I have receipts, homie."

Receiving And Release: The building where all incoming and outgoing convicts pass through in the prison for processing.

Reception Center: Inmates sentenced to state prison in California arrive at one of the several reception centers from jail. The inmates wait to be transferred to their next prison via the "Grey Goose."

Red Flag: Being red-flagged means an inmate is no longer allowed to do drugs. This can happen for several reasons: they have passed the drug debt limit, or maybe the last time they did drugs, they acted foolishly and brought heat to themselves or others. Some gangs have a $200 drug debt limit for their gang members in prison. Some other gangs have a rule that you can only have one drug debt at a time. The penalty for doing drugs after being red-flagged is getting "Poked" or a severe beating.

Red Flagging: When gang members who claim red wear it proudly and don't hide their gang affiliation even if they are outnumbered.

Red-Headed Stepchild Status: An inmate put on the "Shine" by his gang. His gang won't talk or associate with him until he redeems himself by doing a "Cleanup."

Red Liners: There used to be jeans that inmates were issued, which had a red thread running down the outside of the pants leg. They were called Red Liners because of the red thread used on them.

Red Light: When a "Shot Caller" sends word that a person or group of people is off limits to attack. Red light is the opposite of "Green Light."

Restricted Housing Units: Under a new policy in 2024, the

California Department of Corrections and Rehabilitation renamed the "Administration Segregation" and "Security Housing Unit." Both of those longstanding segregated housing facilities have been renamed to Restrictive Housing Units. Only inmates who have engaged in violence or have serious safety concerns are placed in restricted housing under this new policy.

Red Light Zone: A place where fights among convicts are strictly prohibited. The "Visiting Room" is a prime example of a red light zone. If an inmate starts a fight in a red light zone, he will get a "DP" or be "Removed" by his "Car."

Red On Red Conflict: This is when "Northerners" are "Politicking" and fighting amongst themselves.

Red On Red Crime: This is an unauthorized attack on a fellow "Northerner." Red on red crime is a serious offense dealt with harshly by the "Northerner chain" of command.

Reduced Food Rations: Many years ago, some inmates could be placed on a restrictive diet in the "Adjustment Center." In San Quentin, Soledad, and Folsom Prisons, the food they got on this diet was called a "Dog Biscuit." The Dog Biscuit was made by compressing leftover food into a cube and drying it out. This dehydrated mass of slop was then given to the inmates on reduced food rations. The inmates got two Dog Biscuits a day served with a slice of bread.

Reg: Reg is short for "Regular," and it is a convict who is in "Good Standing" with his "Car."

Regain Their Status: In some prison gangs, after a member has been "Deemed No Good," they might be allowed to regain their status and become in "Good Standing." For this to happen, they must "Put In Work" by doing a "Clean Up," and they will be accepted with no restrictions.

Regiment: A group of "Northerners" who control a city or group of convicts in a prison.

Reglas: The rules that the "Southerner" gang members have to follow, or they will be "Checked."

Regs: This stands for regulars; it means the "Solid" homies in prison as opposed to a "Fish" or "New Booty."

Regular: A convict in "Good Standing" with his "Car."

Regular: The correctional officer who is permanently assigned to a post and typically has a good rapport with the convicts under their custody and control. As an officer, you always follow the lead of the regular, even if you are senior to him.

Regulate: When an inmate breaks a gang rule, his homies will discipline him as punishment. This punishment can range from cell or bunk restriction to a violent beating or stabbing. For example, "Check this out: you need to regulate your homeboy and tell him to stop 'Smutting Up' our 'Compas.'"

Regulate The Function: A convict who comes to a yard and, takes control of his "Car" and starts pushing a "Hardline." For

example, "Any yard I 'Land' on I regulate the function."

Regulated: When an inmate breaks "Household Policies," he gets disciplined by his comrades. This punishment usually means the inmate gets physically beaten for a set amount of time.

Relay: This person helps their homie who is "Fishing" a long distance down a tier. They will pull the "Fishing Line" into their cell and then shoot it down the tier to help it get to its intended destination.

Release Date: The specific day an inmate will be released from prison.

Religious Diet: Inmates who require a unique religious diet fill out the CDCR Form 3030 and will get special meals once approved. Inmates can get Kosher and vegetarian meals, among others, once they get their religious diet card.

Removal: When a gang removes a member with extreme violence.

Removal Drill: Some "Factions" in prison conduct drills among their members whereby they practice attacking another person. For example, gang members will post up in their assigned areas on the yard or "Building," and the "Bombers" will make their move and simulate an attack on their victim. Most of the time, the victim in this drill will be one of their members who knows it's just training. However, sometimes, during these drills, they will test one of their homies to see if he is aware and able to detect the attack on him before it happens.

Remove: When a gang removes a member for breaking their "Code Of Conduct." The removal process involves extreme violence. It can range from a severe beating to getting "Poked" numerous times.

Remove Their Letters: When a prison gang demands that other inmates remove any tattoos related to their gang. There could be several reasons, such as an imposter claiming to be a gang member when they aren't and a former member whose membership has been revoked.

Removed: When a gang removes a member for breaking their "Code Of Conduct." The removal process involves extreme violence. It can range from a severe beating to getting "Poked" numerous times.

Removed Off The Line: When a gang removes a member from the "Line" for breaking their "Code Of Conduct." Getting removed off the line involves extreme violence, ranging from a severe beating to getting "Poked" numerous times.

Rent: Profits from illegal activities that go to the "Big Homies" of a particular gang. Usually, 1/3 of profits is paid in rent in this manner.

Rent: When an inmate must pay another person or group of people "Canteen" for him to safely live among them.

Reps: Prison gang leaders wield significant influence among the other convicts due to their power to have you "Smashed" if you disrespect them or their gang.

Reputable: Gang members with a reputation for "Putting In Work" and pushing a "Hardline." For example, "I was put on the 'Set' by four reputable comrades."

Resident: A Mexican inmate who isn't in a gang on the streets, but the "Southsiders" let him run with them in prison.

Respectable: Gang members with a reputation for "Putting In Work" and pushing a "Hardline." For example, "I was put on the 'Set' by four respectable homies."

Respetos: This word translates to respect and refers to the taxes paid to "Mexican Mafia" members by other gang members. Any form of "Contraband" brought into prison by "Southsiders" is taxed by the Mexican Mafia. This tax is usually one-third of the profits made.

Rest Your Neck: Something you say to somebody so they will leave you alone. For example, "Stop running your mouth and go rest your neck."

Restricted Custody General Population Unit: There are three categories of inmates who qualify for this type of facility: (1) inmates whose own safety is at risk in the "General Population," (2) inmates who continually violate prison rules while in the "Step Down Program," (3) and inmates who refuse to take part in the step down program.

Restricted Housing Units: Under a new policy in 2024, the California Department of Corrections and Rehabilitation renamed the "Administration Segregation" and "Security Housing Unit." Both of those longstanding segregated housing facilities have been renamed to Restrictive Housing Units. Only inmates who have engaged in violence or have serious safety concerns are placed in restricted housing under this new policy.

Restrictive Diet: Many years ago, inmates could be placed on a restrictive food diet in the "Adjustment Center." In San Quentin, Soledad, Tracy, Chino, and Folsom Prisons, the food on this diet was called a "Dog Biscuit." The Dog Biscuit was made by compressing leftover food into a cube and drying it out. This dehydrated mass of slop was then given to the inmates on reduced food rations. The inmates got two Dog Biscuits a day served with a slice of bread.

Restrictive Housing: Inmates are placed in restrictive housing for disciplinary, security, or safety reasons. Some of these types of housing might be the "SHU" or "ASU."

Resume Normal Program: This is what the "Tower Officer" says into the microphone after a "Yard Down" command, and this gives the inmates permission to get up off the ground and do what they were doing before the alarm sounded.

Retired: This is a convict doing a life sentence. A life sentence in prison is also referred to as doing "All Day."

Revocation: When a judge places a parolee in custody for violating parole.

RHU: This acronym stands for Restrictive Housing Unit. Under a new policy in 2024, the California Department of Corrections and Rehabilitation renamed the "Administration Segregation" and "Security Housing Unit." Both of those longstanding segregated housing facilities have been renamed to "Restrictive Housing Units." Only inmates who have engaged in violence or have serious safety concerns are placed in restricted housing under this new policy.

Rice Bowl: A meal inmates make that contains rice, chopped sausage, pork rinds, and spices.

Ricochet: When a convict is ordered to "Whack" someone on the yard and it turns out it was a "Bad Call." Those involved in a hit when it turns out to be a bad call now have an issue coming from their comrades. Usually, they will now get "Poked" as punishment for attacking a person who was actually in "Good Standing."

Ride: To attack a person or group in prison. For example, "The 'Pisas' owe us money, and they haven't paid. We are going to ride on them twenty minutes before 'Yard Recall.'"

Ride On Them: To attack a person or group in prison. For example, "Those punk 'Woods' owe us money, and they haven't paid. We are going to ride on them ten minutes before 'Yard Recall.'"

Ride Out That Term: You must do the time you were sentenced, no matter how hard it gets. For example, "I know it's hard, youngster, but you must ride out that term."

Ride Your Own Beef: This means to take your conviction without snitching on your crime partners.

Ride The Rack: When an inmate is constantly in their rack. For example, "Sleepy lives that ride the rack life."

Rider: A rider is a gang member who is always "Putting in Work."

Rider Stripes: The symbolic stripes a gang member has for doing dirt for his gang. For example, "My rider stripes, they have no expiration date. Everything I did lives on in my legend as a rider."

Riders: Another name for the "Northern Riders," aka "Certified Riders."

Riding His Leg: When someone follows someone around and admires them too much. For example, "Check this out youngster, Ran Ran is good people, but you need to stop riding his leg. It's not a good look."

Riding The Fence: When a convict talks to his comrades at the fence that divides the prison yard.

Riff Raff: A lazy, sloppy, and good-for-nothing person nobody respects in prison. For example, "There was nothing but solid homies on the yard. There wasn't any riff raff or 'Lames.'"

Rig: A tattoo gun made from the motor of a Walkman, cassette player, or other electronic device. The rig will use a sharpened guitar string for a needle.

Righteous: When something is very good or "Solid." For example, "Did you see that 'Banger?' It was righteous." or "Did you see that sticking? It was righteous."

Ring Bells: This is when a person or group of people do something so notorious that the streets and the penitentiary will speak about it for a long time. For example, "If we make this move, our names will ring bells."

Ringing Bells: This is when someone is talked about for something they have done. For example, "My name was ringing bells on those streets. I was a 'Ghetto Superstar.'"

Rip: A slang term used by some gangsters for "Crips." For example, "I took out my knife, and the rip started running from me and my four comrades."

Rival: This word refers to a person's enemies.

Rival Row: The "Row" in County Jail where the enemies of your gang are housed.

RJD: Richard J. Donovan Correctional Facility, also known as Donovan Prison.

Road Dog: A homie who has remained steadfast through thick and thin, whether on the streets or in prison.

Robocop: An overzealous correctional officer always sweating the convicts over petty things. A nit-picking control freak officer who needlessly harasses the convicts to make up for their shortcomings.

Rocker: The curved tattoo on the top of an inmate's chest right below his neck.

Rocking: When a prison or prison yard is violent with fights and riots all of the time. For example, "Salinas Valley prison is rocking homie."

Rocking Someone To Sleep: Disarming a target for assault or robbery by making him believe you are friends. Rocking someone to sleep makes them easier to kill or rob because they aren't expecting it.

Rocking The Baby To Sleep: Disarming a target for assault or robbery by making them believe everything is cool. For example, "I was rocking the baby to sleep before I made my move. Scarface never saw it coming."

Rode Him To The Dirt: This refers to stabbing another inmate and continuing to stab them as they fall on the ground. It means to show no mercy and ensure your victim is dead by stabbing them dozens of times as they lay immobilized on the ground. For example, "I caught the dude in the kitchen, and I stabbed him and rode him to the dirt."

Rode The Beef: When a person commits a crime with others but is the only one arrested and doesn't snitch on their homies. For example, "I wasn't alone when I did my crime, but I was the only one arrested and the only one to do time. I rode the beef."

Rogue Move: When a gang member doesn't act according to his gang's rules. For example, "Ken Dog, what our little homie did was a rogue move. We don't condone that."

Roll Call: In the "Hole," the "Shot Caller" will yell out of his cell and speak to each of his people by their "Street Name." He does this in the morning and night. He will "Open The Tier" in the morning and "Close The Tier" at night. Only members in "Good Standing" can participate in the roll call.

Roll Dog: A homie who has remained steadfast through thick and thin, whether on the streets or in prison.

Roll It Up: What an officer tells an inmate when he gets paperwork for a "Bed Move." For example, "Hey Smith, roll it up! You are moving to building 3."

Roll It Up: When an inmate succumbs to fear and intimidation and tells prison administration that he fears for his safety and he needs "Protective Custody."

Roll Up: What an officer tells an inmate when he gets paperwork for a "Bed Move." For example, "Crusher was involved in that alarm. Roll up his property."

Roll Your Mat Up: In prison, some "Cars" require their members to roll up their mattresses as soon as they wake up. Doing this shows they are "Programming" and not a lazy "Dump Truck."

Rolled Up: When an inmate goes into "Protective Custody." For example, "Did you hear about Bullet? He rolled up."

Roller Phone: A pay phone in some jails back in the day that was on a cart and pushed in front of each cell in a "Section" so inmates could use it. When I was arrested as a teenager, the Long Beach City Jail had a roller phone, and it was pushed in front of my cell.

Rollies: A term used for cigarettes.

Rolling It Up: When an inmate goes into "Protective Custody."

Roof: In some county jails in California, the recreational area is on the roof. There are places to play basketball, workout, etc., in the fenced-in yard. For example, "We got roof back at county, and you know we were 'Spinning Laps' with the homies."

Roof Time: In some county jails in California, the recreational area is on the roof. There are places to play basketball, workout, etc., in the fenced-in yard. For example, "We got some roof time back at county, and you know we were playing basketball with the homies."

Rooster Fights: Between 1989 and 1994, it is alleged that officers at

Corcoran State Prison orchestrated confrontations between rival gang members in the Security Housing Unit (SHU). During thisperiod, seven inmates were fatally shot, and 43 others sustained severe injuries due to officers discharging their firearms.

Roster: A list of active prison gang members usually "Hooped" by convicts and then transported from prison to prison.

Rotunda: A narrow hallway in a building that leads outside to the prison yard.

Row: A group of cells in a prison or jail.

Rub Them On Your Chest: A reply to someone when you are fighting over something. For example, "I don't want to use your headphones. Take them back and rub them on your chest for all I care."

Rules & Regulations: The rules and regulations of a prison gang that all of its members must follow. The rules and regulations are also referred to as "Household Policies," "Household Rules," "Constitution," "Code Of Conduct," or "Bible."

Rules Violation Hearing: This is the hearing that an inmate goes to after he has been issued a "Rules Violation Report." A sergeant or a lieutenant adjudicates the hearing, and the Chief Disciplinary Officer is usually an Associate Warden.

Rules Violation Report: This is issued to inmates by the administration for serious misconduct. There are two categories of a rules violation report: serious and administrative.

Run A Fade: To fight with another person. For example, "You talk too much fool. Let's run a fade."

Run A Make: This means to check a person's background, and it usually refers to a new arrival in a prison setting. To run a make includes his government name, street name, age, and criminal record. The new arrival's information will be passed to the homies and checked through the screening process to verify if they are in "Good Standing."

Runback: To fight a person again after losing to them. For example, "You ain't even going to ask for a runback with Knots? Are you scared?"

Rundown: This is when an inmate gives information about a situation in a detailed manner. For example, "Camel, give me the rundown on what happened at Corcoran and why you transferred here."

Run His Vitals: This means to check a person's background, and it usually refers to a new arrival in a prison setting. Vitals include his government name, street name, age, and criminal record. The vitals of a new arrival will be passed around to the homies and checked through the screening process to verify if they are in "Good Standing."

Run It: To start doing something like a chess game, fight, card game, basketball game, etc. For example, "You think you can do more 'Burpies' than me? Run it, comrade."

Run It In: To finish strong on anything that you are doing. For example, "Homie, you have watched me run it in for five years. What's your excuse for not being 'Swole' like me?"

Run Their Family Dry: A dope fiend inmate who constantly lies to his family, so they send money to pay his drug debts. For example, "Those 'Tecatos' are all the same. They run their family dry while they are locked up."

Run With: A group of people whom a person associates with. It means a person's "Faction" or "Car." For example, a "Fish" lands on your yard, and if he is unfamiliar to people, they will ask him, "Who do you run with?"

Runner: A person in the "Free World" who delivers messages to and from gang members in prison.

Runner: A person who brings drugs or other "Contraband" into prison for a person or a group of people. For example, "Yeah, homie, I can get you a runner. What do you need?"

Runners: People who distribute drugs, money, and information to prison gang members.

Running Drag: A false story or scheme used to take advantage of someone or manipulate them. For example. "I gave you the 'Hook Up' to that dude. I don't know enough about the subject to know if he was running drag or not."

Running Our Program: These are the "Big Homies" who dictate what type of "Program" their people will do in jail or prison. For example, "Clever was running our program on Bravo yard when I 'Drove Up.'"

Running Showers: When a correctional officer in a "Housing Unit" gives showers to the convicts in his custody and control. For example, an officer receives a phone call from his "Road Dog," and he tells him, "I can't talk on the phone right now because I'm running showers."

Running Tags: This means to check a person's background, and it usually refers to a new arrival in a prison setting. To run a make includes his government name, street name, age, and criminal record. The new arrival's information will be passed to the homies and checked through the screening process to verify if they are in "Good Standing."

Running The Program: Prison gang leaders wield significant influence among the other convicts due to their power to have you killed if you disrespect them or their gang. No illegal activity or assault is performed without a "Shot Caller's" order or permission. If a convict does any of those activities without a shot caller's permission, he will be "Violated" by his gang. For example, "Puppet was running the program on Bravo yard when I 'Drove Up,' but nobody liked him."

Running Up Debt: Two things in prison that can get an inmate caught up the quickest in some drama are gambling and drug debts. Running up debts in prison is dangerous, primarily when the money is owed to different "Factions." Some factions have a "Zero Debt Policy" to avoid problems that arise from owing other groups of inmates money. For example, "Chico was known on the yard for running up debt; it finally caught up with him, and that's why he got 'Poked.'"

Rushing: This is the term used for someone who injects meth intravenously and gets the rush from the drugs.

Rutina: The exercise routine that convicts do in prison. For example, "The homie Boxer always goes hard in his rutina."

RVR: This is a "Rules Violation Report" issued to inmates by the administration for serious misconduct. There are two categories of an RVR: serious and administrative.

S

S Time: When inmates are about to parole, they are unassigned from their prison job and placed on S Time.

Sabana: A word that translates to sheet, a term used for White inmates. For example, "That sabana owes me $50. He has until Friday to get my money right."

Sack: A term that refers to drugs smuggled into prison. For example, "I had the sack on the yard. I was 'Hitting' every weekend at 'Visiting.'"

Sack: This term refers to drugs smuggled into prison. For example, "Kilo has the sack. He is 'Hitting' every weekend."

Sack Lunch: Convicts receive two hot meals (breakfast and dinner) every day; they receive a sack lunch for lunch. The sack lunch consists of a piece of fruit, four pieces of bread, a small milk, two slices of lunch meat, a small bag of dried fruit, kool-aid, and small condiments. Some lunches come with peanut butter and jelly sandwiches.

Sacramaniacs: A "Peckerwood" gang in prison from Sacramento.

Safe: When a convict places items of "Contraband" in his rectum to avoid discovery by officers. Some convicts become very proficient at this and can do it in seconds. When a "Banger" is placed inside of the prison safe, it will have a protective layer of cellophane to prevent their insides from being perforated. For example, "I stashed the 'Clavo' in the safe homie."

Sally Port: The area of the prison where inmates enter and exit the institution via buses and smaller vehicles.

Sally Port: The narrow passageway in a "Housing Unit" that is used to enter and exit the building.

Sally Port: The secured area of the prison where officers enter the institution and have their lunch bags searched by another officer before entering.

Salt Water Lighter: This is a metal device that plugs into an electrical socket. Salt water is placed near the bottom, and two metal springs attached to the device are submerged in the cup of water to complete an electrical circuit. Once the circuit is complete, a cigarette or "Wick" could be ignited.

San Quentin A's: An inmate baseball team at San Quentin State Prison.

San Quentin Giants: An inmate baseball team at San Quentin State Prison.

San Quentin Six: Six inmates at San Quentin Prison on August 21, 1971, attempted to escape, and as a result, six people were killed in the mayhem, including three correctional officers.

San Quentin Warriors: The name of the inmate basketball team at San Quentin State Prison.

SAP: These are substance abuse programs that prisons offer inmates.

Sat Down: This means to receive a lengthy prison sentence. For example, "Homie, it wasn't until I was sat down for ten years that I looked at my situation and decided to change."

Sat Down: When a gangster with authority is stripped of his power by other high-ranking members. Being sat down can happen for a number of reasons in prison, and it is not that uncommon. For example, "Serio got 'Stripped' and sat down over that 'Bad Call' he made regarding Crow getting 'Whacked.'"

Sat Him Down: When a gangster with authority is stripped of his power by other high-ranking members. Being sat down can happen for a number of reasons in prison, and it is not uncommon. For example, "The 'Big Homie' in the 'Back' sat him down. Shady was doing too much on the yard because the power got to his head."

Say It With Your Chest: To say something proudly and stand behind it. For example, "Say it with your chest, homeboy. Stand behind what you're pushing."

SB: This is short for "Security Blanket," and these are the "Norteños" on the prison yard who are designated to watch over a homie who is on "Freeze." The security blankets are armed with "Bangers," and they will use them without hesitation. The homie on freeze will have a security blanket until they are cleared after the investigation. The purpose of the security blanket is to ensure the homie on freeze doesn't try any activities that might harm the organization.

SCC: Sierra Conservation Center, also known as Jamestown Prison.

Schooled: When an older convict kicks down game to a young "First Termer" to help him navigate the treacherous waters of the penal system. This process allows the youngster to stay away from trouble and getting himself into a "Wreck." It also includes how to make a knife. The "Big Homie" will tell the "Fish" to go make a knife, and then he will grade it. If the knife isn't good enough, he will have him make it again. He will also teach him how to make a "Bomb" to melt plastic for a knife if he has no metal. He will instruct him on how to defend himself and on various exercises.

Schooling: When an older convict kicks down game to a young "First

Termer" to help him navigate the treacherous waters of the penal system. This process helps the youngster stay away from trouble and getting himself into a "Wreck." It also includes how to make a knife. The "Big Homie" will tell the "Fish" to make a knife, and then he will grade it. If the knife isn't good enough, he will have him make it again. He will also teach him how to make a "Bomb" to melt plastic for a knife if he has no metal. He will instruct him on how to defend himself and on various exercises.

Scrap: A derogatory term used by "Northerners" for "Southerners."

Scrapping: When two inmates are fighting each other. For example, "I was in the 'Blood' tank, so homies were scrapping all the time."

Screening: This means to check a person's background, and it usually refers to a new arrival in a prison setting. The new arrival's information will be passed to the homies and checked through the screening process to verify if they are in "Good Standing."

Screw: An old-school term for a correctional officer.

Search & Escort Officer: The two correctional officers assigned to each yard at Centinela Prison that are in charge of escorting inmates to various appointments.

Seating Officer: The correctional officer in the "Dining Hall" who is in charge of seating the convicts and releasing them when they have finished eating.

Second Term: An inmate who is doing his second prison term. For example, "Buzzard is on his second term. He knows what time it is."

Secretary: This is the "Camarada" who works directly for a "Mexican Mafia" member and sends out "Wilas" and does other things that the "Big Homie" wants done.

Section: In a 270 design "Housing Unit," there are three sections: A, B, and C. Each section has an upper and lower tier with cells on each tier. Each section has two sets of showers, one on each tier. B section has two large showers several inmates could shower in at a time.

Section: The people that you associate with or the gang members from your county.

Sectionero: A convict who is in charge of a "Section" in a housing unit, and they report to the "Bloquero."

Security Blanket: These are the "Norteños" on the prison yard designated to watch over a homie on "Freeze." The security blankets are armed with knives, and they will use them without hesitation. The homie on freeze will have a security blanket until they are cleared after the investigation. The purpose of the security blanket is to ensure the homie on freeze doesn't try any activities that might harm the organization.

Security Check: When an officer walks around their post and ensures nothing is amiss with the convicts under their custody and control. They also check the general security of their environment.

Security Housing Unit: The Security Housing Unit is where the most violent and influential convicts are placed due to their threatening institutional security at other prisons. These convicts are in their cells 23 hours a day and are allowed very little personal property due to security reasons. These convicts are given a shower once every three days and exercise on a small yard for an hour daily.

Security Level: When an inmate goes to a "Reception Center," he is eventually given "Points," which determines his security level. These security levels range from Level I to Level IV. The inmate's security level is based on various factors such as their crimes, length of sentence, escape risk, age, and other factors. The points that determine the security level are 0-18 Level I, 19-35 Level II, 36-59 Level III, and 60+ Level IV.

Security Threat Group: A formal or informal group of disruptive inmates. To be validated as a member of a security threat group, three independent source items must indicate an inmate's membership. The "STG Unit Classification Committee" determines if an inmate is a security threat group member.

Security Threat Group 1: These are the current prison gangs certified by the California Department of Corrections and Rehabilitation: "Aryan Brotherhood," "Black Guerrilla Family," "Nuestra Familia," and "Mexican Mafia."

Security Threat Group 2: These are some of the designated "Disruptive Groups" within the California Department of Corrections and Rehabilitation: "Bloods," "Crips," "Skinheads," "Nazi Low Riders," "Sureños," "Norteños," "Fresno Bulldogs," "415 Kumi," "Wah Ching," "SNY Gangs," and outlaw motorcycle gangs.

Seen The Move: When a convict is aware of other inmates subtly sliding up on him to confront him about an issue. Once he recognizes their play, he either goes on the offense with his "Piece," or if it's possible, he plays it cool to survive until he has his homies with him. For example, "Ren Dog seen the move, those cats posted up on his flank and asked him if he wanted any problems, and he said no."

Selective Politicking: This is when the "Big Homies" choose not to discipline or go easy on the punishment of a gang member because of who they are or who they are related to in the hood.

For example, if a well-liked "Comrade" does something worthy of a "Violation," they will probably ignore it, but if any other homie did the same infraction, they would "DP" them.

Selling Woof Tickets: To speak aggressively to someone without intending to back it up with violence. For example, "That 'Cell Soldier' was selling woof tickets, so I let him have it during the next 'Unlock.'"

Send Him Home: When given this coded "Carnival Talk" message from a "Shot Caller," it means to kill the person. For example, "Bandit has got to go. Send him home."

Send My Love: When given this coded "Carnival Talk" message from a "Shot Caller," it means to kill the person. For example, "Send my love to Redwood for me."

Send Out: When a convict sends money from his "Books" for drugs, a gambling debt, or any number of reasons.

Señor: A member of the "Mexican Mafia." For example, "Boxer is a señor. Pay your 'Respetos.'"

Señores: Members of the "Mexican Mafia." For example, "You must pay your 'Tribute' to the señores."

Sensitive Needs Yard: Sensitive Needs Yards are the majority of yards in CDCR now. These yards are considered "No Good" by the "General Population" convicts. The inmates on sensitive needs yards are the natural enemies of the general population convicts because many of them are former members of the gangs on the "Line." SNY yards tend to be more chaotic and violent than the "Mainline" because the gang structure is less rigid than the general population gangs.

Serio: A word that translates to serious. For example, "Chuy locked it up? Are you serio?"

SERT: This acronym stands for Special Emergency Response Team, and it's a group of trained officers who respond to emergencies in the prison. The SERT name has been changed to "Crisis Response Team."

Set: Within some gangs, numerous sets are determined by what street the gangster lives on. For example, a gang claims five streets as their territory, and each street is its own set within the same gang.

Set Tripping: When "Cars" in prison discriminate against their own members due to what gang they are from on the streets. For example, when it's time to give out drugs to their car, they give the lion's share to their gang members from the streets and give the scraps to their homies from other gangs on the streets. Set tripping can apply to anything that is shared with the homies in your car in prison. Another example would be if they "Removed" one of their former homies from the yard and then stole all of the victim's "Canteen" right after the assault. The homies from the same car on the streets will take most of their food and hygiene items and leave very little for their homies from other street gangs.

Set Ups: This old-school term was coined by inmates in the "Adjustment Centers" of San Quentin, Soledad, and Folsom Prisons. They claimed officers would open the cell door of an enemy while they were on the tier so they would be attacked.

Sewed Up: When a "Car" controls a yard or a "Hustle" on a prison yard. For example, "We had that yard sewed up, homie. There wasn't anyone who wanted any 'Problems' with us."

Sewer Rat: A derogatory term used by "Norteños" for "Sureños."

Sex Jerk: This is an old-school term to describe an inmate who has "Bad Charges" pertaining to sex crimes. For example, "Pee Wee is a sex jerk. He has to go."

Sex Play: To joke around in a sexual nature with another person. This type of behavior is highly frowned upon by some "Factions" in prison.

Shadow: Some "Factions" require witnesses for all dealings with officers and other prison officials on high-level yards. They have this requirement to document what was said and verify a homie isn't snitching. This witness is called a shadow.

Shadow Board: A board or cabinet in "Vocational" or "Culinary" areas in prison used for tool storage with shadows painted in the shape of each tool to ensure missing tools are immediately noticeable.

Shakedown: When officers search a cell, housing unit, prison yard, or the entire prison.

Shampoo A Cell: Some inmates use shampoo to clean their cells thoroughly. Most inmates keep their prison cells immaculately clean.

Shamrock Tattoo: When a White convict has this tattoo, it means they are a member of the "Aryan Brotherhood." If a regular White inmate has a shamrock tattoo, they will be ordered to remove it under threat of violence by other White convicts.

Shank: A prison knife made of metal, melted plastic, or any other hard material that can be sharpened to a point.

Shanked: Stabbing someone in prison with a "Shank." For example, "That 'Chomo' got shanked after the 'CO' told us about his charges."

Shared A Vent: This is when two convicts have cells next to each other and can talk to each other via the connected air conditioning vents. For example, "I shared a vent with Clever so we could communicate with each other without having to 'Put It On Paper.'"

Shark Cage: The phone booth-shaped cage that convicts are placed in for short periods. The shark cage looks like a phone booth with mesh wire for walls.

Shark Tank: A name given to "Administration Segregation" by some convicts.

Shine: When people in your "Car" ignore you because of your bad behavior. Your fellow gang members will not associate with you until you redeem yourself, and that is usually accomplished by "Putting in Work" by doing a "Clean Up."

Shine Status: When people in your "Car" ignore you because of your bad behavior. Your fellow gang members will not associate with you until you redeem yourself, and that is usually accomplished by "Putting in Work" by doing a "Clean Up."

Shining Me On: When some inmate is ignoring you and not taking you seriously. For example, "I kept telling Scratch to pay me what he owes me, but he kept shining me on. So I grabbed my 'Piece,' and I 'Poked' him."

St On A Shingle:** This breakfast years ago consisted of gravy with small pieces of meat and some toast. These days, it doesn't even come with bread or real meat. It is a very unpopular meal among convicts these days.

St Status:** When an inmate disrespects an officer, and the officer refuses to give him things. For example, a "Problem Child" asks an officer for a favor, and the officer replies, "You got nothing coming. You're on s**t status."

Shoe War: Some say this started the bloody 45-year war between the "Mexican Mafia" and the "Nuestra Familia." In 1968, at San Quentin Prison, several members of the Mexican Mafia stole a pair of shoes from the cell of a Nuestra Familia member, and this incident kicked off the war that followed.

Shoes On At All Times: Some "Factions" require their members to wear shoes during "Program" hours. This shows that a convict is "Programming" and ready for duty. An inmate will get a "DP" if they walk around without shoes. There is a short exemption when an inmate is taking a shower.

Shoot: It means to give something to another inmate. For example, "Hey homie, shoot me one of those 'Soups.' I'm hungry as a twoheaded shark over here."

Shoot Your Line: Inmates will yell this to people in other cells when they want them to shoot their "Fishing Line" so they can pull it into their cell and attach something they want to give them. For example, "Rifleman, shoot your line homie. I have some soups for you."

Shooter: A convict sent on a "Mission" to "Remove" or "Discipline" other people.

Shooting Gallery: A section of the Corcoran State Prison "SHU" where several inmates were shot during "Cockfights" from 1989 to 1994. The shooting gallery was the SHU yard for buildings 4-A, 4-Left.

Short: When a convict is near the end of their prison sentence.

Short Corridor: At Pelican Bay Prison B Side has ten blocks, and C

Side has twelve blocks, so they call it the short corridor. Many of the prominent "Aryan Brotherhood" members were locked down there.

Short Eyes: This term refers to a child molester. An inmate with "Bad Charges" will be "Removed."

Short Runs: When several brief prison sentences were served at different intervals. For example, "You had five 'CDC Numbers?' You must have done a lot of short runs."

Short-Stopped: To stop someone's hustle or promotion and prevent their "Come Up." For example, "That punk officer gave my 'Porter' job to someone else. He short-stopped me."

Short Stopped: This is when a "Kite" is being passed down the tier, and a person opens the kite and reads it in their cell before passing it to where it is going.

Short Stopped The Call: When an order in prison is nullified by someone of a higher rank in a "Faction." For example, "Whiskey claims that Slugger short stopped the call to 'Wack' Bronco."

Short Talk: The process of disarming a person so that you can easily take advantage of them in some fashion.

Short Termer: When a convict has a short time until he is released from prison.

Short Timer: When a convict is near the end of their prison sentence. For example, "Don't ever cross up a comrade. If the yard has 'Trash,' look for a lifer to take him out. Don't ask a comrade with any 'Date,' especially a short timer, to handle that."

Short Timer Blues: When inmates are "Short To The House," they start getting anxious, and time starts to drag on because they can't wait to get out of prison. For example, "Check this out, homeboy, if you got the short timer blues, you better watch what you say and do around our comrades doing 'All Day.' It's a 'Bad Look,' and they aren't going for any of that type of activity."

Short Timing: When an inmate gets close to his "Release Date," he tries to avoid any "Problems." He will avoid any "Prison Politics" and lay low to go home on time.

Short To The House: A convict with little time to serve before their release date.

Shot Caller: The leader of a prison gang or "Car" who wields significant influence over his comrades. If an officer has a persistent problem with a convict, they usually talk to the shot caller to resolve the issue. Shot callers in prison help keep things in order.

Shot Me A Kite: What an inmate says when someone gives him a "Kite." For example, "Colorado just shot me a kite. He just 'Hit' at visiting, so you know it's good news. It's time to 'Party' homeboy."

Shot Of Coffee: Enough coffee to make a cup in prison. For example, "Hey, comrade, can you slide me a shot of coffee?"

Shot Out: When a person, thing, or situation looks terrible. For example, "I ran into Fangs the other day, and the homie looks shot out."

Shovel: This term refers to a spoon. For example, "That is a bomb 'Rice Bowl.' Can I get my shovel?"

Showed Me How To Jail: When an older convict kicks down game to a young "First Termer" to help him navigate the treacherous waters of the penal system. This process helps the youngster stay away from trouble and getting himself into a "Wreck." It also includes how to make a knife. The "Big Homie" will tell the "Fish" to go make a knife, and then he will grade it. If the knife isn't good enough, he will have him make it again. He will also teach him how to make a "Bomb" to melt plastic for a knife if he has no metal. He will instruct him on how to defend himself and on various exercises. For example, "Mad Man really showed me how to jail when I was a youngster."

Shower Shark: An inmate who is always staring at naked men in the shower. For example, "Watch out for Big Nasty. He is a shower shark."

SHU: The Security Housing Unit (SHU) is where the most violent and influential convicts are placed due to them threatening institutional security at other prisons. These convicts are in their cells 23 hours a day and are allowed very little personal property due to security reasons. These convicts are given a shower once every three days and exercise on a small yard for an hour every day.

SHU Kick Out Yard: This is a yard that inmates get released to after doing time in the "SHU."

Shut The Tier Down: In the "Hole" and the "SHU," the "Shot Caller" will yell out of his cell and say good night to each of his comrades in their cells, and they will reply, good night. Once the tier is shutdown, they must be quiet and can't "Fish" or cause any other disturbance.

Shutdown: To put a stop to something. For example, "The homie wanted to play football with the cats from Compton and Watts, that was an automatic shutdown. You know how those football games get in the pen."

Side Busting: To interrupt a conversion between two people. For example, "Check this out, Lips, you need to stop side busting."

Side Piece: The tattoo a convict gets on the side of his torso.

Sideways: To approach a person disrespectfully. For example, "Wheels came at me sideways, so I 'Smashed' that 'Lame.'"

Sideways: To give a person a strange look because of abnormal behavior. For example, "Big Mike was talking out the side of his neck, so I looked at him sideways."

Sign Language: When inmates in a particular gang talk to each other using hand signs. They do this when they are far away from each other or when they don't want to make any noise. Each "Faction" has its own sign language, so others can't decipher it.

Signed Up: Convicts who are "With The Function" and push a "Hardline." For example, "Those homies in the 'Back' are signed up. Watch yourself, youngster."

Single Cell: When an inmate lives alone in a cell that is designated for two inmates. There can be various reasons an inmate gets a single cell "Chrono."

Single Cell Status: This is when the prison administration determines that an inmate will not be allowed to have a "Cellie." There are various reasons for this. The main one is they often attack their cellie.

Sissy: To be used as a "Punk" by another inmate.

Sit Down: When inmate workers go on strike and refuse to work until the prison administration addresses their grievances. If an inmate dares to cross the picket line and work during a sit down, he will be attacked by the other inmates when they have a chance to "Put Hands" on him.

Sit Him Down: This means that a person or group of people in prison plan to remove a person from a leadership position. For example, "We need to deal with Dozer and sit him down."

Sit In: When inmate workers go on strike and refuse to work until the prison administration addresses their grievances. If an inmate dares to cross the picket line and work during a sit in, he will be attacked by the other inmates when they have a chance to "Put Hands" on him.

Sit To Fart: Some inmates have a rule while living in a cell with another man that if someone has to fart, they need to sit on the toilet and flush it when they fart. For an inmate to fart in a cell without flushing it is very disrespectful and will lead to problems with their cellie.

Sit To Pee: Some inmates require that when they pee in their cells, they must sit down. The reason for this is to avoid pee splashing on the floor and walls around the toilet. Inmates are meticulous about keeping their cells spotless, and if an inmate refuses to sit when he pees in the cell, he will have "Problems" with his cellie.

Sitting Fat: When a person "Comes Up" materially or financially. For example, "Midnight has been 'Hitting' for a few weeks, and he is sitting fat in his cell."

Sitting On Something: This means a convict has something of value on their person, cell, or locker. For example, "A lot of players in the 'Dope Game' don't even go to the 'Chow Hall' because they are sitting on something back at the 'Pad.'"

Six Use Of Force Options: Officers must take these six steps when dealing with inmates. 1. Verbal persuasion. 2. Physical Strengths and holds. 3. Chemical Agents and other immobilization devices.

4. Handheld Baton. 5. Less-Lethal Weapons. 6. Firearms.

Skante: Slang term for methamphetamines.

Skante Warrior: A person who is always taking methamphetamines. For example, "My 'Bunky' was a skante warrior."

Skating: To be somewhere in a prison where you shouldn't be. For example, a convict was "Validated" and then paroled from prison. If he went to prison at a later time and they let him on the "Mainline" instead of placing him back in the "SHU," that is an example of skating.

Skeleton Bay: The nickname for Pelican Bay State Prison.

Skinheads: White inmates who "Push A Hardline" on racial issues and "Prison Politics." If a skinhead needs to be "Violated," only another skinhead can participate. "Peckerwoods" are forbidden from disciplining them because only a skinhead can discipline another skinhead.

Skittles: The term some inmates use for the medication they get from the "Pill Line."

Slam The Program: When inmates are "Locked Down," they get a shower every three days and two hot meals delivered with one "Sack Lunch." For example, "You know the administration will slam the program if we attack that 'Out Of Pocket' officer."

Slammed: When inmates are "Locked Down," they get a shower every three days and two hot meals delivered along with a "Sack Lunch." Being Slammed usually occurs on the "Line" when inmates assault officers or riot amongst themselves. Slammed can also refer to inmates in the "SHU," "Hole," or "Adjustment Center."

Slammed Down: When inmates are "Locked Down," they get a shower every three days and two hot meals delivered with a "Sack Lunch." Being Slammed Down usually occurs on the "Line" when inmates assault officers or riot amongst themselves. Slammed Down can also refer to inmates in the "SHU," "Hole," or "Adjustment Center."

Slamming: When an inmate is using intravenous drugs.

Slave Bus: Some Black inmates refer to the "Grey Goose" as a slave bus and prison as a "Plantation." They believe the prison system is racist, cruel, inhumane, and focused on the oppression of Black men.

Sleep Restriction: When inmates in the "Hole" bang on their toilets with hard cups to keep their enemies awake in the cells next to them. They yell, kick their cell doors, and do anything else to deprive their enemies of sleep.

Sleeper: A member of a prison gang that the California Department of Corrections and Rehabilitation has not "Validated." A sleeper can also be a prison gang member that other inmates don't know is "Tipped Up" or an inmate sent on a "Mission" to assault another inmate at another location.

Sleepers: Inmates who are prison gang members, but their memberships are a secret to most inmates on the "Mainline" yard they are on.

Sleepers: Medications in prison that, one of the side effects is drowsiness. Sometimes, inmates will lace "Pruno" with these sleepers so their victim will become sleepy, and it will be easier to kill them.

Sleeved Down: When a convict has tattoos covering the area from their shoulders to their hands.

Slicer: An inmate-manufactured weapon usually made with a razor to slice others. For example, "I had a slicer when I hit that dude, and I cut his ear in half and got his face good."

Slick: To deceive another person and play them for a fool. For example, "Are you trying to be slick? You better watch yourself, youngster."

Slide: To make a move physically or politically. To push an agenda or to make a move to attack someone. For example, "Sneaky tried to slide his cousin into our 'Car,' but we weren't having that because he is a 'Lame.'"

Slide You: To knock another person out or to beat them in a fight. For example, "Leave cuzz alone. He will slide you for sure in a 'Squabble.'"

Sling That Iron: When a convict uses a "Banger" to "Poke" holes in people. For example, "Watch out for 8-Ball. He will sling that iron and poke a hole in you real quick."

Sling Them Hounds: A person who has a reputation for being able to fight well. For example, "Dane can sling them hounds."

Sling Them Thangs: When people are fighting each other. For example, "I was in the 'Crip Tank,' so I had to sling them thangs all the time."

Sling'em: To fight with another person. For example, "My cellie came at me 'Sideways,' so we had to sling'em."

Slinging Ink: The process of getting a tattoo while in prison. A convict who is a tattoo artist will usually get paid for his services. There is usually one ink slinger for each race in a "Housing Unit" who always has a "Rig" and ink in his possession. "Title 15" section 3063 strictly forbids this practice: "Inmates shall not tattoo themselves or others and shall not permit tattoos to be placed on themselves."

Slip Him Some Steel: An old-school phrase that means an inmate will get stabbed. For example, "That youngster better stop acting a fool because someone is going to slip him some steel."

Slipped Their Cuffs: This is when a convict gets loose from their handcuffs. They could have used a hidden key or pulled their hand out.

Slipping: When a person is caught without their "Banger" on them. For example, "The 'Woods' caught me slipping and 'Poked' me."

Sloppy Program: When inmates in a "Car" aren't representing themselves well because they are sleeping in and not working out. They also have numerous drug debts and "Trash" on the yard that needs to be cleaned up. For example, "Our comrades from 'Dago' are running a sloppy program."

Slot: The small opening in the cell door whereby food is given to the inmates. Inmates are also cuffed through this opening while still inside their cells. For example, "The cops opened my slot and sprayed me after I 'Boarded Up.'"

Slow Dragging: Deliberately taking too much time to do something for someone else. For example, "Why are you slow dragging comrade? You said that you would talk to Bear for me."

Slow Playing: Deliberately taking too much time to do something for someone else. For example, "Why are you slow playing me, homie? You said that you would talk to Big Sluggo for me."

Slow Your Roll: A warning to stop your actions before you get into a "Wreck." For example, "You need to slow your roll homie before Hulk smashes you."

Slung Back: When a convict is covered in prison tattoos. For example, "Homie, have you seen Snoopy? He is slung back now, he is 'A Lame With A Paint Job.'"

Smacked Back: When a person is high on drugs. For example, "Biscuit is in his cell smacked back."

Small Things Become Big Things: The slightest issue can ignite a fullscale riot in prison. Looking at another man "Sideways" in prison can lead to murder and mayhem.

Smash: When a person gets violently attacked.

Smash Out: When a group of inmates violently attack another person, get them on the ground, and then kick and stomp them until they are unconscious.

Smash Them Out: When a group of inmates violently attack another person, get them on the ground, and then kick and stomp them until they are unconscious.

Smashed: When a person gets violently attacked.

Smashed Down: When a person gets violently attacked.

Smashed Out: When a group of inmates violently attack another person, get them on the ground, and then kick and stomp them until they are unconscious.

Smashing Out: When a group of inmates violently attack another person, get them on the ground, and then kick and stomp them until they are unconscious.

Smile Now, Cry Later: This common gang member philosophy means to live life to the fullest today and worry about the consequences later. The tattoo associated with this mindset is two theatrical masks: one is laughing, and one is crying.

Smoked Out: A drug-addicted inmate who constantly lies to his family so they send money under false pretenses so he can pay his drug debts. For example, he will tell them his television broke and he needs money to buy another one. He will use the money they send to pay for his drug debts. If things get desperate and he is about to get "Poked" for owing money, he will tell his family that he will be killed if they don't help. For example, "I ran into Dopey, and he was just a smoked out dope fiend."

Smut: To spread false or damaging information about another inmate. This is usually done when "Politicking" against someone. For example, "Don't let anyone put smut on your 'Jacket.'"

Smut On Their Jacket: When an inmate has any of the following on their "Paperwork;" rape, snitching, molestation, abusing women or the elderly, etc. Most prison gangs will violently attack inmates with these things on their "Black & Whites" and "Remove" them from the yard.

Smut Up: To spread false or damaging information about another inmate. This is usually done when "Politicking" against someone. For example, "Those lames tried to smut up Goldie."

Smutted Up: To spread false or damaging information about another inmate. This is usually done when "Politicking" against someone. For example, "The homie Dynamite got smutted up."

Smutting Up: To spread false or damaging information about another inmate. This is usually done when "Politicking" against someone. For example, "Those 'Dump Trucks' are always smutting up someone."

Snail Mail: This refers to the regular mail inmates get via the postal service.

Snake Pit: This refers to a prison, yard, or building that is very violent, and the "Prison Politics" are extreme. For example, "C-Yard at Centinela is a snake pit."

Snatching Lines: When "Protective Custody" inmates grab other convicts' "Fishing Lines" and pull them into their cells to aggravate them. A "GP" convict would never snatch a line because if they did, their own "Car" would discipline them. For example, "Those 'Pesetas' were snatching lines in the 'Hole.'"

Sniper: An inmate who likes to masturbate while watching female correctional officers or "Free Staff."

Snipes: The cigarette butts that are left on the ground in prison. Some inmates collect snipes, collect the tobacco from them, and make cigarettes.

Snitch: To tell on your gang members and cooperate with the investigation by authorities. The only thing considered worse in prison than a snitch is a "Chomo." The homies used to say, "If you ever call another man a snitch, you better be shooting or stabbing him as you do it." The reason for that is twofold: according to the streets, a snitch should be attacked in that manner. The other reason is if you put a "Jacket" like that on another man, he will shoot or stab you in retaliation. So you better "Get Off" first.

Snitch, Parole, Or Die: A saying used by convicts in the "Security Housing Unit" regarding the only ways to get out of there.

Snot Box: This term refers to a person's nose. For example, "Wild Bill got his snot box rocked for all of that trash he was talking."

SNY: This acronym stands for Sensitive Needs Yard. Sensitive needs yards are the majority of yards in CDCR now. These yards are considered "No Good" by the "General Population" convicts. SNY yards tend to be more chaotic and violent than the "Mainline" because the gang structure is less rigid than the general population gangs.

SNY Gangs: Inmates on "Sensitive Needs Yards" have formed their own groups after renouncing their former gangs on the "Mainline." Many people find it strange that they quit a gang in the "General Population" and then join another. However you may feel about that issue, the gangs on SNY yards are just as violent as the ones on the "Other Side Of The Fence."

Sod Buster: A derogatory term "Southerners" used for "Northerners."

Soft Candy: When inmates break gang rules, they will sometimes be given a soft candy as punishment. A soft candy will usually be getting "Poked" with a knife with only a three-inch or less blade. The knife has such a short blade, so no serious injuries are likely to occur. Sometimes, a "Tomahawk" will be used during a soft candy. It just depends on the yard and who is in charge at the time. A soft candy is usually the result of an unpaid drug or gambling debt.

Soft Check: When inmates break gang rules, they will sometimes be given a soft check as punishment. A soft check will usually be getting "Poked" with a knife with only a three-inch or less blade. The knife has such a short blade, so no serious injuries are likely to occur. Sometimes, a "Tomahawk" will be used during a soft check. It just depends on the yard and who is in charge at the time. A soft check is usually the result of an unpaid drug or gambling debt.

Soft Move: When inmates break gang rules, they will sometimes be given a soft move as punishment. A soft move will usually be getting "Poked" with a knife with only a three-inch or less blade. The knife has such a short blade, so no serious injuries are likely to occur. Sometimes, a "Tomahawk" will be used during a soft move. It just depends on the yard and who is in charge at the time. A soft move is usually the result of an unpaid drug or gambling debt.

Soft Yard: A yard that is easy to do time on because nobody is pushing a "Hardline" when it comes to "Prison Politics."

Soldado: A word that translates to soldiers, which refers to solid homies willing to "Put In Work" for the "Cause."

Soldier: A "Solid" gang member down for the "Cause."

Soledad Brothers: Three inmates charged with the murder of a correctional officer at Soledad Prison on January 16, 1970.

Soleta: When "Homies" do a lengthy prison sentence without a woman to ride the time out with them. It also means to do a lengthy prison sentence in general. For example, "Venom just did a 17-year soleta, and after two weeks on the streets, he caught a 'Hot One.'"

Solid: A respectable and tough convict who can be relied upon by his homies.

Solitary Confinement: This is another term for the "Security Housing Unit." The security housing unit (SHU) is where the most violent and influential convicts are placed due to them threatening institutional security at other prisons. These convicts are in their cells 23 hours a day and are allowed very little personal property due to security reasons. These convicts are given a shower once every three days and exercise on a small yard for an hour every day. For example, "I was given a 12-month solitary confinement term for distribution of narcotics in a state facility."

Solo Dolo: When people don't associate with a gang or homies and do their thing on their own. For example, "I'm not involved in all that drama, homie. I'm solo dolo."

Sopas: This word translates to soups. For example, "Hey homie, slide me and my cellie some sopas."

SOS: This acronym stands for "S**t On A Shingle." This breakfast years ago consisted of gravy with small pieces of meat and some toast. These days, it doesn't even come with bread or real meat. It is a very unpopular meal among convicts.

Souls On Ice: This is an old-school term used by some inmates in the 1960s through the 1970s to refer to Black inmates in the California Department of Corrections.

Sounds Good: When a person tells you a false story, you say to them when they are finished, "Sounds good." It is also used when a person threatens you, and when they are done, you disdainfully reply, "Sounds good."

Soup: Name for instant noodles, which are the convict's most popular food in prison. Soups are also used to wager with. For example, "I'll bet you five soups the Raiders will beat the Chargers."

South Side: When "Southerners" attack another person. For example, "That fool has a south side coming."

South Siding: This is a discipline by "Southerners" in prison where the person in violation will be violently attacked by his comrades. For example, "Check this out, homie, next yard, you got a south siding coming."

Southern Raza: The term is used for "Southerners."

Southerner: A Southerner is a Hispanic gang member from Southern California.

Southsider: A Southsider is a Hispanic gang member from Southern California.

Southsider Spread: A unique community meal for all "Southsiders" that everyone contributes to. Then, when it's done cooking, everyone eats together like a barbecue at a park.

Sparking Up: When inmates stick prison-made devices into electrical sockets so they can light their cigarettes and joints. Due to this dangerous process, the electrical socket will have burn marks around it from the electricity arcing. For example, "The homies are over there sparking up."

Speaking Out Of Turn: When a gangster speaks on things he has no business or authorization to give his public opinion on.

Spear: An inmate-manufactured weapon that is similar to a spear. The shaft will usually be made of tightly rolled magazines or newspapers, and the tip will be made of metal or hardened plastic.

Spearing: When an inmate uses a "Spear" to stab someone through the little openings in their cell door. When they do this, they will call their victim over to ask a question. Usually, they will speak softly so the victim gets closer to the door so they can hear. When they get close enough, they stab them in the neck or face with the spear.

Special Isolation Diet: Back in the day, some inmates could be placed on a Special Isolation Diet in the "Adjustment Center." In San Quentin, Soledad, and Folsom Prisons, the food they got on this diet was called a "Dog Biscuit." The Dog Biscuit was made by compressing leftover food into a cube and then drying it out. This dehydrated mass of former slop was then given to the inmates on reduced food rations. The inmates got two Dog Biscuits a day served with a slice of bread.

Special Purchase: Special Purchases are for procuring various musical instruments, electronics, televisions, and radios that would not fit into a "Quarterly Package." Inmates are allowed four Special Purchases a year along with their Quarterly Packages.

Special Services Unit: This unit of special agents works for the California Department of Corrections and Rehabilitation but are neither parole agents nor corrections officers. SSU agents perform criminal investigations on parolees and prison inmates.

Speeding Ticket: A notice of a rules violation for inappropriate behavior. For example, "Homie, I was in visiting kissing my girl, and that punk officer gave me a speeding ticket."

Spensa: A word that translated to "my bad." For example, 'Spensa home. I meant no disrespect."

Spike: This term refers to the Folger Adams brass keys the officers use to open doors in prison. For example, "The spike makes a distinctive sound when it hits the key jam."

Spike: A hypodermic needle and other supplies used to "Mainline" drugs while in prison.

Spiking The Doors: This term refers to an officer who is opening the cell door on a "Section" of a "Tier." For example, "The officer is spiking the doors on the tier."

Spill: This is when a person gives their opinion on a subject, and they go into great detail. For example, "That was a good spill, comrade."

Spin: When an officer searches an inmate and the inmate quickly spins around to assault or move away from the officer. If an inmate ever spins on an officer, they have every right to grab them because they don't know if the inmate is attacking them.

Spin A Lap: To walk or run around the track on the prison yard. For example, "High Top, let's go spin a lap, homeboy."

Spin The Track: To walk or run around the track on the prison yard. For example, "Dizzy, let's go spin the track, homie."

Spinning Laps: This is when a convict runs or walks around the "Track" on the yard. For example, "Fast Eddie is spinning laps. He isn't in his cell."

Spitting Drag: A false story or scheme used to take advantage of someone or manipulate them. For example. "I sent you the 'Hook Up' to Big Rob. I don't know enough about it to know if he was spitting drag."

Split Tier: This system of yard and "Dayroom" release only allows the same tiers in all buildings to go to yard and dayroom. Each "Housing Unit" at Centinela Prison has two tiers, with five housing units on each yard. On even days, the lower tier went to the yard; on odd days, the upper tier went to the yard. Split tier was also implemented for the dayroom so inmates only hung out with people from their same tier during these activities.

Sports Rules: This general prison concept refers to when inmates are watching television in a "Dayroom." If sports are being televised, they will be watched over anything else.

Spot: Another name for a prison cell. For example, "I got those soups I owe you, comrade. They are at the spot."

Spread: A spread is a meal prepared by a group of convicts in a large trash bag filled with several "Soups" and other food items. After the items are cooked, the meal is spread out on a table, and the group eats together, similar to a barbeque at a park. For example, "We are going to bust a spread with the homies from our area."

Spread Your Hustle: This is said to a person who is always asking for stuff because they don't have enough game to get it themselves. For example, "You need to spread your hustle, homie. I just gave you a 'Soup.'"

Spun: A mentally ill inmate. Someone who is acting like a "J Cat."

Spun Out: When someone is high on drugs and acting crazy. For example, "Speedy is spun out and running around the yard."

SQ: The nickname for San Quentin State Prison.

Squab: When two people fight. For example, "Big D and Dre are about to squab in the 'Blind.'"

Squab It Out: When two people fight to settle their differences. For example, "Check this out, homie. You and Maniac need to squab it out if you can't resolve your issues."

Squabble: When two people fight. For example, "Smurf and Looney got their squabble on."

Squabble Up: To fight with another person. For example, "Win, lose, or draw, I'm going to squabble up. I'm not afraid of a fight."

Squabbles: Someone who can fight well. For example, "Ray Ray got them squabbles, homie."

Squabbling: When two inmates are fighting each other. For example, "I was in the 'Crip Tank' so homies were squabbling all the time."

Squad: The squad is similar to the detectives of the prison, and they investigate inmates and officers alike for alleged nefarious activities. They are commonly referred to as the "Goon Squad."

Squad Leader: The squad leader is a "Norteño" who is the "Shot Caller" for a "Housing Unit" in prison.

Square: A "Punk" who gets no respect from their peers. A worthless, good-for-nothing person who does not stand up for themselves.

Squashed: When two inmates or groups agree to stop fighting over a current dispute. For example, "Playboy got with my old lady when I was locked up in county jail. It's squashed now."

Squat & Cough: This is the convict term for the prison "Strip Search" process. During the strip search process, the convict will be naked with his back to you and ordered to squat and cough while spreading his butt cheeks open. This is done so the officer can see if he has any "Contraband" in his anal cavity.

Stab It Out: When two people in prison can't resolve their differences, they agree to go into a cell with "Pieces" and stab it out until one man is left standing. This process is similar to a pistol duel in the Old West.

Stabbed Off The Yard: When an inmate violates a serious gang rule and as punishment, his "People" will "Poke" him.

Stabbing Up: When an inmate "Pokes" another inmate with some prison steel. For example, "Stranger caught that 'Chomo' in the 'Blind' and he was stabbing up that fool."

Staff Assault: This is the official term used in reports when an inmate physically assaults a correctional officer.

Staff Assistant: This staff member assists inmates during an "RVR" hearing.

Staff Entrance: The entrance to the secure area of the prison that all officers must pass through, show their identification, and have their lunch bag searched before they enter.

Stall Him Out: To make someone stop doing something. For example, "Stall him out, don't let him do cuzz like that."

Stall Out: This means to stop doing something. For example, "I had to stall out on eating those honey buns because I need to look good for my 'Conjugal Visit.'"

Stamps: Books of stamps are a form of currency in prison. Books of stamps are used to pay off debts, pay for tattoos, pay for drugs, and many other things.

Stand At The Cell Door To Fart: Some inmates have a rule while living in a cell with another man that if someone has to fart, they must go stand by the cell door to let one rip. For an inmate to fart in a cell without standing by the cell door is disrespectful and will lead to "Problems" with his "Cellie."

Stands On His Business: A respectable and tough convict who can be relied upon by his homies. For example, "Cowboy stands on his business. He ain't playing around."

Stand On His Square: When a gangster stands his ground and doesn't back down from a confrontation. For example, "I told you the homie was going to stand on his square. He isn't a punk."

Stand Point: To watch for officers or enemies from other gangs.

Stand Tall: To do your time through hardships and find a way to endure even though it's hard. For example, "Prison is rough. There is nothing nice about it. You got to stand tall, 'Ten Toes Down.'"

Stand Tall Through It All: To do your time through hardships and find a way to endure even though it's hard. For example, "The only thing I can do in the penitentiary is stand tall through it all."

Stand Up: A well-respected convict who honors his word and handles himself with respect. For example, "Gremlin is a stand up guy. If he gave you his word, he will come through, homie."

Stand Up Convict: A well-respected convict who honors his word and handles himself with respect. For example, "Sapo is a stand-up convict. If he gave you his word, he will come through, homie."

Stand Up Guy: A well-respected convict who honors his word and handles himself with respect. He will handle his business when it's time to kick things off.

Standing Count: This type of "Count" in prison requires the inmates to stand until an officer counts them.

Starvin Marvin: To be extremely hungry while in prison. For example, "I missed 'Store' again, and I was starvin Marvin in the cell during 'Lockdown.'"

Starving: A term used in prison that means a person doesn't have a lot of "Groceries" in their cell, and they get hungry between the meals served in the prison. For example, "I was starving and going without when I was in the 'Hole.'"

Stash Box: A term used to describe the anal cavity of a convict. A convict places items of "Contraband" in his rectum to avoid discovery by officers. Some convicts become very proficient at this and can do it in seconds. When a "Banger" is placed inside of the stash box, it will have a protective layer of cellophane to prevent his insides from being perforated. For example, "Don't trip homeboy. The cops will never find it because it's in the stash box."

Stash Box: This refers to an area where contraband is stored. For example, "Don't trip homie, the 'Clavo' is in the stash box."

Stash Spot: A secret storage area inmates use to hide "Contraband," such as cell phones, drugs, money, knives, tattoo rigs, hype kits, etc.

State Blues: The blue-colored clothes that inmates are issued in prison.

State Crack: When a person gets convicted of a state crime and has to go to state prison. For example, "Bandit just caught a state crack."

State Food: The food that the state of California provides for the inmates. Inmates receive two hot meals and one sack lunch daily in California state prisons.

State Issue: The allotted number of items a convict can possess and the services the state must provide daily according to the "Title 15."

State Raised: A gangster who spent most of their formative years in the "California Youth Authority."

Status: The influence that a person has to get things done in prison. For example, "How did Rockhead get moved from Housing Unit Alpha-3 to Alpha-2?" The answer is, "He used his status with the captain."

Status: The status a convict has among his peers. The respect a convict is given by the other members of his "Car."

Stay Down: This means to carry yourself with honor and never let anyone disrespect you. For example, "When I came up, the 'Big Homies' always taught us to stay down, don't 'Mark Out.'"

Stay Down For Your Crown: This means to carry yourself with honor and never let anyone disrespect you. For example, "When I came up, the 'OG' always taught me to stay down for my crown."

Stay In Your Lane: In prison, you don't involve yourself in other people's business or things that don't concern you. For example, "Hey homie, why did Tio order the hit on Termite?" The answer is, "Stay in your lane, homie. You are asking too many questions."

Stay On Your P's And Q's: This means always watching your back and being ready for anything. For example, "Prison life is ruthless. You must always stay on your P's and Q's homie."

Stay Out Of The Mix: To do your own time and not get involved in other people's drama. For example, "Freckles, you need to stay out of the mix, comrade. Those cats 'Play For Keeps.'"

Stay Solid: To do your time through hardships and find a way to endure even though it's hard. For example, "Prison is tough. There is nothing nice about it. You have to stay solid."

Steel Garden: An area on the prison yard where convicts bury their knives for easy access to their "Car." For example, "We strategically buried our knives in our steel garden on the yard for easy access when things 'Kicked Off' between us and the Blacks."

Steel Only Yard: Most gangs have a "No Hands Policy" on level IV prison yards. This means gang members cannot fight each other with fists. If they can't resolve their issue, they can grab a "Banger" and go into a cell and "Stab It Out." This is because gangs need all their soldiers on level IV yards and don't want to lose them to the "Hole" for petty fights. If a gang lost soldiers to petty fist fights amongst its members, they would become easier targets for other gangs, hence the no hands policy.

Step Back: When a gang member retires from gang life for whatever reason. For example, "Once you step back, you stay back. You don't get to come back."

Step Down: When a convict in a leadership position voluntarily gives up his role in his gang. Stepping down can be on his own accord or under pressure from his "Car" under the threat of his removal from his position by force. For example, "We told Bandit to step down or be 'Removed.' He got out of the way just like we knew he would."

Step Down Program: The California Department of Corrections and Rehabilitation program assisted the "SHU" inmates in transitioning to the "General Population." This program was at Pelican Bay and Corcoran prisons.

Stepped Away: When a gang member retires from gang life for whatever reason. For example, "I just got tired, homie. I stepped away, and it was the best decision I ever made."

Stepped Back: When a gang member retires from gang life for whatever reason. For example, "Once I had kids, I stepped back and laid down my flag."

Stepping On Toes: This means disrespecting someone by interfering with something they are doing. For example, "Check this out, youngster, you must stop stepping on my toes! If you do that again, we are going to have problems."

STG Unit Classification Committee: This committee decides whether an inmate is part of a "Security Threat Group."

Stick: This is a rolled marijuana cigarette. For example, "Me and my 'Cellie' hit a stick once we got into the 'Pad' after yard."

Stick: A prison knife made of metal, melted plastic, or any other hard material that can be sharpened to a point.

Stick & Move: This is the aggressive concept of striking fast and getting out of the area before the enemy can counterattack. When convicts go on a "Mission," many use this combat philosophy to get away after quickly "Poking" another inmate with a "Banger."

Stick To The Code: When a person is down for theirs and won't let anyone disrespect them. For example, "Check this out, little homie. You need to stick to the code behind these prison walls."

Stick To The Script: To carry yourself with respect. For example, "There is nothing nice about prison. If you want to survive, you must stick to the script, homeboy."

Sticking: When someone gets stabbed in prison. For example, "There was a sticking on A yard. They are saying one of our 'People' was hit."

Still On Paper: When a released inmate on the streets is still on parole. For example, "I have to watch myself, homie. I am still on paper."

Stinger: An electrical device inmates use to heat water for coffee or "Soups."

Stomped Down: When a person or group gets physically attacked violently. For example, "We rushed the 'Nortenos' and to be honest, we got stomped down. They had their way with us."

Store: "Canteen" where an inmate may purchase food and other items in prison.

Store Draw: These are the weeks inmates are allowed to go to

"Canteen" and get their "Commissary." The 1st draw is the first week of the month, the 2nd draw is the second week, and the 3rd draw is the third week. The inmates are assigned draws by the last two numbers of their "CDCR Number."

Straight: This means everything is good. It can be a question to a friend: "Are we straight?" It can also be an accusation, "I thought we were straight?"

Strains On Their Jacket: When an inmate has any of the following on their "Paperwork;" rape, snitching, molestation, abusing women or the elderly, etc. Most prison gangs will violently attack inmates with these things on their "Black & Whites" and "Remove" them from the yard.

Strap: A prison-made knife. For example, "There's Risky right there. Get your strap homie!"

Strapped: When a convict has his knife on him. For example, "Homie, you better be strapped today because those 'Peckerwoods' are tripping about that 'White Crip' on the yard."

Strapped Down: When a convict has a knife on them. For example, "I'm strapped down, and so is my crew. We are ready to 'Go Up.'"

Strapped Up: When an inmate has a knife on him. For example, "Bolo was 'Wolfing' while I was strapped up, so I 'Poked' him."

Street Code: The standard guidelines a gangster must follow to remain in "Good Standing" with his peers. For example, testifying in court or cooperating with law enforcement goes against the street code.

Street Name: A convict's nickname that all gang members call him by. For example: Flaco, Termite, Trouble, Casper, Downer,

Cowboy, Rocky, Hatchet, Redwood, Blazer, Maniac, Bandit, Popeye, Tarzan, Snail, Bolo, Twist, Bozo, Pirate, Snoopy, Thumper, Tricky, Bugsy, Pelon, Stranger, Tyson, Nasty, Menace, Red, Blue, etc.

Street Politics: These are the politics that govern gangsters on the streets, and they are different in many ways from "Prison Politics," which is more strict. On the streets, gangsters have more freedom in what they can do, but in prison, some activities won't be tolerated by their "Car."

Street Regiment General: This person oversees all of the "Nuestra Familia's" criminal street operations.

Street To Street: A form of payment for a drug deal or wager inside of prison when a convict's people on the streets send money to another convict's outside people.

Stress Box: The nickname for the prison phones. For example, "Is Trippy on the stress box arguing with his girl again?"

Stretch: Doing a set amount of time locked up. For example, "I did a twoyear stretch in the 'SHU,' so this punk little lockdown doesn't faze me."

Stretched: When a person gets convicted of a crime and receives a lengthy prison sentence. For example, "Back in county jail, we knew we were going to get stretched. So we started our time before we even got found guilty."

Stretched Him Out: When a convict attacks someone, and the victim ends up lying on the ground. For example, "I caught him with a good one and stretched him out."

Stretched Out: When a person gets convicted of a crime and receives a lengthy prison sentence. For example, "Munchie got stretched out, and his old lady got with the homie. He is feeling some type of way about that."

Strict Politics: When a prison yard has rigorous politics and severe consequences for breaking "Household Policies." Level IV yards have strict politics.

Strict Program: When convicts in a "Car" are up early, working out hard, on point, and representing themselves well in prison based on their conduct. For example, "The homies were running a strict program at Kern Valley."

Strike Me Up: When a convict wants you to write him, he might say, "Strike me up when you get some free time."

Strike Up: When gang members represent their gangs via graffiti. For example, "Hey, homie, slide me those clippers so I can strike up the set on the cell door."

Strike Up: To write or contact another person. For example, "I'm going to strike up Tricky about that issue we are having with Lil Joker."

Strike Up Paperwork: This means filling out paperwork to report an incident in prison. An officer can strike up paperwork on an inmate or an inmate could strike up paperwork on an officer via a "602" Inmate Appeal Form.

Striker: A convict convicted under the California Three Strikes Law.

Strip Cell: This type of cell was in places like San Quentin, Folsom, and Soledad Prisons back in the day. A strip cell was a cell in the "Isolation Wing" of the prison that didn't have anything but a hole in the floor to be used as a toilet. This hole on the floor was referred to as an "Oriental Toilet." The inmate was allowed a small hard mat to sleep on the concrete floor. As the name suggests, the inmate was usually naked in a strip cell. A strip cell had a regular cell door, a small vestibule, and another solid steel door to isolate the inmate. According to court documents filed on September 6, 1966, the inmate in a strip cell was rationed 2 cups of water daily.

Strip Him Of His Jersey: When gang members remove a member for breaking their code of conduct. Getting stripped of a jersey involves extreme violence, ranging from a severe beating to getting "Poked" numerous times. For example, "Tiny is 'No Good,' we are going to strip him of his jersey."

Strip Out: An order given to inmates when an officer is going to perform a "Strip Search."

Strip Search: When convicts have to take off all their clothes to be searched, and while they are naked, they are visually checked under their nut sack and inside their anus for drugs, "Shanks," or other "Contraband."

Stripes: The reputation a gang member earns by "Putting in Work" and "Doing Dirt." For example, "I have stripes for putting in work. You better ask somebody!"

Stripped: When a gangster with authority is stripped of his power by other high-ranking members. Being stripped can happen for several reasons in prison, and it is not uncommon. For example, "Stranger got stripped and 'Sat Down' over that 'Bad Call' he made regarding Bouncer getting 'Whacked.'"

Strolling The Yard: This means walking the yard. For example, "When we came out of the 'SHU' and were strolling the yard, those punks 'Broke It Down' and didn't want any problems."

Stronghold: A prison or prison yard where a particular gang has a tight grip on running the "Program." For example, "The Black inmates have a stronghold at Lancaster Prison" and "The White inmates have a stronghold at High Desert State Prison."

Struck Out: When a person in California is convicted of their third serious or violent felony, they will get a 25-year-to-life sentence.

Structure: The "Politics" that govern a particular group of gangsters on the streets or in prison. For example, "Snitching and stealing from a homie violates our structure."

Structured: When a person or "Faction" carries themselves with the utmost respect and doesn't play games. For example, "The homies are structured. They don't play around."

Structured Up: When a "Car" controls a yard or a "Hustle" on a prison yard. For example, "We had that yard structured up, homie. There wasn't anyone who wanted any 'Problems' with us."

Stuck Up: To get stabbed with a "Banger." For example, "They caught Blue on the second tier, and he got stuck up."

Sucked Up: When a person looks skinny after losing weight. For example, "Flaco, you look sucked up, homie."

Suicide Watch: Anytime an inmate is deemed a threat to himself, he is placed in a cell in the "Infirmary" under constant watch to ensure that he doesn't hurt himself. The inmate is stripped of all clothes and property except for a thin cotton hospital gown. The only thing in his cell is a mattress on the floor and an extra thick blanket that cannot be used to hang himself.

Suitcase: A term used to describe the anal cavity of a convict. A convict places items of "Contraband" in his rectum to avoid discovery by officers. Some convicts become very proficient at this and can do it in seconds. When a "Banger" is placed inside the suitcase, it will have a protective layer of cellophane to prevent their insides from being perforated. For example, "Don't trip homie. The officers will never find it because it's in the suitcase."

Suited & Booted: When a convict expects smoke, he will be ready for battle. They will stay ready, so they don't have to get ready. For example, "When in prison, you better be suited and booted and ready to handle your business."

Super Blood: A "Blood" who pushes a "Hardline" and is "Turned Up." The bad part about having these homies in prison was they had no diplomacy. Having them around usually leads to issues because they don't know how to talk to people.

Super Crip: A "Crip" who pushes a "Hardline" and is "Turned Up." The bad part about having these homies in prison was they had no diplomacy. Having them around usually leads to issues because they don't know how to talk to people.

Super II: An old-school boom box radio made by General Electric that some inmates had.

Super III: An old-school boom box radio made by General Electric that some inmates had.

Super Tuner: An old-school boom box radio made by General Electric that some inmates had.

Supercop: An overzealous correctional officer always sweating the convicts over petty things. A nit-picking control freak officer who needlessly harasses the convicts to make up for their shortcomings.

SUR: This acronym means a soldier under-recognition. This title refers to "Sureños." A Sureño is a "Southerner" highly regarded by their peers. This means they have "Put In Work" in jail or prison for the "Cause" and earned the title of Sureño.

Sureño: A Sureño is a "Southerner" highly regarded by their peers. This means they have "Put In Work" in jail or prison for the "Cause" and earned the title of Sureño. They are a soldier under-recognition; that's what "SUR" stands for.

Susie's House: A nickname for Susanville State Prison.

Suwoop: Some say this originally started as a warning about approaching police by "Brims." Others say this was originally a greeting between Brims and later adopted by other "Bloods."

SVP: The Sexually Violent Predator Unit reviews the history of inmates in the California Department of Corrections and Rehabilitation to determine those likely to be sexually violent predators. If the inmate meets the criteria of a sexually violent predator, he is then referred to the Department of State Hospitals for a thorough examination.

SVSP: Salinas Valley State Prison.

Swap: When two correctional officers switch workdays to get three days off instead of two. When this happens, they must work a 16-hour shift to work their buddies' post in exchange for their extra day off. Some officers are on permanent swaps with their "Road Dogs," and they have 3-day weekends.

Sweating: When a person harasses or pressures another inmate. For example, "That punk officer is always sweating me about not having a shirt on during 'Dayroom.'"

Sweating His Program: This is when someone confronts another person in prison when they feel they are doing things wrongly. For example, "That youngster has the homies sweating his program because he hasn't learned how to do time yet."

Sweating My Program: This is when a person is on your case, harassing you, or asking too many questions. For example, "Don't be sweating my program. Stay out of my mix."

Swimming: When a person in a fight puts their head down and starts wildly swinging their arms like they are swimming. For example, "That punk can't fight a lick. He put his head down and started swimming like Michael Phelps."

Switchboard: This is when a member or "Associate" of a prison gang sets up avenues of communication on the streets for gang members in prison. For example, "Big Turk is going home next week. Make sure he sets up that switchboard."

Swole: A very muscular or "Yoked" person.

Sword: A very long knife in prison that is the size of a small sword or machete.

SWP: This is a tattoo that some White convicts get that means Supreme White Power.

Sympathizer: A person who hangs around gangs and even does things of a criminal nature with them, but they aren't a bonafide member.

T

Tagger: A Tagger is a person who usually runs with a small group called a "Tagging Crew," and they go around their area doing graffiti. It's not uncommon for a tagger to join the local street gang.

Tagging Crew: This group of "Taggers" go around their area doing graffiti. It's not uncommon for members of a tagging crew to join the local street gang.

Take A Little Off That: Usually, this saying is told to a convict pressing a "Hardline" on an issue others feel isn't necessary. For example, "Candy Man, take a little off that homie. You are doing too much, 'Pump Your Brakes.'"

Take Care Of The House: Profits from illegal activities that go to the "Big Homies" of a particular gang. Usually, 1/3 of profits is used to take care of the house. For example, "You need to take care of the house. The house gets broke off first, homie."

Take Flight: To physically attack someone. For example, "If that punk officer trashes my cell again, I will take flight on him."

Take Him Out The Hat: This means a person was once "In The Hat," but for some reason, the "Big Homies" took him off of the "Bad News List." The "Southsiders" had a "Buyback Policy" whereby a homie in "Bad Standing" could pay $10,000 to get off of the hit list.

Take His Air: This means to make a person stop breathing. For example, "We just got word that Kermit is 'No Good.' During the next 'Unlock,' they are going to take his air."

Take His Wind: This means to make a person stop breathing. For example, "We just got the 'Green Light' regarding Lefty. They want us to take his wind."

Take It Home: This is an order for a convict to go into his cell and "Lockup." For example, "Cricket, take it home!"

Take It To The Hoop: This means a convict will place some "Contraband" inside his anal cavity so officers don't discover it. For example, "When we had weapons, and the police were doing searches, we would wrap it up in plastic and take it to the hoop. You have to watch how you sit and move to avoid getting poked. All of the homies do it. If they have a weapon, it's going up there."

Take It To The Stall: To settle a dispute among convicts in the shower area of the "Dorm" through mutual combat. For example, "Quit running your mouth and take it to the stall."

Take Off: To physically attack someone. For example, "If that fat officer ever comes in our cell again, I'm going to take off on him."

Take This To The Box: When an inmate denies the deal from the district attorney and wants a jury trial. For example, "Nah, I'm not accepting that twelve-year plea deal. I will take this to the box."

Talk Crazy: To come at another person "Sideways" and disrespect them with your words. For example, "If Charlie Brown starts to talk crazy to me, I'm going to 'Poke' him."

Talk Him Off The Fence: To reason with a homie so he doesn't do something foolish and get into a "Wreck." For example, "I had to talk him off the fence because the homie was about to 'Take Off' on the homie."

Talking Out Of The Side Of Your Neck: To tell stories that aren't true or to speak aggressively to someone without intending to back it up with violence. For example, "Jackal, quit talking out the side of your neck. We all know you aren't going to 'Bust A Grape.'"

Tank: In county jail or "Receiving And Release," it's the large cell in which numerous inmates are locked while they await the next step in whatever they are doing. In a tank, there is usually a toilet in the corner and some benches for some inmates to sit on while others stand. I had heard numerous stories from convicts who say they were attacked in a tank when an enemy "Slipped Their Cuffs," pulled a razor from their mouth, and started slashing them.

Tank: In most county jails in California, the housing units that inmates live in are called tanks. For example, "What tank were you in back in county?"

Tap In: To check in with a higher authority in your "Car" to ask permission for something or to request advice. It also means to check in with your comrades to let them know you have "Landed."

Tap Out: When a prison gang member stops gang banging and lays down his flag. For example, "Did you hear about Trey? He plans to tap out because of his old lady."

Tatted Back: When an inmate is covered in tattoos all over his body. For example, "Downer is tatted back."

Tax Free: These "Southerner" gangs refuse to pay "Taxes" to the "Mexican Mafia." Because they refused to pay taxes, the Mexican Mafia placed a "Green Light" on them.

Taxes: The profits from illegal activities that go to the "Big Homies" of a particular gang. Usually, 1/3 of profits is paid in taxes in this manner.

Team Fell Off: When the people who once supported an inmate by visiting, sending packages, and putting money on his "Books" stop supporting them for whatever reason. For example, "My team fell off after my 'Second Term.' This prison life is 'For The Birds.'"

Tear His Sheets: To call someone's bluff or to reveal damaging information about them. For example, "I am going to tear Sinbad's sheets about what he did to the homie."

Tecato: A word that some inmates use for a heroin addict. For example, "Who cares what Gumby says? He is just a tecato."

Tell: To "Snitch" on your gang members and cooperate with the investigation by authorities.

Telling: The act of snitching on someone.

Telling Line: Where snitches go to tell on others. For example, "Where is Mugsy?" The answer "Mugsy is at the head of the telling line. He is 'No Good.'"

Ten Toes Down: This means a person stands defiantly in the face of adversity. For example, "Ten toes down, homeboy. There ain't no other way to go about it."

Tension: When a person or group of people in prison causes other "Cars" to "Group Up" or get upset because of their actions. For example, "Homie, you need to stop being so loud at night in your cell. You are causing tension with the Blacks."

Tent: When a convict in a "Dorm" setting hangs sheets around his bunk for privacy.

Term: A prison sentence. For example, "I'm on my second term homeboy."

Test Your Water: To physically confront someone to see if they will fight or "Pee On Themselves." For example, "Listen up, young homie, dudes in the penitentiary are going to test your water to see what type of time you are on."

That Guy: An inmate always acting hardcore and ready to fight over any situation they think they were disrespected. For example,

"Malo thinks he is that guy with the way he is getting at people."

That's What's Up: This is said when you are impressed or agree with what another person did or is telling you. For example, "You did good homeboy when you 'Took Off' on that 'Chomo.' That's what's up!"

The Back: The "SHU" or the "Hole" where the "Heavy Hitters" are "Locked Down." Basically, it is a prison within the prison. It's where convicts are placed when their presence on the "Mainline" is deemed problematic to the administration. For example, "The 'Big Homie' Chico is in the back."

The Back Runs The Front: A prison saying that simply states the "Big Homies" in the "SHU" run the "Mainline" prison yards.

The Bay: Term used by convicts for Pelican Bay State Prison.

The Big Four: The four original main prison gangs in the California Department of Corrections and Rehabilitation. These gangs are: "Aryan Brotherhood," "Mexican Mafia," "Nuestra Familia," and "Black Guerrilla Family."

The Box: This is another term used for the "Security Housing Unit." The security housing unit is where the most violent and influential convicts are placed due to them threatening institutional security at other prisons. These convicts are in their cells 23 hours a day and are allowed very little personal property due to security reasons. These convicts are given a shower once every three days and exercise on a small yard for an hour daily.

The Brand: This is another name for the "Aryan Brotherhood" prison gang. The Aryan Brotherhood is a White prison gang formed in San Quentin Prison in 1967. The Aryan Brotherhood started as the "Blue Bird Gang" in the 1950s, and as a result of a vicious war with the "Black Guerrilla Family," they joined forces with other smaller White gangs to form the Aryan Brotherhood.

The Brass: The leaders of a prison gang or "Car" who wield tremendous influence over their "Faction." For example, "Scarface came to my door and told me, "I need you to pass this 'Filter' to the homies. It's coming from Pelican Bay, it's coming from the 'Brass.'"

The Cause: The mission and goals of a "Faction." It's supposed to be all about the cause at the expense of the individual's wants, needs, or desires. The cause comes first, and if one individual goes "Against The Grain," the leadership won't hesitate to make an example out of them to keep other members in line.

The Code: This is the standard guidelines a gangster must follow to remain in "Good Standing" with his peers. For example, testifying in court or cooperating with law enforcement goes against the code.

The Collective: In prison gangs, it's supposed to be all about the group at the expense of the individual's wants, needs, or desires. The group comes first, and if one individual goes "Against The Grain," the leadership won't hesitate to make an example out of them to keep other members in line.

The Dad: Term used by convicts for Soledad State Prison.

The Fellas: The leaders of a prison gang or "Car" who wield tremendous influence over their "Faction."

The Hatch: A nickname for Tehachapi State Prison.

The Hotel: In "CRC" Prison, a notorious building called the Hotel houses about 400 inmates. There is a rumor that the Eagles song Hotel California is about this building.

The House of Dracula: The old-school nickname for Folsom State Prison.

The House That George Jackson Built: A nickname used by some "Factions" to describe San Quentin State Prison.

The Ins: This refers to things inside of prison. For example, "Nothing I did on the streets counted. It wasn't until I hit the ins and got my name to the right people by 'Putting In Work' that my name started 'Ringing Bells.'"

The Jungle: This was the nickname of my "Housing Unit" Charlie 5 on the Level IV yard at Centinela State Prison. It was called this because it was "Rocking," and bloodshed was very common inside its walls. On my day off, my partner was stabbed in the neck by a "Crip." On another occasion during this same time, two Crips violently beat an officer, and they tried to pull him into cell 217 and close the door so they could kill him. That officer barely escaped with his life, and I visited him at his home a few days later. He looked terrible because of the injuries on his face. Even the "Booty Bandit" in Charlie 5 would threaten officers with beatings if he didn't get his way. I was assigned to this building as a "Fish" because the "Regular" officers either quit or were off because of stress or injuries.

The Line: The "General Population" of inmates who have little restrictions placed on their activities and privileges.

The Man: A slang term for a correctional officer.

The Mob: This term is used for the "Mexican Mafia" by some people.

The Movement: The mission and goals of a "Faction." It's supposed to be all about the mission at the expense of the individual's wants, needs, or desires. The mission comes first, and if one individual goes "Against The Grain," the leadership won't hesitate to make an example out of them to keep other members in line.

The Outs: This is how inmates in prison refer to things outside of the prison walls.

The Pass: In a prison setting, this is when "Contraband" is discreetly passed from one person to another. For example, when a visitor in the "Visiting Room" passes drugs to the inmate, they are there to see that day.

The Pit: The nickname for Old Folsom State Prison.

The Q: The nickname for San Quentin State Prison.

The Ride: Another name for the "Nazi Low Rider" prison gang.

The Sharks: This is an alleged gang of violent officers at Corcoran State Prison in the 1990s. Several members of this gang were either fired or demoted after being investigated by authorities.

The Struggle: The mission and goals of a "Faction." It's supposed to be all about the struggle at the expense of the individual's wants, needs, or desires. The struggle comes first, and if one individual goes "Against The Grain," the leadership won't hesitate to make an example out of them to keep other members in line.

The System: The entire criminal justice system, from the local police and prosecutors to the California Department of Corrections and Rehabilitation. For example, "I have 20 years in the system, youngster. If you don't want to listen to me, that's on you."

The Table: The three "Shot Callers" who ran the "Nuestra Familia" prison gang in its old structure. It is also referred to as "La Mesa."

The Unholy Alliance: This is used by some factions in prison to describe the alliance between the "Aryan Brotherhood" and the "Mexican Mafia."

The Walk: The walkway in a prison that leads from one place to another. Most walks contain yellow lines on either side. Inmates must walk on one side of the line depending on their direction.

The Walking Dead: This refers to inmates who have life sentences without the possibility of parole. For example, "Ghost just got 'Broke Off.' He is the walking dead."

There Are No Secrets In Prison: This statement is very accurate, and "Smut" spreads just as quickly. Even officers will spread lies to inmates about fellow officers because they want to damage their reputations and make their jobs harder. Once one person knows something in prison, everyone knows.

There Is No Honor Among Tecatos: Those "Tecato" homies only care about their high and nothing else at the end of the day. So many righteous homies have been done dirty and "Crossed Up" by tecatos. A gangster can give his freedom and loyalty to his organization, yet in the end, he is thrown away like trash just because some tecato only cares about his next high.

There You Go: This is what you say to a person when they start running their mouth.

They Don't Want To See Us: This means another "Faction" fears a conflict with your "Car." For example, "Those 'Woods' are scared.

They don't want to see us."

They Got To Go: This means a person or group needs to be "Removed" from the prison yard. For example, "Word just came down from the 'Big Homie' about those dudes we got an issue with. They got to go."

They Left Correctly: When two factions go to war in prison, and one loses the war and valiantly fights until the end without "Rolling It Up." For example, "Those 'Woods' were outnumbered 8 to 1 at Lancaster when the 'Crips' 'Moved On' them. They left correctly, even against those odds."

They On Them: When a group of inmates violently attack another person or group and "Smash" them. For example, "There was 'Bloods' everywhere. They were 'Beating The Brakes' off those White boys. They on them."

Third Term: An inmate who is doing his third prison term. For example, "Smiley is on his third term, we should make him the 'MAC Rep.'"

This Is Their House, I'm Just Passing Through: This means the big homies doing "All Day" run the show in prison. They are never getting out, so they have nothing to lose. If you have a "Date," do your time and try to get home to your family. This also applies to officers. We had a saying in my day that relates to this, "They live here; I'm just here for eight hours."

Three Strikes Law: When a person in California is convicted of their third serious or violent felony, they will get a 25-year-to-life sentence.

Three Way: When associates of convicts in the "Free World" accept the collect phone calls of two different convicts at his home. Doing this allows them to talk to each other.

Three Way: When three correctional officers are talking on the prison phones to pass the time. A code on the prison phone at Centinela Prison allowed these types of group conversations, and some officers at my prison would sit and talk for hours while neglecting their duties during their eight-hour shifts.

Threw His Date: When a convict commits a crime in prison, that gets more time added to his sentence, and as a result, he misses his parole "Date."

Throw The Bar: This means an officer is going to deactivate the "Bar" so the inmates will be able to get out of their cells once their doors are opened.

Throw Yourself Out There: To put yourself in a vulnerable position. For example, "You shouldn't throw yourself out there like that dog."

Throwing It Out There: This is what you say when you want to inform somebody of something important. For example, "I'm just throwing it out there, but Nutcase just 'Hit' at visiting."

Thug Hug: This is when two gangsters greet each other by shaking hands and simultaneously putting the other hand on the shoulder.

Thumbs Down: The extreme disapproval of a person's actions or orders to attack another person.

Thunderdome: A name given to "Housing Units" or "Dorms" that are "Off The Hook." For example, "Charlie 5 at Centinela was a Thunderdome homie. Fools were getting 'Smashed' daily in there."

Tia Rita's House: This is the nickname for the Santa Rita Jail in Dublin, California. The Santa Rita Jail has a design capacity of over 3,400 inmates, which makes it larger than many California state prisons.

Tienda: This word translates to store, and in prison, it refers to a person's "Canteen" items.

Tier: A row of cells in a prison or jail.

Tier Channel: The "Norteño" who is responsible for all messages and reports on his tier that must be relayed to other "Channels" in his chain of command.

Tier Name: "Norteños" in the "Hole" pick a fake "Street Name" to confuse enemies who might report which Norteños were in the hole while they were there. For example, a Norteño nicknamed Trippy goes to the hole and picks a temporary name of Bird. Their information would be incorrect if his enemies reported which Norteños were in the hole at the time.

Tier Security: In every "Housing Unit," the "Norteños" have an inmate designated tier security for each tier. Tier security screens new arrivals and gives them the "New Arrival Application," which asks numerous questions, including name, "CDC Number," age, what prisons he has been to, his "Street Name," etc. This information is then run through their channels to see if the new arrival is "No Good."

Tier Tender: A convict whose job is to clean up a specific area and usually gets paid for this job by the state. The average pay for a Tier Tender is about .25 an hour. A tier tender is also referred to as a "Porter" or "Trustee."

Tier Time: The time spent by inmates walking the "Tier" and talking to their homies. During this time, they will also pass things from cell to cell for their "People."

Tight: A convict who is "With The Business" and they are familiar with all of the "Prison Politics."

Tight Program: When convicts in a "Car" are up early, working out, "On Point," and representing themselves well in prison based on their conduct. For example, "The homies were running a tight program at High Desert Prison."

Time Credits: When a convict is assigned to a job, he will earn credits that take time off their sentence.

Timeout: When a prison gang member is investigated by his comrades for wrongdoing. He will be kept to the side, and no gang business or "Politics" will be shared with him until he is cleared of any violations.

Tio: A nickname used by "Southerners" for an associate of the "Mexican Mafia."

Tip: A prison gang in the California Department of Corrections and Rehabilitation.

Tipped Up: When an inmate is a member of a prison gang. For example, "Thumper is tipped up. Be careful what you say around him, homie."

Title 15: A compendium of rules that govern the treatment of convicts, their behavior, discipline, rights, and anything else that might apply to them while they are in prison. The Title 15 is also referred to as the "Director's Rules."

Tlatoani: This is a "Nahuatl" word that literally means speaker and refers to a "Mouthpiece." This person has the authority to speak for the "Big Homie." For example, "Silent is the Tlatoani; you better pay attention to what he says."

To The Gate: How many days a convict has to serve until he is released from prison. For example, "Bats has 20 days to the gate."

To The House: How many days a convict has to serve until he is released from prison. For example, "I got two months to the house."

Tomahawk: An inmate-manufactured slashing device usually made with a razor melted onto a toothbrush.

Tomb: What the convicts call the "Security Housing Unit."

Too Hard For The Yard: An inmate always acting hardcore and ready to fight over any situation they think they were disrespected. For example, "Cuete thinks he is too hard for the yard with his bad attitude."

Took A Dive: When a convict starts working with the police as an informant. For example, "I was talking to Gumby about our 'Pipeline,' and I didn't know that he took a dive and was working for the Feds."

Took Off: To physically attack someone. For example, "That punk officer trashed my cell, so I took off on him."

Toothpick: A thinly rolled cigarette or joint.

Top Of The Morning: This is a greeting that some people use in prison. For example, "Top of the morning, homeboy."

Torcido: This word means to get caught or busted. For example, "I didn't know you were torcido, homeboy."

Tore Up: When a person, thing, or situation looks terrible.

Tore Up From The Floor Up: When a person, thing, or situation looks terrible. For example, "That new officer thinks she is all that, but she is tore up from the floor up."

Torpedo: A convict who is sent on a "Mission" to "Remove" or "Discipline" other people.

Touchdown: This means you received something that someone else sent to you. For example, "Hey homie, touchdown on that. Good looking out!"

Touched: A place that you have been in the past. For example, "I touched a couple of Level IVs, I was in Pelican Bay twice, and I touched Calipatria."

Touched: When a person gets physically attacked. For example, "Someone had to pay, and the only one reachable was Toro. That's why he got touched."

Tough: This means to do something to the extreme. For example, "I used to chop it up tough with Lunatic Frank back in Old Folsom."

Tower: In each yard, a designated tower houses an officer who oversees inmates when they are outside their respective "Housing Units." This officer uses the public address system to summon inmates to the yard or for appointments as necessary. In the event of an emergency, the tower officer will instruct inmates to take cover by shouting "Get Down." Additionally, a "Mini-14" rifle is present in the tower, intended for use solely to protect lives during instances of violent assault.

Tower Officer: This officer is assigned to the "Observation Tower" on the prison yard. This officer will call out inmates on the yard via the public address system for various purposes when their presence is needed on the yard or for appointments. The tower officer will yell for the inmates to "Get Down" during an emergency. There is a "Mini-14" rifle in the tower to be only used to save a person's life during a violent attack.

Track: This is the oval-shaped concrete pathway used for walking and jogging. About four laps around the track would equal a mile at my prison. Inmates were only allowed to walk counterclockwise on the track because keeping inmates moving in the same direction is more orderly and safe. When inmates were jogging on the track and approached others who were walking, they would yell as they came up behind them, "On your left or your right," to give proper warning because nobody in prison appreciates people running towards their back unexpectedly.

Tracy: This is the nickname for the prison Duel Vocational Institution. This prison has a storied history in the California Department of Corrections and Rehabilitation. It was shut down on September 30, 2021.

Traffic Ticket: A notice of a rule violation for inappropriate behavior. For example, "I was in visiting kissing my girl, and that punk officer gave me a traffic ticket."

Trailer: The name for the building where inmate's wives stay the night with them on prison grounds during a "Conjugal" visit. For example, "I have a trailer visit with my wife next week."

Trailer Visit: When the wife of an inmate stays the night with him on prison grounds at the "Love Shack." The Love Shack is a small building surrounded by a secure fence with a small kitchen, bedroom, and seating area. The visitors can bring food to cook in the kitchen during their short stay.

Train: When inmates "Fish" through several "Sections" in a "Housing Unit," it's called a train because it's such a long distance.

Training Academy: The California Department of Corrections and Rehabilitation training academy is located in Galt, California. The academy has a 13-week duration, and housing and food is provided.

Transitional Housing Unit: This is a special "Housing Unit" for gang members going through the "Debrief" process. Basically, after a gang member has renounced his gang, he will be placed in the transitional housing unit for observation for a period of time.

Transitional Housing Unit Program: The THP is a residential program for parolees that provides food and housing for up to 180 days. In other words, when inmates parole, this gives them a place to live while they get on their feet.

Transpack: This is when an inmate is transferred to another prison. Before they leave their current prison, their "Property" will be shipped several days ahead of them on the "Grey Goose" to their new destination.

Transport Jewelry: When convicts are transported on the "Grey Goose" between prisons or to court, they are shackled in waist chains and leg irons. The waist chains and leg irons are referred to as transport jewelry by the "Transportation Officers."

Transportation Officers: These California Department of Corrections and Rehabilitation officers are the ones who drive the buses to transport inmates all around the state of California. They wear black jumpsuits; on average, they have been officers for at least ten years to get that job. They have a reputation with the inmates for being no-nonsense and not the ones to play with. Transportation officers have many ways to cause problems to an unruly inmate, so the inmates tend to follow orders when on the "Grey Goose."

Transportation Team: These California Department of Corrections and Rehabilitation officers are the ones who drive the buses to transport inmates all around the state of California. They wear black jumpsuits; on average, they have been officers for at least ten years to get that job. They have a reputation with the inmates for being no-nonsense and not the ones to play with. The Transportation Team has many ways to cause problems to an unruly inmate, so the inmates tend to follow orders when on the "Grey Goose."

Trash: When an inmate has any of the following on their "Paperwork;" rape, snitching, molestation, abusing women or the elderly, etc. Most prison gangs will violently attack inmates with these things on their "Black & Whites" and "Remove" them from the yard.

Trash On Their Jacket: When an inmate has any of the following on their "Paperwork;" rape, snitching, molestation, abusing women or the elderly, etc. Most prison gangs will violently attack inmates with these things on their "Black & Whites" and "Remove" them from the yard.

Trashed My Cell: When a correctional officer does a cell search and leaves the inmate's cell in total disarray. For example, "The officer trashed my cell, and now I can't find my pictures that were on the wall."

Tray: The thick plastic tray that food is served to inmates on.

Tray Slot: The small opening in the cell door or wall whereby food is given to the inmates. Inmates are also cuffed through this opening while still inside their cells.

Tree Jumper: This term refers to a rapist. Most "Factions" will attack them once they learn about their "Foul Charges."

Trenches: An active area where the homeboys hang out. For example, "This is the trenches homeboy. You better have that 'Banger' on you at all times."

Tribute: The "Taxes" that prison gangs collect from those in prisons and the streets. If you don't pay your tribute, you will get a visit from several gangsters to put some fear in you. If you don't pay your tribute after that visit, you will be "Whacked."

Trick Bag: When someone else manipulates or takes advantage of an inmate. For example, "Don't let them put you in a trick bag, homeboy."

Trip On This: This means pay attention while I tell you this story. For example, "Trip on this homie, that crooked officer just brought me a cellphone."

Triple-CMS: Informally to the average officer or convict, any inmate labeled Triple-CMS is a "J Cat." Officially, Triple-CMS is the Correctional Clinical Case Management System. It is an outpatient medical care for inmates with mental health issues. There are currently about 30,000 inmates in the Triple-CMS program in the California Department of Corrections and Rehabilitation. These medications are also referred to as "Heat Meds."

Trophy: A person who is a high-value target on the enemy side. If you "Smash" or "Poke" a high-ranking member of your enemy's gang, they are a trophy, and you earn "Stripes" in your gangster "Career." For example, "You don't want to become a trophy to those 'Lames' homeboy."

Trustee: A convict whose job is to clean up a specific area in prison, and they usually get paid for this job. The average pay for a Trustee is about .25 an hour. A Trustee is also referred to as a "Porter" or "Tier Tender."

Tube: The nickname for the television.

Tubo: A slang term used for a television. For example, "Homie, turn on the tubo because the football game is on."

Tuck: The process of putting a knife in a hiding spot. For example, "You need to tuck that 'Pick' so the police don't find it."

Tuck Your Flag: When a gangster is caught in the wrong area, they hide their "Flag" to avoid conflict.

Tucked: The process of putting a knife in a hiding spot. For example, "I tucked the knife in my waistband and went looking for that 'Chomo.'"

Tumbler: The name for the cups that convicts use in prison.

Tune-Up: When officers beat up a convict. For example, "I was 'Fat Mouthing' those pigs, so they gave me a tune-up."

Tune-Up: This term refers to a short stay in prison or county jail. For example, "I had a six-month tune-up at the county last year."

Turf: The area a gangster hangs out at and claims as his own. For example, "This is our turf. No other race will walk through here!"

Turn-ins: This is anything a convict must turn into prison officials to get another one. A turn-in could be a razor, clothing, television, or shoes. For example, if a convict receives a "Quarterly Package" and a new pair of shoes is in it, he has to bring his old shoes to turn-in to get the new ones.

Turn Key: An old-school term for a correctional officer.

Turnaround: When an inmate is doing prison time for a parole violation, and he isn't going to be there very long.

Turnaround: This is a short stay a convict has at a prison while being transported to another destination. For example, "I had a turnaround at Corcoran on my way to court."

Turned On: When a gang member goes to the extreme in gang banging or other issues. For example, "Have you heard of Red from Queen Street? That homie is turned on."

Turned Out: This is when an inmate is forced to be someone's "Punk." For example, "I turned him out and had him grabbing his ankles."

Turned Out: When a convict manipulates an officer to bring "Contraband" into prison. For example, "I turned out that 'Lame' officer and she is bringing in 5 cellphones every month."

Turned Up: An inmate pushing a "Hardline" in prison. He is always in the mix "Kicking Up Dust." For example, "Iceman is turned up!"

Turtle Squad: This term refers to the officers who wear protective clothing to perform a "Cell Extraction." The protective items include helmets, a large plexiglass shield, and other safety equipment. When the officers are all geared up with this equipment, they look like turtles, hence the name.

Twacked Out: An inmate who is out of his mind because he has been awake for several days high on methamphetamines. For example,

"Watch out for Psycho. He is twacked out."

Twinkies: A derogatory name for the "25" "SNY" prison gang.

Twist One Up: This is when a convict rolls up a cigarette. For example, "I see you, comrade, twist one up for me."

Twisted Up: When a gangster is betrayed by his homies. When a gangster fails to understand "Prison Politics" and falls victim to a savvy comrade looking to move up the ladder in the organization.

Two At All Times: Some "Factions" require witnesses for all dealings with officers and other prison officials on high-level yards. They have this requirement to document what was said and verify a homie isn't snitching.

Tycooning: When a person "Comes Up" materially or financially in prison, and they are living very "Comfortable." For example, "Ace is 'Sitting On Somehting' in his cell. He is tycooning. His shelves are stocked with 'Groceries.'"

Type Of Time He Is On: This describes how a convict does his prison time. For example, "I don't mess with Crazy Chuck. You see what type of time he is on."

U

Under The Gun: When a correctional officer is watching inmates on the yard with a Mini-14 and other less lethal weapons such as a "40mm Launcher." Under The Gun usually refers to Level IV yards or yards in the "Hole," "SHU," or "Adjustment Center."

Unit: A concrete and steel structure with 100 cells that hold two convicts each at Centinela Prison. Each unit has four phones, twelve benches, eighteen metal tables, one clothes iron, two sinks, two water fountains, two televisions, and eight showers. Two "Floor Officers" supervise all 200 convicts in the unit, and they ensure that all inmates receive their "State Issue," i.e., showers, phone calls, yard, "Dayroom," mail, medical appointments, visits, and meals.

United Blood Nation: United Blood Nation is an old-school organization consisting of "Blood" gangsters that were started in California prisons.

United Society Of Aryan Skinheads: A White prison gang that had a "Green Light" put on them by the "Aryan Brotherhood." The Aryan Brotherhood ran them off the "Line."

Unlock: When inmates are allowed out of their cells to engage in designated activities.

Unnecessary Force: The utilization of physical force by an officer in situations where it is deemed unnecessary or unsuitable.

Up North: This refers to the prisons that are in the Northern California region. For example, "I spent five weeks at Chino waiting to catch the 'Grey Goose' for my ride up north."

Upstairs: When a person or thing is above you in a "Housing Unit" or "Pod." For example, "Pelon was right upstairs from me when I was at Tehachapi SHU."

Upstate: It is an old-school term that refers to going to prison. For example, "When I first got upstate, I didn't like what I saw in my 'People.' These dudes were walking around doing what was easy all of the time. They were sleeping in every chance they got and always trying to get out of working out. They were also doing drugs and drinking 'Wine' all the time."

Upstate Sureño: A "Sureño" who is gang-banging in Northern California.

Upstater: A "Southerner" who is gang-banging in Northern California.

Uptown: These are stimulants in prison, chiefly "White," which is methamphetamine. For example, "I got some uptown homeboy if you need a boost."

Usalama: This word means security in Swahili, and some Black inmates use Swahili words in prison to get back to their cultural heritage. For example, "The homies need some usalama while doing their 'Burpees' on the yard."

USAS: This acronym stands for United Society Of Aryan Skinheads. They are a gang that the "Aryan Brotherhood" put a "Green Light" on and went to war with in prison. The Aryan Brotherhood ran them off the "Line."

Use Of Force: This is when a correctional officer uses force on an inmate. When a use of force happens, a report must be written by all officers involved in any way, or who witnessed this incident.

Uso: This word means brother in Samoan and is used in prison to refer to the Samoans. For example, "Those uso's in prison 'Run With' the 'Others.'"

V

Validate: Many years ago in the CDC, they needed three points to validate an inmate as a prison gang member. Once the CDC had those three points, the inmate would get an "Indeterminate SHU Sentence" in one of these prisons: Pelican Bay, Corcoran, or Tehachapi. CDC needed three of these items to validate an inmate: a tattoo, drawings, emblems, or a letter, and if these contained anything about the gang, they would be "Slammed Down" in the SHU indefinitely.

Validated: Many years ago in the CDC, they needed three points to validate an inmate as a prison gang member. Once the CDC had those three points, the inmate would get an "Indeterminate SHU Sentence" in one of these prisons: Pelican Bay, Corcoran, or Tehachapi. CDC needed three of these items to validate an inmate: a tattoo, drawings, emblems, or a letter, and if these contained anything about the gang, they would be "Slammed Down" in the SHU indefinitely.

Validation Packet: This file is the evidence the California Department of Corrections and Rehabilitation uses to try and "Validate" a convict as a member of a "Security Threat Group." This packet is sent to the "STG Unit Classification Committee," and they decide if there is enough evidence to validate the convict.

Valley Fever: A fungal virus that affects inmates in the Central Valley area of California. The inmates most involved are at Pleasant Valley and Avenal prisons. The fungal infection is incurable and can be fatal. The condition also causes severe joint pain, skin lesions, and difficulty breathing.

Vampire Slayer: A "Banger" made out of wood. For example, "The homie gave me a vampire slayer as soon as I 'Drove Up.'"

Vanguard: An old-school prison organization consisting of Black inmates who wanted to organize and educate other Black inmates.

Varrio: A word that means neighborhood.

Vato: A word that translates to homeboy, dude, or guy.

Vault: When a convict places items of "Contraband" in his rectum to avoid discovery by officers. Some convicts become very proficient at this and can do it in seconds. When a "Banger" is placed inside of the prison safe, it will have a protective layer of cellophane to prevent their insides from being perforated. For example, "I stashed the 'Black' in the vault, homie."

Vendor: The companies that the families of inmates order "Packages" from quarterly to be sent to them in prison. These vendors sell food, "Hygiene" items, and just about anything else an inmate needs to make themselves a little more "Comfortable" in prison.

Vent: Convicts in prison cells can communicate with their neighbors by talking in the vent for the air conditioning. This is a common form of communication, and convicts are careful not to speak too loudly so they won't disturb the "Program" of other people in their cells.

Verbal: To pass a message verbally to another person. For example, "Give Mayhem a verbal that I want to meet him in the chapel so we can settle this issue."

Verbal Judo: A skill used by officers to gently persuade an inmate to comply with their directives.

Verdes: This is when a "Shot Caller" gives a "Green Light" for their "Soldiers" to assault or kill somebody. This "List" is "Hooped" and then transported to different prisons.

Veterano: A well-respected gangster who has been through the wars and always handled himself like a "Soldier."

Victim Yard: This term refers to a prison yard where most inmates were "Removed" from other yards for not upholding the standards of their "Faction."

Vietnam: This is the nickname for the brutal war between the "Crips" and "Mexican Mafia" at San Quentin in the summer of 1984. This war started after a Crip was murdered by the Mexican Mafia while trying to broker a peace deal with them. He went to the negotiating table without a knife and was murdered because he could not defend himself adequately.

Violate: When a gang member is investigated by his comrades for violating a gang rule. The punishment for the convict who broke "Household Policies" can range from writing 1,000-word essays, going on "Bunk Status," going on the "Burpee Line," getting a "DP," getting a "Soft Check," to getting "Stabbed Off The Yard."

Violated: When a gang member is investigated by his comrades for violating a gang rule. The punishment for the convict who broke "Household Policies" can range from writing 1,000-word essays, going on "Bunk Status," going on the "Burpee Line," getting a "DP," getting a "Soft Check," to getting "Stabbed Off The Yard."

Violation: When a gang member is investigated by his comrades for violating a gang rule. The punishment for the convict who broke "Household Policies" can range from writing 1,000-word essays, going on "Bunk Status," going on the "Burpee Line," getting a "DP," getting a "Soft Check," to getting "Stabbed Off The

Yard."

Visiting: This is where the convicts meet family members and friends in prison. Most of the drugs brought into prison come through the visiting room. A widespread method is a female visitor will place drugs in little balloons in her vagina. She will take them out at the visit and put them in her mouth or pocket. One way to transfer them is while kissing her incarcerated loved one, and during the kiss, she will push the drugs into his mouth, and he will swallow them. Once in his cell, the inmate will pick them out of his poop. Another method is to drop the little balloons of drugs into a bag of chips, and the inmate will pick them out and swallow them.

Visiting Room: This is where the convicts meet family members and friends in prison. Most of the drugs brought into prison come through the visiting room. A widespread method is a female visitor will place drugs in little balloons and insert them in her vagina. She will go to the bathroom, take them out, and put them in her mouth or pocket. One way to transfer them is while kissing her incarcerated loved one, and during the kiss, she will push the drugs into his mouth, and he will swallow them. Once in his cell, the inmate will pick them out of his poop. Another method is to drop the little balloons of drugs into a bag of chips, and the inmate will pick them out and swallow them.

Visiting Room Porter: A highly coveted job among convicts because he helps bring drugs in from the "Visiting Room." It is mandatory for a visiting room porter to help bring in drugs. If he refuses to, his "Car" will take his job away from him, one way or another.

Voc: The short version of "Vocational Training." For example, "I liked working in voc as an officer because I got weekends and holidays off."

Vocation: The "Vocational Training" area of the prison is where convicts learn a trade like working on cars, woodworking, silk screening, or welding. This place is commonly referred to as "Behind The Wall."

Vocational Training: The area of a prison where inmates learn a trade like welding, woodworking, silk screening, working on cars, etc. This place is commonly referred to as "Behind The Wall."

Voluntary Inline: This is the set time for convicts on the yard to enter their "Housing Units" voluntarily.

W

W Wing: This is the "Administration Segregation" at Vacaville State Prison.

Wah Ching: This Chinese street gang was founded in San Francisco, California, in the 1960s. They have a minimal presence in CDCR.

Waist Restraints: These restraining devices are used when inmates travel outside the prison for various reasons. The handcuffs are secured to the waist chain on each inmate's side.

Waiting For The Chain To Come: When an inmate in county jail waits to catch the "Grey Goose" for a ride to prison. For example, "Back in county, my homie Trippy was always waiting for the chain to come. Every night, he would get ready and wait for his name to be called. He was ready to do his 'Bid' and get it over with."

Wake Up: A convict's release date from prison. For example, "My wake up ain't for ten more years."

Walk Alone: This term is used for an inmate who has to be kept away from the "General Population" due to various issues.

Walk Alone Cage: The small cage in the "SHU" that one inmate is placed in for an hour to get some sun, talk, and exercise.

Walk & Talk: This is said to another inmate when you want to walk with them and talk privately. For example, "Cisco, let's walk and talk, comrade."

Walk Away: A walk away is an escape from a low-level prison facility that doesn't have walls, such as a "Fire Camp." Since 1977, 99 percent of all people who have walked away from an adult institution or camp have been apprehended.

Walk With Me: This is said to another inmate when you want to walk with them and talk privately. For example, "Cornfed, walk with me brother."

Walked Off: When an officer is fired, the "Goon Squad" walks them off prison grounds. The offending officer's identification card and badge are taken from them, and they are no longer allowed onto prison grounds for any reason. For example, "Did you hear about Jackson? He got walked off for bringing a cell phone and drugs to some inmates."

Walkers and Talkers: These refer to inmates designated by a "Faction" to go around the prison yard during "Lockdowns" and inform their people of important information. These walkers and talkers also negotiated with other factions to broker peace treaties before inmates were released from being "Slammed."

Walking: When an officer is doing their rounds in a prison. For example, "Dumbo caught me on my cell phone last night. That 'Dump Truck' shouldn't have been walking."

Walking Laps: Walking laps is when inmates walk around the track on the prison yard.

Wall-A-Vision: This refers to when convicts sit in their cells and stare at the walls for hours on end while in deep thought. For example, "I don't get bored in my cell, homeboy. I have wall-a-vision."

Wallet: A term used to describe the anal cavity of a convict. A convict places items of "Contraband" in his rectum to avoid discovery by officers. Some convicts become very proficient at this and can do it in seconds. When a "Banger" is placed inside the wallet, it will have a protective layer of cellophane to prevent his insides from being perforated. For example, "Don't trip homie. The officers will never find it because it's in the wallet."

Want The Funk: This means a convict is willing to push a "Hardline" on someone. For example, "If you want the funk, let's catch that 'Fade.'"

War Bird Tattoo: This tattoo is of the Nazi Bird symbol, one of the most recognizable Third Reich images. To earn this tattoo in prison, a White Convict must shed the blood of an enemy.

War Chest: An emergency supply of food that some inmates have and store in their cell in case their race goes on an extended "Lockdown." A sample of what they might have in their war chest: 20 bags of beans, 100 soups, and 5 jars of coffee.

War Dog: Someone you have been in fights, shootings, stabbings, robberies, and riots with. A trusted homie you know will "Hold His Mud" no matter the situation. For example, "Bloodhound is my war dog. We were giving those 'Woods' the blues back in county."

War Shield: This is a tattoo of an Aztec war shield that a "Camarada" earns by "Putting In Work" for a member of the "Mexican Mafia." It is also called the "3-Step Shield," and it has three steps to it. Each step is earned by committing an act of violence for a "Pilli."

War Stories: These are exciting and often violent stories about the gang life that homies tell each other in prison to help pass the time. For example, "Me and Soldier Boy were in our cell killing time and telling war stories."

Warpaint: These are tattoos that can only be earned in prison. These types of tattoos, for the most part, are for shedding the blood of your rivals. These tattoos are taken very seriously, and if an inmate gets one without having earned it, his gang members will discipline them and make him remove them, cover it up, or earn it. For example, "See that 'Shinhead' with all of that warpaint? When things 'Go Up' with the 'Gabachos' that's the 'Trophy.'"

Wasco Prison Bell: There is a bell at Wasco Prison Reception Center that new arrivals can ring to go to "Protective Custody." It's similar to the bell at BUDs training on Coronado Island that the SEAL candidates ring when they quit, except this is the prison version.

Wash Him Up: When a convict does something his homie thinks makes him "No Good," and he goes on a campaign to "End His Career." For example, "Wolf was pushing the issue on Pancho, and he was trying to wash him up and end his career."

Washed Up: When a person gets a lengthy prison sentence. For example, "Shaggy just got washed up. They gave him 'All Day' for that 'Hot One.'"

Watch Office: The Watch Office is the coordination center of the prison. The "Watch Sergeant" and the "Watch Search & Escort Officers" are based in this area.

Watch Search & Escort Officers: The Watch Search and Escort Officers work directly for the "Watch Sergeant." Some of their duties include escorting convicts, testing alarms around the prison, checking the electric fence, and many other tasks.

Watch Sergeant: The Watch Sergeant is in charge of making sure correctional officers fill all positions, and they are also in charge of assigning overtime positions. If the Watch Sergeant was your "Road Dog" and you were a rookie officer without a set job, they would always hook you up with the good posts. Conversely, if the Watch Sergeant didn't like you, they would assign you the worst and most dangerous jobs. If a correctional officer calls in sick, they must talk to the Watch Sergeant.

Watching From My Window: When an inmate is standing at his cell door looking through his window into the "Dayroom" or other area of the prison. For example, "I was watching from my window when Looney got 'Poked.'"

Water Bag: A large trash bag filled with water convicts use as a dumbbell. These bags can get very heavy, and they are an excellent substitute for the weights that were taken away from the California prisons in 1997. Water bags are not allowed, but if a convict was a "Programmer," I would not take it from him.

Watered Down: This means things aren't as serious as they used to be in certain situations. For example, "The game is watered down. Back in the day, the homie would have been dealt with for doing that."

Way Out: When something is very hard to believe. For example, "Did you hear about Lefty? It's way out, homie. He has been an informant for over a year."

Wayside: One of the correctional facilities included within the Los Angeles County Jail system.

We Did Our Homework On You: When a convict does a background check on another person, they will use a cell phone and search their name on Megan's Law database or call convicts in other prisons to ask about the new convict. For example, "We did our homework on you. Nobody from the 'Set' knows you."

We Got A Live One: When a person is acting "Out Of Pocket" and coming at people "Sideways." For example, "We got a live one. We are going to have fun with this officer tonight."

Weak: This term is used to describe the actions of somebody when you believe they are being soft. To be called weak in prison is a great insult. For example, "Superman, I can't believe you are giving showers to the inmates. You are being weak."

Weak As Puppy Piss: A "Lame" coward who always lays down whenever the tension rises. For example, "Don't trip off that punk. He's as weak as puppy piss."

Weapon Stock: A piece of material crafted by an inmate intended for use as a weapon. Weapon stock remains unfinished due to the absence of a handle or a sharpened point.

Weenie: A person who gets no respect from their peers. A worthless, good-for-nothing person who doesn't stand up for themselves. For example, "Mad Dog is a weenie. He is just 'Woofing.'"

Weight Pile: The weightlifting area on the prison yard. The weights were removed in 1997 from the "Mainline" (They have weight machines in "Fire Camps") in California prisons. I have heard two reasons why they were removed. The first reason I heard was because the inmates were getting too big and strong, so the administration took them away out of fear. The second reason for removing the weights was that inmates were seriously injured when attacked with dumbbells and bars. As an officer who walked the mainline level III and IV yards for several years, I believe they took them away because officers and administration were getting intimidated by the massive size of the "Swole" convicts. The administration used reason two to justify their fear of the muscle-bound convicts who spent all their free time driving iron on the weight pile. When the weights were removed, the "Yard Crew" loaded them onto the back of the trucks. Numerous convicts have stated they were angry at the inmates for helping them remove the weights. I don't know if they were attacked for helping, but it definitely caused tension.

Weird Charges: When an inmate has any of the following on their "Paperwork;" rape, snitching, molestation, abusing women or the elderly, etc. Most prison gangs will violently attack inmates with these things on their "Black & Whites" and "Remove" them from the yard. For example, "Creeper has weird charges, that's why he was 'Removed.'"

Weirdo: A person who gets no respect from their peers. A worthless, good-for-nothing person who does not stand up for themselves.

Welfare Check: This is when an inmate is at risk of committing suicide or housed in the "Administrative Segregation Unit," "Security Housing Unit," "Psychiatric Services Unit," or "Condemned Housing Unit," an officer must check on them every 35 minutes to ensure they are alive and well.

Welfare Envelopes: These are the "Indigent" or free envelopes that the California Department of Corrections and Rehabilitation gives inmates who have had less than $25 on their "Books" for 30 consecutive days.

Went Belly Up: When an inmate can't take the pressure on a prison yard and tells the officers they need "Protective Custody." For example, "Turtle went belly up after talking all of that 'High Power' nonsense."

Went Out Backwards: When an inmate "Rolls It Up" and goes "SNY" or "PC." For example, "I heard that Blazer went out backwards."

Went Out Negative: When an inmate "Rolls It Up" and goes "SNY" or "PC." For example, "I heard that Joker went out negative."

Went Out Sideways: When an inmate "Rolls It Up" and goes "SNY" or "PC." For example, "I heard that Felony went out sideways."

Wet Him Up: When an inmate stabs another person with a "Banger." For example, "I caught that 'Chomo' in the 'Blind,' so I wet him up."

Wet Work: Spilling blood with your "Banger" or "Tomahawk." For example, "I did a lot of wet work back at Tracy."

Wet Your Steel: To "Book" somebody and get blood on your "Banger." For example, "Check this out! You got to wet your steel, homeboy!"

Whacked: When an inmate gets "Blasted" in prison. For example, "Did you hear about Warlock? He got whacked coming out of the chow hall."

Whacked Out: To have a letter, number, color, or gang crossed out on a tattoo or "Strike Up." In some "Factions," if another gang member in prison sees an inmate with their gang whacked out on a tattoo they have, they will challenge them to a "Fade." For example, if a "Blood" lands on a yard with a C whacked out on one of his tattoos, a "Crip" might go to his cell door and say, "Crack your door, I need that 'Fade.'"

Wham Whams: Candy or snacks in prison.

What Kind Of Time He's On: This describes how a convict does his prison time. For example, "I don't mess with Psycho. You see what kind of time he's on."

Whatever Is Clever: A phrase that means a person is just saying something to get over on someone or look good in a particular situation. For example, "I didn't mean what I told my old lady on that phone call. I was just saying whatever is clever."

When The White Folks Let Me Come Home: This is an old-school reply by some Black inmates when asked, "When are you coming home?"

Whip: This term refers to a mustache. For example, "Pharoh is the comrade on the right, the one with the whip."

Whiskey: A potent form of alcohol that sells for $20.00 a cup or $40.00 a quart. To check the quality of the whiskey, an inmate will light it with a flame.

White: Term used for methamphetamines in prison.

White Blood: In California state prisons, the "Peckerwoods" were notorious for starting riots with Black inmates if a White "Blood" ever "Landed" on the yard. These attacks by the "Woods" took place between the 1980s-2020. The reason given by some White convicts for doing these types of attacks is because they felt that their numbers were so small in prison that they believed those White inmates were traitors for running their "Program" with another race. These days, in California state prisons, the White inmates don't attack White inmates who are Bloods.

White Crip: In California state prisons, the "Peckerwoods" were notorious for starting riots with Black inmates if a White "Crip" ever "Landed" on the yard. These attacks by the "Woods" took place between the 1980s-2020. The reason given by some White convicts for doing these types of attacks is because they felt that their numbers were so small in prison they believed those White inmates were traitors for running their "Program" with another race. These days, in California state prisons, the White inmates don't attack White inmates who are Crips.

White Elephant: This was the nickname for the "PC" yard at Chino back in the 1980s.

White Farmer: Many years ago, a group of White inmates in Tracy prison feared the "Norteños" and Black inmates. They would give them information on the other White inmates to get on their good side. The other White inmates figured this out and started killing those White traitors. They called them White Farmers because Norteños were called "Farmers." The White Farmers were also called the White Mistress and The New White Family.

White House: The location at a prison where orders from the "Shot Callers" come from. The White House can be a prison where gang leaders are housed. It can also be a "Cell" on a yard where the "Heavyweights" live. For example, "This order is coming from the White House."

White Lighting: A potent form of alcohol that sells for $20.00 a cup or

$40.00 a quart. To check the quality of the white lighting, inmates light it with a flame.

White Men: A term used by White convicts to describe "Solid" White men in prison. Basically, the term White Men and "Peckerwood" are synonymous.

Who's Who In The Zoo: This saying refers to knowing who the "Heavy Hitters" and people with the "Clavo" are at a given prison facility. It basically means knowing who to talk to in order to get something done. For example, "When you first 'Drive Up,' you need to know who's who in the zoo."

Whoopty Woot: When you are talking to somebody about another person, and you describe what they were saying. For example, "This punk was running his mouth claiming all of this work that he had done, whoopty woot. I told him that he should stop 'Fronting.'"

Whore Bath: When convicts use water from their sink to clean themselves with soap and water.

Wick: A tightly rolled-up piece of toilet paper or paper towel that burns very slowly and is used as a source of fire. A wick can also be used as incense if it has been dipped in a fragrance.

Wife: To be used as a "Punk" by another inmate.

Wig Split: To be rendered a bloody mess from a severe beating. For example, "Shaggy got his wig split for claiming to be something he wasn't."

Wiggle: How a person conducts themselves and handles their business. For example, "In prison, all eyes are on you. The homies observe how you wiggle, how you handle your business."

Wilas: A written letter from one convict to another. According to some "Household Policies," wilas are to be shared between "Cellies," who are gang members. Trouble usually starts if cellies refuse to share their wilas because suspicion instantly arises.

Wilding: When an inmate acts rambunctious and draws too much attention to himself and his "Car." For example, "Payaso, you are clowning around too much, fool. You need to stop wilding."

Willie Lump Lump: Someone who gets beat up badly, and their face is full of lumps. For example, "Did you see that punk after they were done with him? He looked like Willie Lump Lump."

Wind: This term refers to how much stamina a person has. For example, "Check this out, youngster, these 'Burpees' help build up your wind. You will need that when fighting for your life on the yard or in your cell."

Window Hopper: A female who visits different convicts in order to get together with them. For example, "Lucy is just a window hopper. She has been with three of my homies already."

Wine: A fermented alcoholic beverage that can be produced by blending various ingredients, including apples, oranges, fruit cocktails, ketchup, and sugar. The mixture is then cooked in a plastic garbage bag for three days to facilitate fermentation. Wine possesses a disgusting taste and odor, and its color varies depending on the type of fruit used, ranging from red to orange. In correctional facilities, a single cup of wine is typically sold for $8.00, while a cup of the more potent "White Lightening" commands a price of $20.00.

Wing: In old-school prisons like Tracy and Soledad, inmates' buildings are called wings. In most newer prisons, the buildings are called "Housing Units." For example, "When I was at Tracy, I stayed in J-Wing."

Winning: When a convict gets drugs regularly from a visitor, "Free Staff," package, mail, or corrections officer. For example, "Ace has been winning the last two weeks during visits."

Wino Time: This is a short sentence or a short amount of time left to do before getting released. Usually, three years or less is considered Wino Time. For example, "I have two 'Balas' left, I am on wino time."

Winos: These are the shoes worn by some old-school gangsters.

Wire: A wire is a means of communication that utilizes various channels. It may be a message conveyed through a "Kite" or a phone call. For example, "I can't talk to you right now, homie. Send me a wire."

Wish Sandwich: A sandwich with nothing of consequence between the pieces of bread. For example, "I'm going to have a wish sandwich. I wish there were something in there."

With The Business: This describes a well-respected convict who honors his word and handles himself with respect. He will handle his business when it's time to kick things off. For example, "Yeah, I have heard of Wild Child. He is a savage who has put in work. He is with the business."

With The Function: This describes a well-respected convict who honors his word and handles himself with respect. He will handle his business when it's time to kick things off. For example, "Yeah, I have heard of Trooper. He is with the function."

With The Funnies: A person who is always joking around and playing games. For example, "Joker plays too much. He is with the funnies."

With The St:** This describes a well-respected convict who honors his word and handles himself with respect. He will handle his business when it's time to kick things off. For example, "Yeah, I have heard of Stinky. He is with the s**t."

Wolf Tickets: To speak aggressively to someone without intending to back it up with violence. For example, "Dreamer was selling wolf tickets, so I smashed him."

Wolfing: When a person is running their mouth and being

disrespectful. For example, "When I walked out of the chow hall, Fangs started wolfing at me."

Wolfpack Skinheads: This is a group that the "Aryan Brotherhood" put a "Green Light" on and went to war with in prison. The Aryan Brotherhood ran them off the "Line."

Wood: A name used for White inmates, and it's short for "Peckerwood."

Woodpile: A term used to describe all the "Peckerwoods" on a prison yard or cell block. For example, "Hey, Woody, you're making the woodpile look bad with your drug debts to the homies."

Woods: A name used for White inmates, and it's short for "Peckerwood."

Woof Tickets: To speak aggressively to someone without intending to back it up with violence. For example, "Cane was handing out woof tickets. So I let him have it."

Woofing: When a person is running their mouth and being disrespectful. For example, "When I walked out of the chow hall, Pug started woofing at me."

Woofing Out The Side Of Your Neck: To tell stories that aren't true or to speak aggressively to someone without intending to back it up with violence. For example, "Akita, stop woofing out the side of your neck."

Woot Woot: When you are talking to somebody about another person, and you describe what they were saying. For example, "Maniac was running his mouth claiming all of this work he had done, woot woot. I told him that he should stop fronting."

Work Change: This is the prison's "Vocational Training" area, where inmates learn a trade like welding, woodworking, silk screening, working, and cars. All inmates must submit to a "Strip Search" when leaving this area.

Work Programs: These programs train inmates in various industries to gain the necessary skills to work in those fields after their release from prison.

Work Strike: When inmate workers go on strike and refuse to work until the prison administration addresses their grievances. If an inmate dares to cross the picket line and work during a strike, he will be attacked by the other inmates when they have a chance to "Put Hands" on him.

Work Time Credits: When a convict is assigned a job, they will earn credits that take time off their sentence.

Work With Me: Instead of saying please, an officer will use this phrase to get some cooperation from a convict. For example, "You need to work with me, man. I'm just trying to do my job."

Worked Under: This is the prison gang member a person worked for on the streets or in prison. The person that you "Check In" to is who you work under in a criminal organization. For example, "Yogi worked under Spider on the streets."

Worker Building: A "Housing Unit" where most convicts work in "Vocation." Inmate workers need their "Worker Showers" before 1645 hours every weekday.

Worker Showers: Convicts who work during the day are allowed to shower before the evening meal. Both of my "Housing Units" on the "Mainline" Level III Yards were "Worker Buildings." About 7080 convicts needed their showers from 1530 hours to 1645 hours every weekday.

Working The Corners: When an inmate makes moves, connections, and business relationships on the prison yard. For example, "Sinbad was working the corners on the yard."

Working With Feelings: When a person is easily offended. For example, "My bad, I didn't know you were working with feelings."

Workout Monster: A convict who stays in top physical shape and they are always working out. For example, "Ripper is a workout monster. He lives for those 'Burpees.'"

Wreck: When an inmate's bad behavior is going to get them into trouble. For example, "Blazer is heading for a wreck. You might want to have a talk with him."

Wrecked Up From The Neck Up: When a person, thing, or situation looks terrible. For example, "That new officer thinks she is all that, but she is wrecked up from the neck up."

Write Up: The official paperwork regarding an incident in prison. For example, "I got the write up in my cell if you want to read it."

Writing An Essay: In some prison gangs, inmates who violate the "Household Policies" must write an essay as punishment. The report will discuss the gang, its history, rules, etc.

WSP: Wasco State Prison.

X

X3: This number represents "Southerners" and is a common tattoo among them.

X4: This number represents "Northerners" and is a common tattoo among them.

XIII: This number represents "Southerners" and is a common tattoo among them.

XIV: This number represents "Northerners" and is a common tattoo among them.

Y

YA: This is where juvenile offenders, ages 12-25, went when they got convicted of crimes in California. The California Youth Authority is notorious for being very violent, with the wards of the state fighting each other every day.

YA Baby: An inmate who spent a lot of time in the "California Youth Authority" when he was young.

Yank: The influence a convict has to get something done in prison or on the streets. For example, "Mack Truck is a righteous 'Big Homie,' and he has a lot of yank."

Yank His Coat: To call someone's bluff or to reveal secrets about them. For example, "Flash is getting on my nerves. I'm going to yank his coat about that drug debt he owed at High Desert."

Yard Bird: A tattoo of a Peckerwood bird that White inmates get for "Putting in Work."

Yard Clean Up: When a "Faction" goes on a mission to "Remove" all of the "Degenerates" and "Basura" belonging to their "Car."

Yard Crew: A group of inmates who work on the prison yard and keep it maintained.

Yard Dogs: These are a convict's workout shoes. For example, "Greyhound, you need some new yard dogs, homeboy."

Yard Down: This is what some officers yell into the microphone when there is a fight on the yard. When this happens, all inmates on the yard are supposed to prone out on the ground.

Yard Officer: The correctional officers assigned to a particular prison yard.

Yard Rat: An inmate on a prison yard with a "Jacket" for being a snitch. For example, "Mappy is a yard rat. Watch what you say around him."

Yard Recall: When convicts must exit the yard and return to their respective "Housing Units."

Yard Security: The "Norteños" designate a member as yard security; his job is to keep a headcount of his homies and enemies. Yard security also ensures weapons are in place on the yard and ready for use.

Yard Sweep: When the officers search an entire yard for weapons and other "Contraband." The officers will use metal detectors and search every square inch of the yard and "Housing Units."

Yard Time: The time a convict spends on the prison yard.

Yard Work: This is when a convict does his workout routine on the yard. For example, "You wanna come do some yard work with me, homie?"

Yardero: This is the "Sureno" or "Camarada" who is in charge of a prison yard for the "Southerners." The yardero directly communicates with a "Mexican Mafia" member he works for. The yardero is in charge of the "Mesa" on the yard.

Year Flat: When you have to do a full year of prison time without any "Half Time."

Yoked: A very muscular or "Swole" person.

You Are Doing Too Much: This saying is sometimes told to a convict pressing a "Hardline" on an issue others feel isn't necessary. For example, "Berserker, 'Take A Little Off That' comrade. You are doing too much."

You Got More Nerve Than A Broken Tooth: When an inmate has no shame in his game. For example, "Fat Pat, I just gave you a honey bun, and now you want a soup? You got more nerve than a broken tooth!"

You Got To Go: This means an inmate needs to be "Smashed" or "Stabbed Off The Yard." For example, "If we find out anyone in our 'Car' is a 'Chomo,' you got to go."

You Got To See Me: This means you are challenging another inmate to a "Fade." For example, "Check this out. You were real disrespectful. We got to get down tomorrow. You got to see me."

You Know What I Mean: Many inmates say this after they finish a sentence while talking to you. For example, "I just got done at the 'Weight Pile,' and I'm feeling good. You know what I mean?"

You Know What You Signed Up For: This saying is used on gangsters who have a problem with something related to gang life. They could be complaining about a prison sentence, a "DP," missing his family, being stuck in his cell, or other issues. For example, "You know what you signed up for, homie. You got to 'Stand Tall' youngster."

You Owe The House: Profits from illegal activities that go to the "Big Homies" of a gang. Usually, 1/3 of profits are owed to the house.

You Owe The House: This means a homie messed up, and he owes 113 to 1,300 "Burpees" to the house, depending on the severity of his infraction.

You're Not A Virgin Anymore: This is said to a "First Termer" after he has "Hooped" a "Banger" for the first time. For example, "You aren't a virgin anymore. Don't make any sudden movements, and watch how you sit."

You're Running: This is said to an inmate whose peers believe he is hiding behind something because he is scared. Maybe an inmate suddenly wants to be a Christian in prison, and other people think they joined the Christian "Car" because they feared "Prison Politics." The skeptical observers will scrutinize every move of the professed Christian, and if they see him gamble or drink "Pruno," they will say, "See, you're running. You aren't a Christian. You are just scared."

Young Rider: A young gang member eager to "Put In Work." For example, "Baby Face is a young rider. He is good people."

Your People: The people in prison who belong to your race and "Car." For example, "Listen up youngster, you have to back the play of your people in prison, or it will be you getting 'Poked.'"

Youth Offender: To qualify as a youth offender, the primary offense an inmate was sentenced on had to be committed when they were under 26.

Z

Z Status: When a prison gang member is placed under investigation by his comrades for wrongdoing. He will be kept to the side, and no gang business or "Politics" will be shared with him until he is cleared of any violations. For example, "Spike is on Z status. It's all bad."

Zapatistas: A violent group of inmates on the "SNY" prison yards. They function under a "No Hands Policy" against their enemies, which means they only attack with weapons. The Zapatistas use the red star as a symbol for their movement.

Zapato: A word that translates to shoe, but in prison, it refers to the "SHU."

Zero Debt Policy: Certain "Factions" have implemented a zero debt policy as a preventative measure against potential issues arising from drug users and gamblers accruing debts and failing to repay them. Failing to settle debts with rival "Cars" often leads to violent confrontations.

Zip Gun: A one-shot gun made in prison where match heads are used for powder and shredded zippers are stuffed down the barrel. The match heads are lit, and the explosion propels the metal out of the barrel.

Zipper: The significant scar resembling a zipper that remains on an individual following an assault with a weapon. For example, "The homie rushed that fool with a 'Tomahawk' and put zippers all over him."

Zoom Zooms: A name for candy or snacks in prison.

NUMBERS

1 Up 1 Down: When inmates must watch out for various reasons, one homie will stay awake while the other sleeps. After a few hours, they will switch so the other homie can rest.

100 Paper: A small square of paper containing heroin valued at $100.

115: This is a disciplinary report that was issued to inmates. There are two types of these reports: Administrative and Serious.

12:01: These numbers represent when a convict will be paroled. For example, "Numbers is getting his 12:01 tonight."

12/12: These numbers represent when a convict serves his entire sentence and is discharged from the system.

128-B: The CDCR Form 128-B records pertinent details regarding inmates and their conduct. It is commonly known as the "General Chrono."

128-G: The 128-G is a formal document that contains a comprehensive record of an inmate's criminal history, personal information, and other pertinent details. Gang members utilize this document to ascertain an individual's status as "No Good." Additionally, the 128-G is commonly referred to as an inmate's "Driver's License."

10 Piece: A ten-year prison sentence.

13: This number represents "Southerners" and is a common tattoo among them.

14: This number represents "Northerners" and is a common tattoo among them.

114-D: This document serves as a detention directive, detailing the reasons and justification for placing an inmate in "Administrative Segregation." In accordance with the instructions of prison gang leaders, all members assigned to the "Hole" must provide their CDC Form 114-D for review to ensure that their placement is not due to any dishonorable behavior.

17 Hit Policy: This was a mandate at one time by a "Car" in prison that whenever a person was targeted for death, the "Hitters" had to "Book" them at least 17 times. This edict aimed to ensure the victim would be incapacitated and instill fear in other people and groups.

1030: CDCR 1030 is a confidential report in prison where "Snitches" make allegations against other "Convicts," which then go into their "C-file."

14/88: The 14 represents these 14 words, "We must secure the existence of our people and the future for White children." The 88 stands for Heil Hitler. White inmates earn these tattoos in prison by "Putting In Work" for their "People."

15/03: These numerical values represent Orange County, with the fifteenth letter of the alphabet corresponding to the letter "O" and the third letter corresponding to "C."

180: This is a "Building" design in some California prisons that is used for maximum security Level IV inmates. Level IV inmates can be housed in a 270 or 180 design building, but the 180 design buildings are reserved for the most violent Level IV inmates.

187: The California Penal Code for murder.

19/04: These numerical values represent San Diego, with the nineteenth letter of the alphabet corresponding to the letter "S" and the fourth letter corresponding to "D."

1968 Shoe War: It has been suggested that the theft of a pair of shoes from a "Nuestra Familia" member's cell by several members of the "Mexican Mafia" at San Quentin Prison in 1968 was the catalyst for the 45-year-long conflict between the two groups. This incident is believed to have sparked the war that ensued.

1st Draw: Inmates can access the facility's "Canteen" and obtain their "Commissary" during specific weeks. The first draw is scheduled for the initial week of the month, the second draw for the second week, and the third draw for the third week. The allocation of draws is determined by the last two digits of the inmate's "CDCR Number."

1st Watch: The designated work hours for these officers are from 2200 to 0600 hours.

2 Piece: To deliver a two-punch combination with accuracy and power to another person. For example, "I gave that 'Punk' a 2 piece and broke his jaw."

23 Seconds: This is how long the "Woods" will beat one of their homies when he has broken a rule that requires a "DP." For example, "Bronco, you messed up. You got to go get your 23 seconds."

23/16: These numerical values represent White Power, with the twenty-third letter of the alphabet corresponding to the letter "W" and the sixteenth letter corresponding to "P." White inmates earn these tattoos in prison for "Putting In Work."

270: The architectural design commonly employed in several California correctional facilities. It is named as such due to the 270-degree view afforded to the "Control Booth Officer" overseeing the inmates within the structure. The building is configured in a "U" shape, with cells on three sides of the control booth.

2nd Draw: Inmates can access the facility's "Canteen" and obtain their "Commissary" during specific weeks. The first draw is scheduled for the initial week of the month, the second draw for the second week, and the third draw for the third week. The allocation of draws is determined by the last two digits of the inmate's "CDCR Number."

2nd Watch: The designated work hours for these officers are from 0600-1400 hours.

3 Piece: To deliver a three-punch combination with accuracy and power to another person. For example, "I gave Snoopy a 3 piece and broke his nose."

3 Piece Suit: It is customary to restrain a convict with handcuffs, a belly chain, and leg irons while transporting them via vehicle. This is called a 3 piece suit.

3 Step Shield: This is a tattoo of an Aztec war shield that a "Camarada" earns by "Putting In Work" for a member of the "Mexican Mafia." It has three steps to it, and each one is earned by committing an act of violence for a "Pilli."

30 Hit Policy: This was a mandate at one time by a "Car" in prison that whenever a person was targeted for death, the "Hitters" had to "Book" them at least 30 times. This edict aimed to ensure the victim would be incapacitated and instill fear in other people and groups.

30/60 Days On The Beach: When an officer is suspended for 30 or 60 days without pay. For example, "I got 30 days on the beach for 'Holding My Mud' during that investigation."

38: This is Prison slang for a hypodermic needle used to inject drugs.

3rd Draw: Inmates can access the facility's "Canteen" and obtain their "Commissary" during specific weeks. The first draw is scheduled for the initial week of the month, the second draw for the second week, and the third draw for the third week. The allocation of draws is determined by the last two digits of the inmate's "CDCR Number."

3rd Watch: The designated work hours for these officers are from 1400 to 2200 hours.

4 Piece: When an inmate is fully restrained and under the supervision of an officer carrying a firearm. This is typically done during transportation to court or while traveling on the "Grey Goose."

40 MM Launcher: This is a weapon utilized by officers that shoots various types of projectiles to break up fights. This is commonly referred to as "Big Bertha" or the "Knee Knocker."

415 Kumi: This is a highly structured prison gang in California comprised of Black inmates.

4 B 1 Left: Years ago, at the Corcoran "SHU," this was the section where the California Department of Corrections and Rehabilitation placed the "Heavy Hitters." At that time, they wanted all the leadership from the "Big Four" prison gangs in one area.

50 Paper: A small piece of paper containing heroin valued at $50. This is the standard quantity of heroin sold in prison.

50/50 Yard: These yards started in 2018, and they are supposed to be half "General Population" and half "SNY."

602: The Inmate Appeal form provided by the CDCR enables prisoners to file grievances regarding the behavior of correctional officers. A 602 complaint will then prompt an official investigation by the prison administration.

7K: All officers are required to attend a mandatory four-hour training session once a month, which must be completed during their personal time.

812: This is the form in prison that is submitted by an inmate who claims other inmates on the yard are his enemies and members of a "Security Threat Group."

88: These numerical values represent Heil Hitler, with the eighth letter of the alphabet corresponding to the letter "H" and the eighth letter corresponding to "H." These tattoos are earned in prison by White inmates for "Putting In Work."

979: These numbers represent "IGI" which is the "Institutional Gang Investigators."

BONUS SECTION

Inmate Weapons

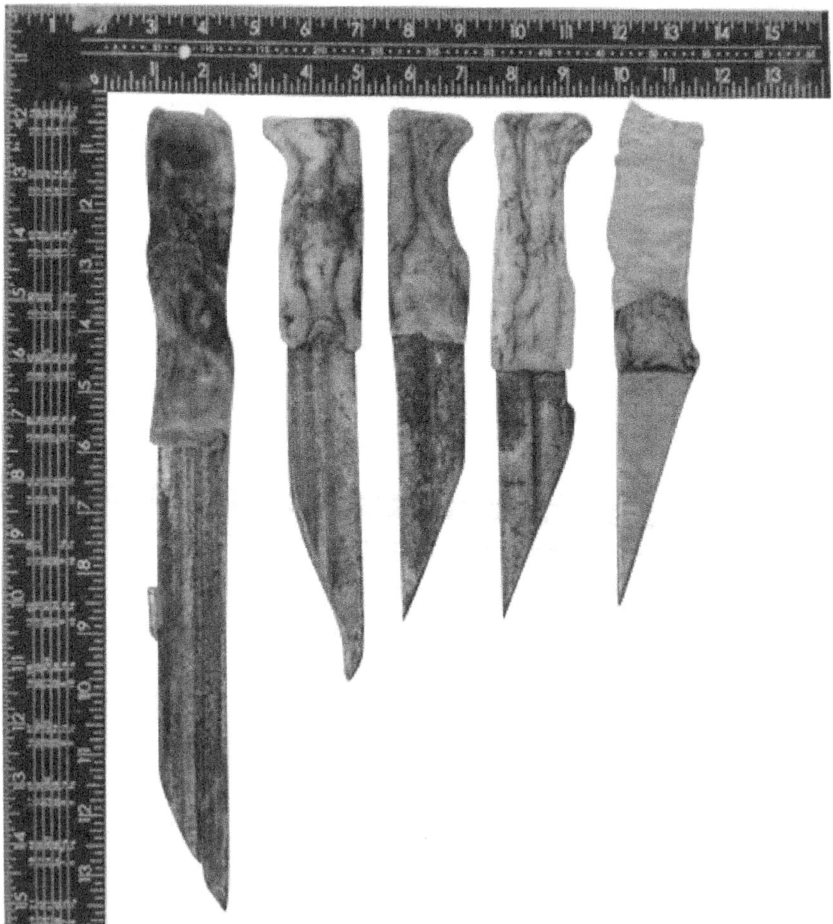

INMATE WEAPONS

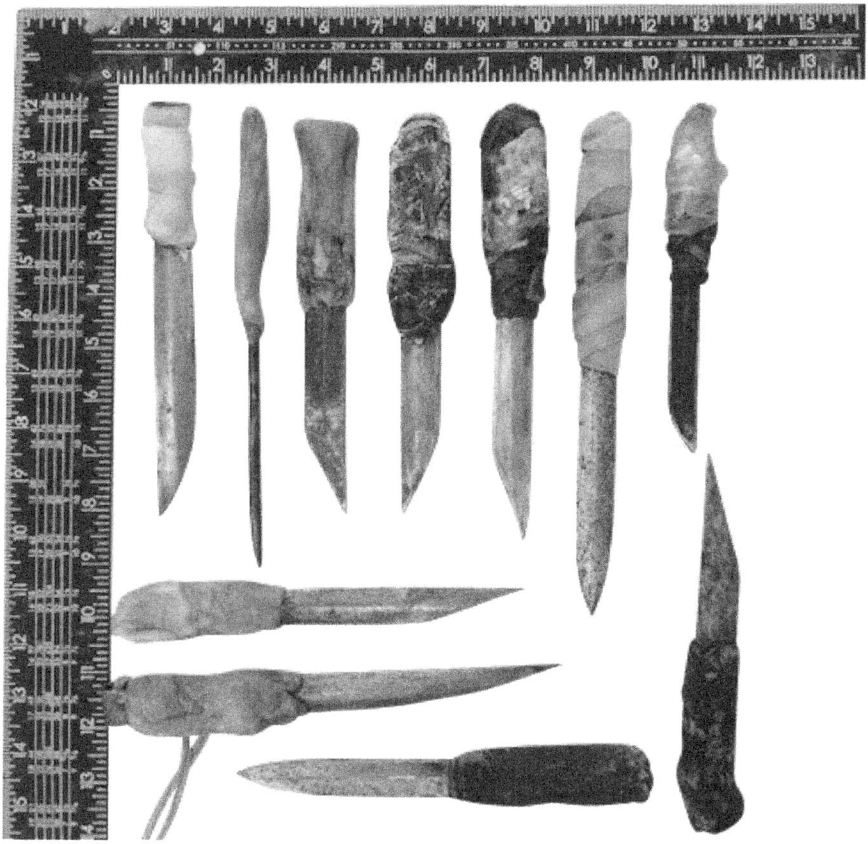

TATTOO GUNS

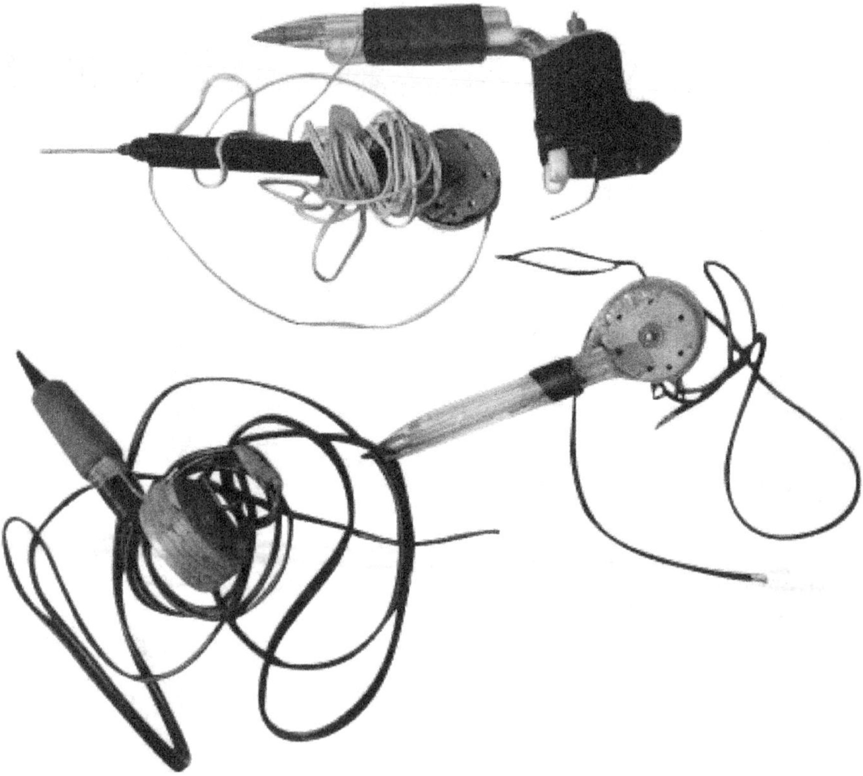

PRISON KITES

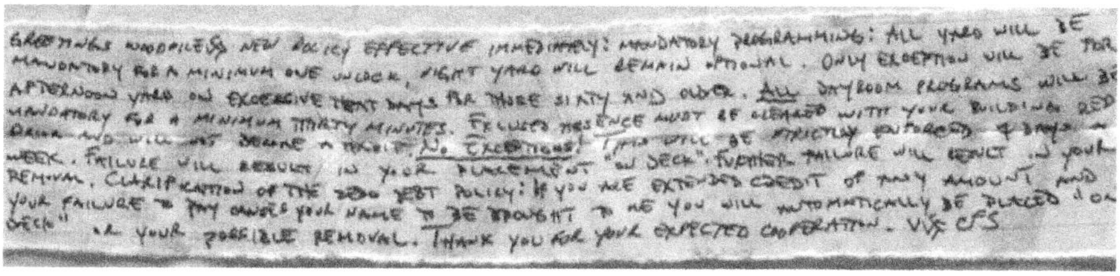

"Greetings Woodpile. New policy effective immediately: mandatory programming: all yard will be mandatory for a minimum one unlock, night yard will remain optional. Only exception will be for afternoon yard on excessive heat days for those sixty and older. All dayroom programs will be mandatory for a minimum of thirty minutes. Excused absence must be cleared with your building rep prior and will not become a habit. No exceptions! This will be strictly enforced seven days a week. Failure will result in your placement on deck. Further failure will result in your removal. Clarification of the zero debt policy: if you are extended credit of any amount and your failure to pay causes your name to be brought to me you will automatically be placed on deck or your possible removal. Thank you for your expected cooperation."

The shot caller for the woods reiterates the household rules for the woodpile on this yard. When an inmate is placed on deck, he will have to attack the next person who needs to be disciplined in their car. This is called a cleanup when you smash another inmate to clear your name among your faction. Unpaid drug debts are a severe matter in prison, and their household has a zero-debt policy. A zero-debt policy means you can't have any outstanding drug debts. To be removed means your homies will violently attack you, so you get taken off the yard in bad standing.

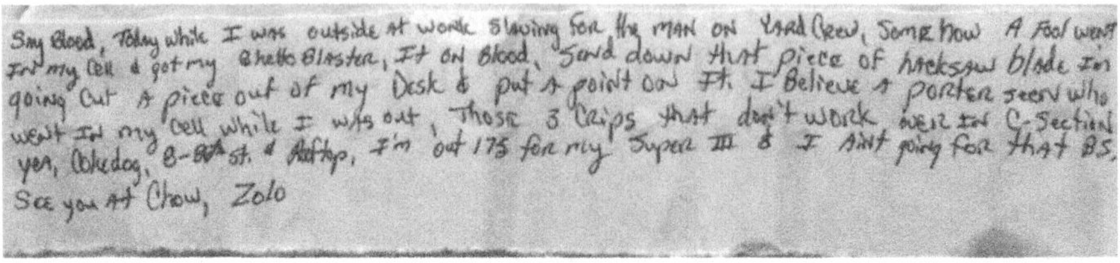
Say Blood, Today while I was outside at work slaving for the man on Yard Crew, Some how A fool went In my Cell & got my Ghetto Blaster, It on Blood, Send down that piece of hacksaw blade I'm going Cut A piece out of my Desk & put A point on It. I Believe A porter seen who went In my cell while I was out, Those 3 Crips that don't work over In C-Section yea, Cokedog, 8-[illegible] st. & [illegible], I'm out 175 for my Super III & I Ain't going for that BS, See you At Chow, Zolo

"Say Blood, today while I was outside at work slaving for the man on the yard crew, somehow a fool went in my cell and got my ghetto blaster. It's on Blood! Send down that piece of hacksaw blade, I'm going to cut a piece out of my desk and put a point on it. I believe a porter saw who went in my cell while I was out. Those 3 Crips that don't work over in C-Section…I'm out $175 for my Super III and I'm not going for that. See you at chow, Zolo."

This inmate was at work on the yard crew, and someone went into his cell and stole his radio. A porter might have seen who did it, and they think it was 3 Crips on the other side of the housing unit. Those radios are valuable in prison and worth $175 to him. He wants his homie to give him a hacksaw blade so he can cut out some weapon stock from his desk and make him a banger to poke the thieves.

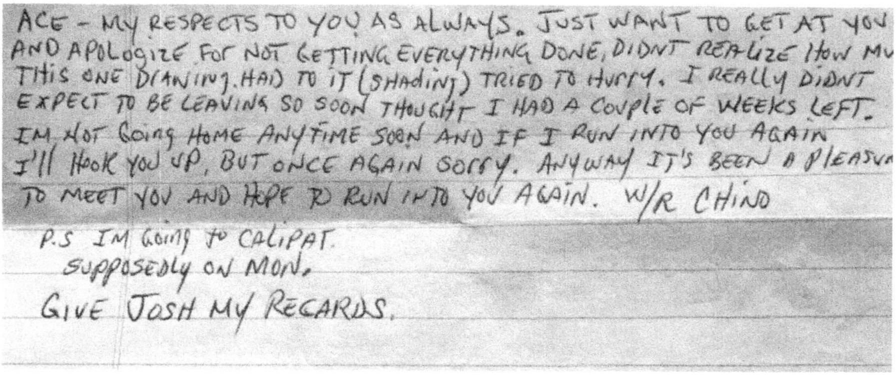
ACE - MY RESPECTS TO YOU AS ALWAYS. JUST WANT TO GET AT YOU
AND APOLOGIZE FOR NOT GETTING EVERYTHING DONE, DIDNT REALIZE HOW MU
THIS ONE DRAWING HAD TO IT (SHADING) TRIED TO HURRY. I REALLY DIDNT
EXPECT TO BE LEAVING SO SOON THOUGHT I HAD A COUPLE OF WEEKS LEFT.
IM NOT GOING HOME ANYTIME SOON AND IF I RUN INTO YOU AGAIN
I'LL HOOK YOU UP, BUT ONCE AGAIN SORRY. ANYWAY IT'S BEEN A PLEASU
TO MEET YOU AND HOPE TO RUN INTO YOU AGAIN. W/R CHINO

P.S IM GOING TO CALIPAT.
SUPPOSEDLY ON MON.
GIVE JOSH MY REGARDS.

"Ace, my respects to you as always. I just want to get at you and apologize for not getting everything done. I didn't realize how much work this one drawing had (shading). I tried to hurry. I really didn't expect to be leaving so soon, I thought I had a couple of weeks left. I'm not going home anytime soon and if I run into you again I will hook you up. But once again, sorry. Anyway, it's been a pleasure to meet you and I hope to run into you again. With respect, Chino.

P.S. I'm going to Calipatria Prison on Monday. Give Josh my regards." Chino was going to draw for his homie, but he couldn't finish on time because he got word that he was being transferred to Calipatria State Prison. He is trying to make it right with his homie so he doesn't try to smut up his name after leaving for not keeping his word about the drawing.

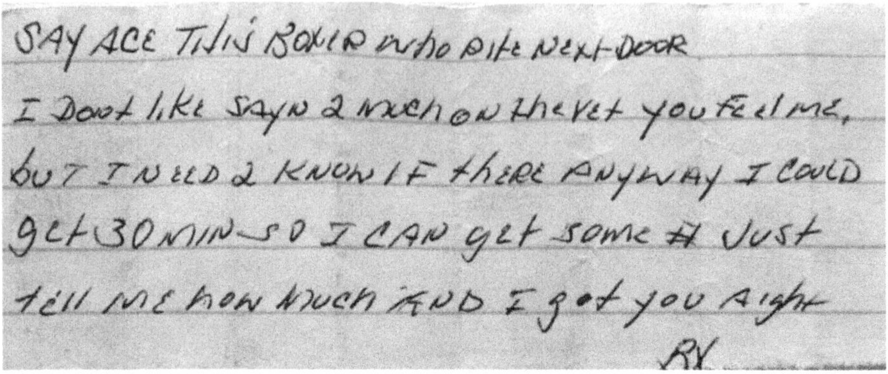

SAY ACE THIS BOXER WHO BIte NEXT-DOOR
I Dont like sayn 2 much on the vet you Feel me,
but I need 2 know if there anyway I could
get 30 min so I can get some # Just
tell me how much AND I got you Aight
RY

"Say Ace, this is Boxer who is next door. I don't like talking in the vent, feel me? But I need to know if there is anyway I could get 30 minutes so I can get some. Just tell me how much and I got you, aight? Boxer."

Boxer is trying to buy some time on the horn (Phone) from Ace to call his people on the streets. Boxer doesn't like talking on the vent because people in other cells can hear you speaking when you do that. Inmates in different cells can talk to each other through the air conditioning vents. In the 270 design prisons in California, four different cells can hear when neighbors talk to each other through the vents. To call someone via a vent, they will yell, "Ace, get on the vent!"

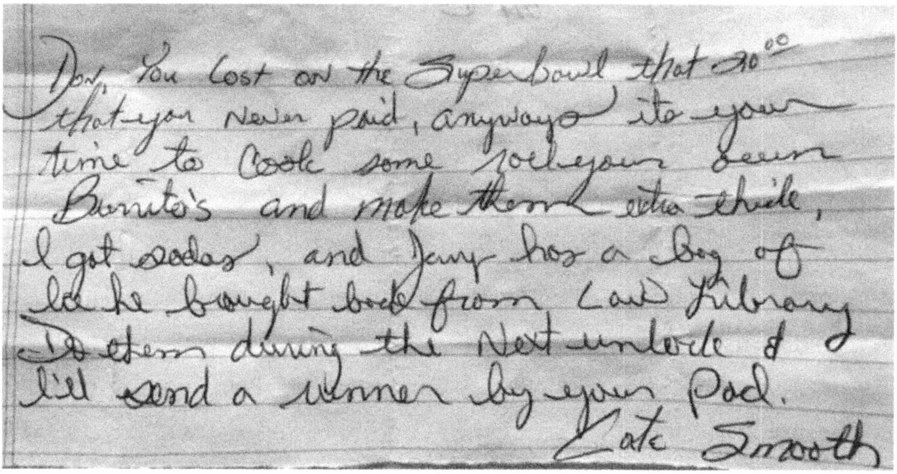
Don, You Lost on the Superbowl that 20.00 that you Never paid, anyways its your time to Cook some of your bean Burrito's and make them extra thick, I got sodas, and Jerry has a Bag of Ice he brought back from Law Library Do them during the Next unlock & I'll send a runner by your Pad.
Late Smooth

"Don, you lost on the Super Bowl that $20 that you never paid. Anyways, it's your time to cook some of your bean burritos and make them extra thick. I got sodas and Jerry has a bag of ice he brought back from the Law Library. Do them during the next unlock and I will send a runner by your pad. Late, Smooth."

This kite is self-explanatory. Don needs to pay his debts before Smooth loses his patience with him. Don better make those burritos extra thick like Smooth wants, or he will get mad and bring up his gambling debt to make an issue out of it.

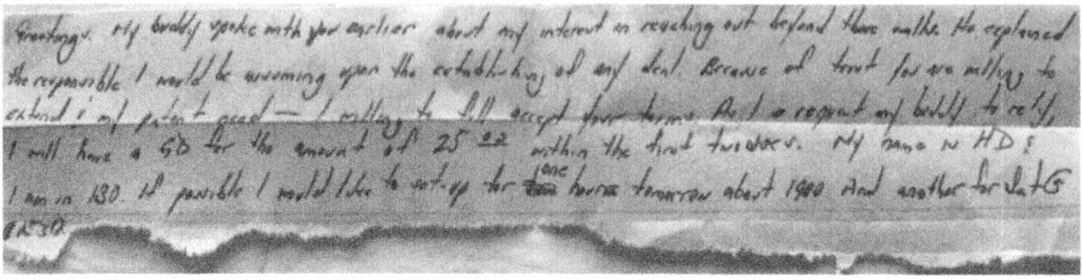
Greetings, my buddy spoke with you earlier about my interest in reaching out beyond these walls. He explained
the responsibility I would be assuming upon the establishing of any deal. Because of trust you are willing to
extend & my patent need — I willing to fully accept your terms. As I request my buddy to reply,
I will have a GD for the amount of 25 within the first two uses. My name is HD &
I am in 130. If possible I would like to set-up for one hours tomorrow about 1900 And another for Sat@
1530

"Greetings, my buddy spoke with you earlier about my interest in reaching out beyond these walls. He explained the responsibility I would be assuming upon establishing of any deal. Because of the trust you are willing to extend and my patent need I am willing to fully accept your terms. As I request my buddy to reply, I will have a GD for the amount of $25 within the first two uses. My name is HD (Half Dead) and I am in cell 130. If possible I would like to setup for one hour tomorrow at about 1900 hours and another for Saturday 1530 hours."

Half Dead is trying to broker a deal to use the horn (phone) with another inmate. The responsibility he is talking about is if he gets caught with the phone or loses it, he must pay for it. A contraband cell phone of good quality goes for about $1000-$1,500 each in the penitentiary. Inmates who have cell phones in prison will sell time to other inmates.

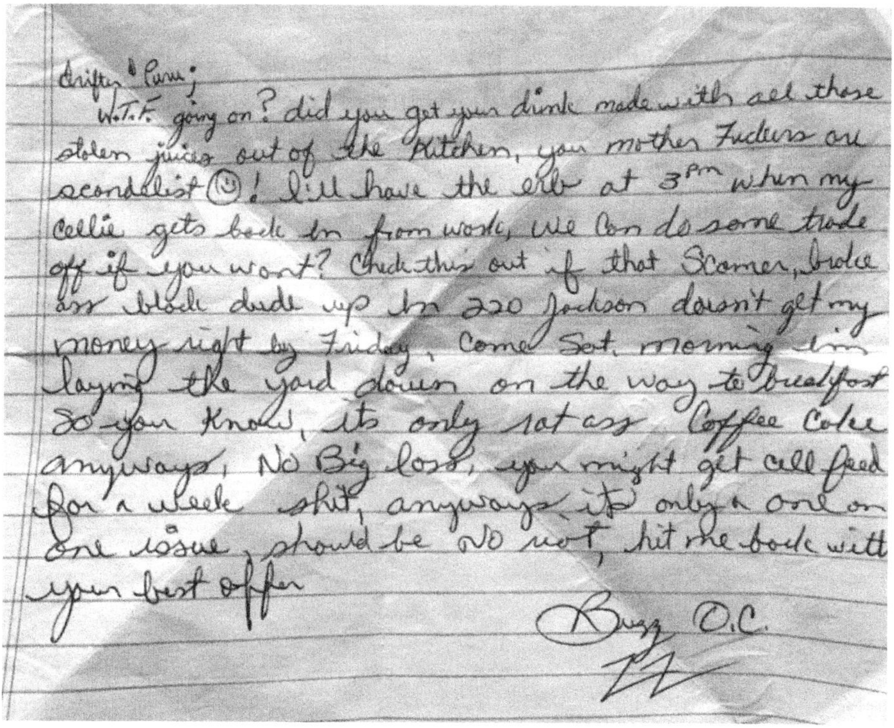
Drifter & Guru;
W.T.F. going on? did you get your drink made with all those stolen juices out of the kitchen, you mother fuckers are scandelist ☺! I'll have the erb at 3pm when my cellie gets back in from work, we can do some trade off if you want? Check this out if that Scamer, broke ass black dude up in 220 Jackson doesn't get my money right by Friday, Come Sat. morning i'm laying the yard down on the way to breakfast So you know, its only rat ass Coffee Cake anyways, No Big loss, you might get cell feed for a week shit, anyways its only a one on one issue, should be no riot, hit me back with your best offer

Buzz O.C.

"Drifter, What is going on? Did you get your drink made with all those stolen juices from the kitchen? You dudes are scandalous! I will have the herb at 3pm when my cellie gets back in from work. We can do some trade off if you want. Check this out, if that scammer broke Black dude Jackson up in cell 220 doesn't get my money right by Friday, come Saturday morning I'm laying the yard down on the way to breakfast. So you know, it's only garbage coffee cake anyway. No big loss! You might get cell fed for a week. Anyways, it's only a one on one issue, there shouldn't be a riot. Hit me back with your best offer. Buzz, O.C."

This dude's homies stole juice from the kitchen to make inmatemanufactured alcohol (pruno). When his cellie gets back from work, he will have some weed because he hit from his pipeline. He wants to trade some weed for something the dude he is writing has.

A Black inmate named Jackson owes him money for some weed that he fronted him, but he hasn't paid his debt yet. If Jackson doesn't pay him, he will attack him on Saturday when the inmates walk to breakfast at the chow hall. He doesn't think there will be a riot when he attacks Jackson because it is just an issue regarding a drug debt.

Monica
Each day that
goes by, Is filled with
misery and hate... But
theres one joyfull thought, That
helps me keep my faith... The
thought of a featherwood, that's down for
a white knight... One that stands by my
side, weather I'm wrong or I'm right. One such
as you Monica, my featherwood friend... Your down
for all cause, and respected too the end... A friend-
ship such as ours, I will cherish and hold tight...
I'am just as proud to be your friend, as I am
proud to be white... Because your the finest
of all women, and your sweeter
than wine... Your a true
featherwood, and your one
of a kind. I Love
You homegirl
Long Love + Respect
Larry

"Monica, Each day that goes by, is filled with misery and hate...But there's the joyful thought, that helps me keep my faith...The thought of a featherwood, that's down for a White knight...One that stands by my side, whether I'm wrong or right. One such as you Monica, my featherwood friend...You're down for the cause, and respected to the end...A friendship such as ours, I will cherish and hold tight...I am just as proud to be your friend, as I am proud to be White...Because you're the finest of all women, and you're sweeter than wine...You're a true featherwood, and you're one of a kind. I love you, homegirl. Long love & respect, Larry."

When convicts send letters to family and friends, they call it "Flying a kite." That is why I included a personal letter dedicated to prison kites in this section. This little letter is a prime example of subtle manipulation from an experienced convict. The goal of every convict is to live as comfortably as possible while in prison. One of the prime ways to do this is to have a female on the outside ride that time out with them by writing, accepting their calls, sending packages, and putting money on their books.

A featherwood is a term that Peckerwoods call their women who are down for the cause and support them in their criminal endeavors. Larry is no low-level dummy; his compulsion skills are above average, and I would venture to guess he has a lot of status in prison among his peers. If this woman hasn't already, she is being set up to start bringing in contraband to prison, via visitation. Larry thanks her for being down for the cause, which is subtle coercion to have her continue to help or pressure her to do more. Larry has his hooks in this featherwood and wants her to do even more. The trap is set, and now he shrewdly applies even more pressure.

GANG CREEDS & OATHS

Prison gang creeds, constitutions, or household policies help keep members in line and let them know what is expected of them. Prison gang oaths are just brief summaries memorized and passed among gang members.

A Northerner Code of Conduct

1. Respect yourself and others.
2. Treat everyone equally.
3. Have a positive attitude.
4. Be well-mannered.
5. Have proper hygiene.
6. No false rumors or gossip.
7. No sex play.
8. No horseplay.
9. No racial talk.
10. No loud talk.
11. No profanity.
12. No boasting or bragging.
13. No cell soldiering.
14. No lying.
15. No bullying.
16. No abuse of drugs or alcohol.
17. No fraternizing with the K-9 or enemies.
18. No punk activities are allowed.

A SOUTHERNER CODE OF CONDUCT

1. There is to be no fighting.
2. There is to be no horseplay.
3. No getting in the cop's faces unless you are disrespected.
4. If one of the homies feels disrespected and attacks a cop, all homies will follow.
5. Keep conversations in your cell.
6. No yelling down the tier.
7. No disrespecting or name-calling on the tier.
8. All South Side business or anything else discussed on the tier remains on the tier unless told.
9. All homies are responsible for weapons or drugs.
10. Guard your conversations on the phones.
11. Mandatory workout of your choice, a minimum of one hour.
12. Keep the tier clean. No trash unless the tier is being swept.
13. Keep your cell clean, and your mattress rolled up during the day.
14. All reps are to run down the rules to the new arrivals on their tier.
15. No illegal activity is allowed until the last chain has gone to visiting on visit days.
16. Keep yourself and your clothes clean at all times.

17. Carry yourself with respect.
18. No punk activities are allowed.

If I ever break my stride,
or falter at my comrades side,

this oath will kill me.

If ever my word should be untrue,
should I betray this chosen few,
this oath will kill me.

Should I be slow to take a stand,
should I show fear to any man,
this oath will kill me.

Should I misuse the people's trust,
should I submit ever to greed or
lust, this oath will kill me.

Should I grow lax in discipline,
in time of strife refuse my hand,
this oath will kill me.

Long live George Jackson,
long live the spirit of the
Black Guerrilla Family.

Aryan Brotherhood Oath

I will stand by my brother.

My brother will come before all others.
My life is forfeit should I fail my brothers.
I will honor my brother in peace as in war.

If I lead, follow.

If I stumble, push me.
If I fall, avenge me.

If I betray you, kill me.

Nuestra Raza 14 Bonds

1. All Norteños will strive for a better education, respect, and social status of equality. This includes and goes beyond acquiring any incentives and privileges entitled to an inmate.
2. All Norteños will take a strong positive attitude towards aiding and assisting those of Latin descent and any other minority group worthy of our cause. We must work in harmony and unite those forces in alliance with us to reach our goals.
3. All Norteños will do everything they can to acquire mainline status. These are the grounds we must secure for our fellow Norteños and all those who live for the cause to have a strong established pinta to go to without the threat or interference of the opposition.
4. In order to continue our struggle with far fewer difficulties, there shall be no tolerance created by internal confrontation, individualism, or homeboy favoritism. No Norteño will spread false rumors or gossip about a fellow Norteño. At no time will a Norteño attempt to take advantage of, or disrespect, a fellow Norteños ruca or familia. To do so will result in serious repercussions.
5. All Norteños will acknowledge and respect the authority in charge at all times. No Norteño will feel inferior to one who holds rank or position. Nor will a Norteño holding rank or a position of some type feel superior over his fellow Norteños because of his status.
6. All data pertaining to a new arrival shall be reported through its proper channels immediately. See Household Procedures,

especially that which endangers a life or is contrary to the cause.

7. At no time will a Norteño jeopardize the life of a fellow Norteño. There shall be no fighting amongst Norteños, Nor shall any cowardice dealing with the K-9 or enemy be tolerated. To do so will be dealt with accordingly.
8. No Norteño will lie or boast about his status, rank, or title. He will take high regard for his physical and mental well-being, always strive to better himself, and become more aware and educated in all aspects relevant to the accomplishments of our set goals.
9. Should a Norteño be transferred from one facility to another, it is his sole duty to establish a branch in union with procedures set henceforth and work hand-in-hand with other Norteños at said facility and parallel with other pintas.
10. Every chapter and stronghold of Norteños will keep track of all enemies and enemy activities behind enemy lines.
11. A Norteño will protect and defend his household to the fullest, regardless of circumstances or consequences. This means standing next to a fellow Norteño or the cause in battle and struggle. To abandon such responsibilities will be considered an act of treason.
12. It is each Norteños' responsibility aware of our struggle to teach and school all those destined for the pinta. No Norteño should enter the pinta blind or unaware of our struggle behind the walls.
13. A Norteño leaving to the streets is encouraged to assist his fellow Norteño behind the walls in whatever form or fashion

he chooses. This is not mandatory. Failure to assist in this manner will hurt his status upon return to prison. This is a necessary step towards the elite circle of dedicated Norteño Soldados we strive for.

14. A Norteño shall stay abreast of all new laws, policies, and procedures. No portion of this format is to be misinterpreted or abused for personal gain. To do so will be considered as an act of treason.

Notable California Prison Riots and Other Incidents

November 7, 2024: Six officers were injured and three inmates were relocated after a disturbance at Kern Valley State Prison on Thursday. An inmate attacked an officer, leading staff to use chemical agents and physical force to subdue him. Two other inmates then assaulted staff, prompting further use of force. The situation was eventually controlled, and a weapon made by an inmate was recovered. The injured officers were treated at a hospital and have since been discharged.

February 1, 2024: On Thursday, authorities reported that eight corrections officers and one inmate were injured during a riot involving about 200 inmates at Ironwood State Prison in Blythe, Southern California. The disturbance began around 10 a.m. Wednesday during a contraband investigation when an inmate headbutted a staff member, leading other inmates to attack officers with fists and rocks. Officers responded with a warning shot and deployed chemical agents and non-lethal rounds. The injured were treated at an external hospital before returning to the prison, with the severity of their injuries undisclosed. Thirty inmates have been identified as directly involved, and the investigation is ongoing.

August 10, 2023: A riot broke out at Salinas Valley State Prison between the Blacks and Southerners. Four inmates received stab wounds and were transported to outside hospitals for treatment. The Southerners approached the Blacks and asked them to remove a Crip for stabbing a Mexican Mafia member a few weeks prior at another prison. The Blacks refused, so the Southerners stabbed the Crip with whom they had an issue, and the riot followed.

August 11, 2022: A riot at Tehachapi Prison left six inmates receiving treatment at outside hospitals. Officers used chemical agents and less-lethal rounds to help quell the disturbance. Several inmate-manufactured weapons were recovered from the scene.

October 29, 2020: Twenty inmates were involved in a riot at Folsom Prison. Five inmates were transported to nearby hospitals to treat their injuries.

August 30, 2019: A riot involving 40 inmates erupted at Susanville Prison, resulting in nine inmates and four officers being transported to area hospitals for treatment.

August 29, 2019: A riot involving 50 inmates jumped off at California Men's Colony. Officers fired rounds from the Mini-14 rifle to stop the disturbance. Two inmates were taken to area hospitals for treatment.

August 28, 2019: A riot involving 40 inmates erupted at California Men's Colony. Four inmates got stabbed and slashed.

August 24, 2019: A riot involving 80 inmates kicked off at Richard

J. Donovan Correctional Facility. Five inmates were injured and transported to area hospitals.

August 14, 2019: A riot involving 200 inmates at Soledad State Prison resulted in eight inmates getting treatment for injuries at area hospitals, and 50 others suffered minor injuries. Four inmate-manufactured weapons were recovered, and the tower officer fired rounds from the Mini-14 to help quell the violence.

July 18, 2019: To quell a riot involving 41 Salinas Valley State Prison inmates, guards discharged rounds from the Mini-14 rifle. Three inmates were stabbed and treated at outside hospitals.

July 18, 2019: A riot kicked off at Pleasant Valley State Prison involving 41 inmates. Guards fired rounds from the Mini-14 rifle to help quell the disturbance. Three inmates were stabbed and treated at area hospitals.

July 8, 2019: A riot involving 25 inmates jumped off at Salinas Valley State Prison. Four inmates were stabbed and transported to outside hospitals for treatment. Five inmate-manufactured weapons were recovered from the scene.

June 4, 2019: A riot involving 40 inmates broke out at Alder Creek Conservation Camp. Three inmates were taken to outside hospitals for treatment.

November 14, 2018: A riot involving 134 inmates jumped off at Pleasant Valley State Prison. Five inmates were transported to local hospitals.

November 14, 2018: A riot involving 80 inmates kicked off at Avenal State Prison. Six inmates were taken to area hospitals.

September 29, 2018: A riot at Avenal Prison left eleven inmates getting treatment at outside hospitals. Three of those inmates were lifeflighted to the hospital during that Saturday morning.

March 25, 2018: A riot involving 65 inmates broke out at California Correctional Institution. Guards fired several rounds from the Mini-14 rifle to stop the rampage. One inmate was shot in his buttocks. Five inmates were transported to area hospitals for treatment.

September 24, 2017: Guards used rubber bullets to help stop a riot involving 160 inmates at California Men's Colony. Nine inmates were stabbed and were transported to an area hospital. One inmate later died from his wounds.

August 17, 2017: A riot involving 350 inmates kicked off at Sierra Conservation Center. Guards fired several Mini-14 rounds to stop the melee. Seven inmates were transported to area hospitals for treatment.

July 12, 2017: A riot involving 20 inmates erupted at Salinas Valley State Prison, resulting in five inmates getting treatment at area hospitals.

May 24, 2017: 97 inmates rioted at Pelican Bay State Prison, resulting in five inmates getting shot. Eight officers and seven inmates were taken to area hospitals for treatment after the battle.

March 15, 2017: A riot at Susanville Prison left six officers and one inmate injured. An inmate attacked an officer in the dining hall, and then 30 inmates joined the attack and smashed food trays on the heads of some officers.

March 7, 2017: A riot involving 110 inmates erupted at California State Prison, Corcoran.

February 8, 2017: A riot involving 125 inmates erupted at Kern Valley State Prison. Five inmates were injured and taken to area hospitals for treatment.

February 7, 2017: A riot involving 125 inmates broke out at Kern Valley State Prison. Seven inmate-manufactured weapons were recovered.

December 22, 2016: A riot at Susanville Prison erupted that involved 100 inmates. Four inmates were hospitalized due to the violence, with one suffering from a gunshot wound to his buttocks.

May 27, 2016: A riot at High Desert State Prison involving 65 inmates resulted in five inmates being transported to outside hospitals for treatment. The riot started on the recreation yard of Facility D, which houses Level IV inmates. 21 inmate-manufactured weapons were recovered from the scene.

August 27, 2015: A riot involving 90 inmates happened at Salinas Valley State Prison in the morning. Two inmates were sliced with tomahawks and had to be treated at area hospitals.

August 16, 2015: A riot at Susanville Prison involving 45 inmates in the dining hall resulted in one inmate getting killed by an officer with a Mini-14 rifle after four warning shots.

August 12, 2015: Following the murder of inmate Hugo Pinell by White inmates, a riot erupted between them and the Black inmates. Seventy inmates were engaged in the disturbance, necessitating several warning shots from the Mini-14 rifle to suppress the turmoil.

March 20, 2015: 60 inmates rioted for five minutes at Calipatria State Prison during the evening yard. Two inmates were taken to area hospitals for treatment.

January 8, 2015: A riot at Calipatria State Prison left 30 inmates and 20 officers wounded; 1 inmate was killed after being shot in the abdomen. The mayhem lasted for about 45 minutes before being quelled. Twenty minutes after getting the riot under control, another group of inmates attacked the officers again.

June 3, 2013: 40 inmates were involved in a riot on the exercise yard at Wasco State Prison that left one dead. Three inmates were taken to a nearby hospital.

December 8, 2012: 115 inmates were involved in a riot at Calipatria State Prison, leaving nine inmates getting treatment at area hospitals.

October 6, 2012: A riot involving more than 460 Blacks and Southerners occurred at Ironwood State Prison, resulting in seven inmates going to area hospitals.

September 19, 2012: 65 inmates were involved in a riot on the New Folsom Prison exercise yard, leaving 13 hospitalized. Eight inmates were stabbed, and one was shot by an officer.

February 10, 2012: 175 inmates were involved in a riot on the exercise yard at San Quentin. Dozens of inmates were stabbed and sliced during the violent melee.

December 7, 2011: 50 inmates were rioting at "New Folsom" Prison on the Level 4 yard. Seven rounds from the Mini-14 were fired to try and stop the violence. Nine inmates were taken to area hospitals for treatment; several were stabbed.

June 7, 2011: A riot involving 50 inmates at Avenal Prison resulted in five receiving medical care at outside hospitals.

May 23, 2011: A riot at San Quentin involving 200 inmates erupted in the chow hall, and four were stabbed.

May 20, 2011: 150 inmates were involved in a riot at Folsom Prison. Two inmates were stabbed and numerous others were taken to area hospitals for treatment.

October 19, 2010: 120 inmates were involved in a riot at Calipatria State Prison, and 14 were injured. The Mini-14 rifle was used to help suppress the violence.

August 27, 2010: 200 inmates were involved in a riot at Folsom Prison.

The fighting started at the handball court and escalated quickly. Seven inmates were taken to area hospitals for treatment.

June 12, 2010: 39 inmates were involved in a riot at Calipatria State Prison, and 37 were injured. One inmate died as a result of the fighting.

September 21, 2009: 193 inmates rioted at Avenal Prison, resulting in 24 inmates receiving treatment at outside hospitals. 30 inmatemanufactured weapons were recovered from the bloody scene.

August 15, 2009: A riot at Avenal Prison, involving 70 Blacks and Southerners, resulted in several inmates getting stabbed.

August 8, 2009: A large riot at Chino State Prison between the Black inmates and the Southerners left more than 240 injured and two buildings destroyed. 55 inmates were hospitalized. The violence left the prison in a state of emergency.

June 21, 2009: A riot broke out at Corcoran State Prison involving 75 inmates. 11 inmates were stabbed and treated at area hospitals. 28 inmate-manufactured weapons were recovered. This melee is commonly referred to as the Father's Day Massacre, and it was a battle between the Southerners and Northerners.

December 30, 2007: 200 Blacks and Southerners were involved in a riot at Chino State Prison that lasted for 90 minutes. 27 inmates were taken to local hospitals. Inmates wrapped six shards of glass with cloth on one end and used them as bangers.

January 13, 2006: A riot at San Quentin in the chow hall injured 23 inmates and two correctional officers.

September 22, 2005: A riot at Chino State Prison involving 200 Blacks and Southerners resulted in 8 injuries.

August 18, 2005: A vicious riot erupted at Calipatria State Prison, leaving one inmate dead, 16 officers wounded, and 25 inmates wounded. At around 1500 hours, an inmate was being searched by an officer, and when an inmate-manufactured weapon was discovered on him, the inmate used it to stab the officer in the head. After the officer was stabbed, dozens of his fellow gang members attacked the rest of the officers. The mayhem lasted for about four hours until it was quelled. Two inmates were shot during this uprising, one in the stomach and one in the head.

August 9, 2005: A riot at San Quentin involved 80 White and Mexican inmates, in which 42 were injured. One inmate received a large gash on his face from a tomahawk, and several lock-in-a-sock weapons were found.

February 24, 2005: A riot at Tehachapi Prison involving 400 Blacks and Southerners lasted about 40 minutes. Several inmatemanufactured weapons were recovered.

April 8, 2002: A riot at Folsom Prison between 80 Northerners and Southerners resulted in 25 of them getting injured. For 12 weeks prior, these warring factions had been separated, but on April 8, they were released on the main yard together.

December 21, 2001: 400 inmates rioted at Lancaster Prison for 15 minutes. 26 homemade weapons were recovered, and six inmates were stabbed. Several warning shots were fired to help quell the violence. Two inmates suffered collapsed lungs after being stabbed.

July 29, 2000: 120 Southerners and Peckerwoods rioted at Lancaster Prison, resulting in ten injuries.

February 23, 2000: 200 Blacks and Southerners were involved in one of the bloodiest riots in California history. The riot occurred on Bravo Yard and lasted 30 minutes at Pelican Bay Prison. There were 24 rounds fired from the Mini-14 to help stop the outbreak of violence. Nineteen inmates were stabbed, 15 were shot, and one was killed. 89 inmatemanufactured weapons were recovered. 16 ambulances arrived at the prison to help transport the injured.

June 5, 1995: Five Crips rushed into the program office while the door was unlocked at 0930 hours and attacked the officers inside with inmate-manufactured weapons. Eight officers were taken to outside hospitals for treatment, with several getting stabbed. A female sergeant suffered severe stab wounds during the violent attack. The motive for this attack is unknown, but officers shot and killed an inmate two months prior during a fight. This attack changed the California Department of Corrections and Rehabilitation's policy on Level IV yards because, after this, they installed fences separating the program office from the rest of the prison yard. They also sectioned the yard off with two buildings in one section and three in the other.

November 1986: An unclassified FBI document states that an inmate was discovered with dynamite at Tehachapi Prison. The FBI believes the dynamite was for use against other inmates.

December 1985: An unclassified FBI document states that large quantities of C-4 explosives were smuggled into Folsom Prison. Correctional officers discovered these explosives but believed more was still circulating in the prison.

June 20, 1982: One of the largest riots in San Quentin's history resulted in injuries to 22 inmates and four correctional officers. Seven inmates got stabbed, and 15 had injuries from shotgun blasts from officers. Three prison gangs were involved in this riot.

December 6, 1979: Two inmates were killed and 17 injured in a riot involving 80 inmates at Soledad State Prison. A group of Black inmates attacked the Whites and Southerners.

August 21, 1971: This marks the deadliest day in San Quentin's history, with three officers and three inmates losing their lives on this fateful afternoon.

January 13, 1970: On this day at the max row yard at Soledad State Prison, three Black inmates were shot and killed. One of these inmates was W. L. Nolen, a prison boxing legend and a plaintiff against the California Department of Corrections in a civil case. This watershed incident sparked violence, leading to 19 more killings of officers and inmates.

September 24, 1937: During a riot at Folsom Prison, inmates stabbed Warden Clarence Larkin 12 times, leading to his fatal injury. In the course of this incident, inmates held Warden Larkin hostage. Officer Martin endeavored to rescue him but was killed by inmates. The aftermath of this riot saw the loss of four lives: two staff members and two inmates.

November 24, 1927: A riot among 1,200 inmates at Folsom Prison resulted in the National Guard being called in along with two tanks. The inmates took five officers hostage. Company "E" of the 184th Infantry Division entered the prison with bayonets on their rifles in a skirmish line. The rioters quickly surrendered after this show of force by the 184th Infantry Division.

March 3, 1925: Two inmates died over ten days of riots at San Quentin Prison. Guards were ordered to shoot to kill over any new signs of trouble by Warden Smith.

Convict Art

Old School

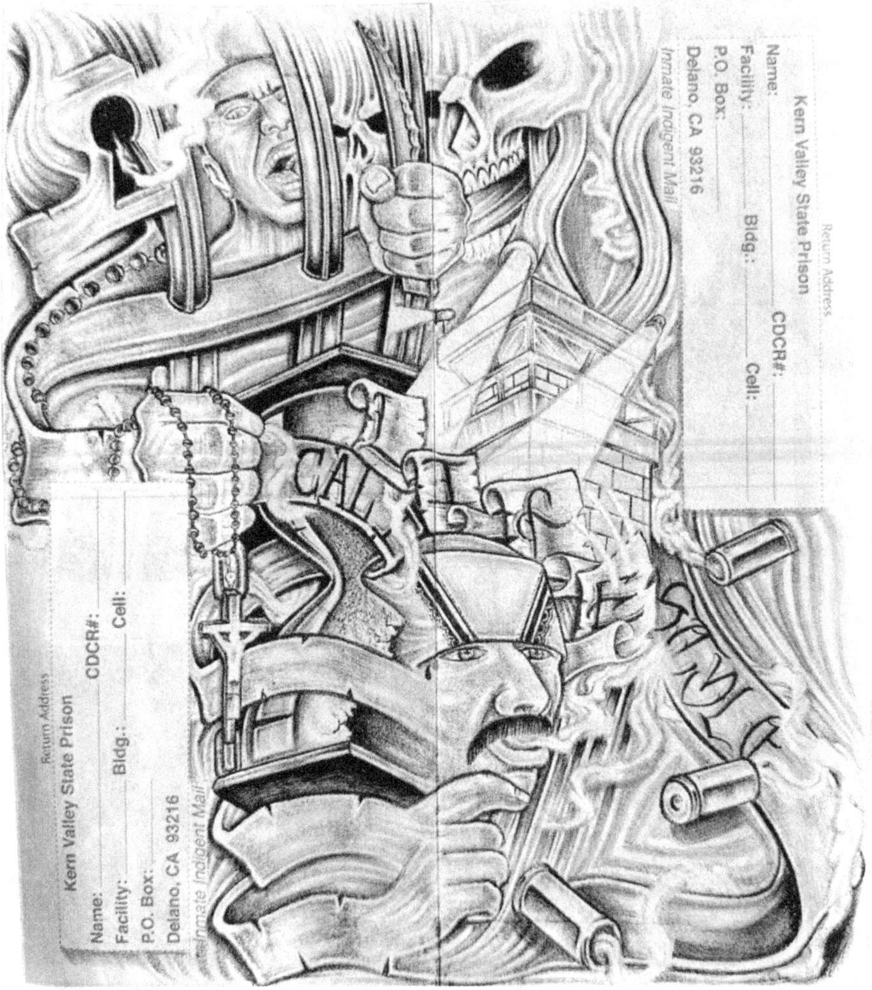
Return Address
Kern Valley State Prison
Name: CDCR#:
Facility: Bldg.: Cell:
P.O. Box:
Delano, CA 93216
Inmate Indigent Mail

CORCORAN STATE PRISON
NAME
CDCR NUMBER
HOUSING
PO BOX
CORCORAN, CA 93212
STATE PRISON
GENERATED MAIL

CORCORAN STATE PRISON
NAME
CDCR NUMBER
HOUSING
PO BOX
CORCORAN, CA 93212
STATE PRISON
GENERATED MAIL

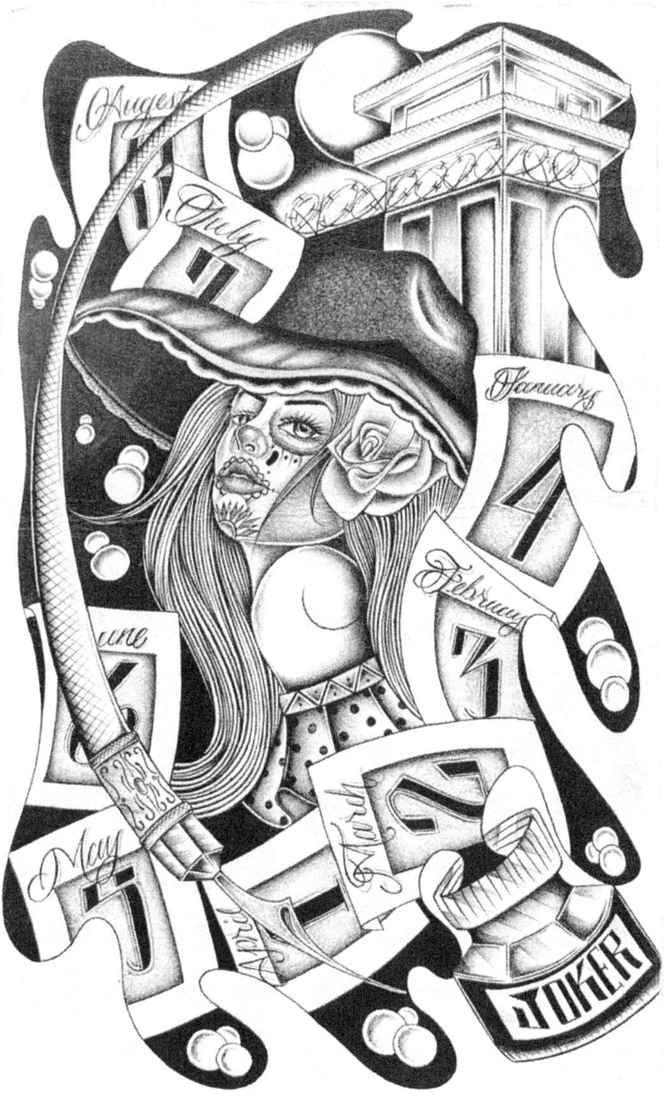
August
July
January
4
February
3
June
6
May
5
April
March
2
JOKER

BRIGHT LIGHTS, BIG CITY

FROM RETIRED TO FIRED

After several years of working at Centinela Prison, I was deemed unable to return to work by doctors employed by the State of California due to my injuries sustained in the line of duty as a correctional officer. About nine years later, I received a certified letter from the retirement agency, which had been paying my monthly check all that time. The letter stated I had to see a doctor employed by them to determine if I was physically capable of returning to work as a correctional officer again.

I had moved three states away from California, so I had to drive back to see their doctor, who was undoubtedly biased since they were paying him. After his examination, the doctor told me I could not return to work as a correctional officer due to my diminished physical ability.

A few months later, when I received the doctor's medical report, it stated that I could return to work. Why did this doctor lie to me during my medical examination? I just found it odd he said one thing to my face, and then he had a change of heart when it came time to formulate his medical report regarding my examination. On page twelve of the doctor's report, there are several question-and-answers, and here is an excerpt:

"Question 3: Is the member cooperating with the examination and putting forth the best effort, or do you feel that there is an exaggeration of complaints to any degree?

Answer 3: The claimant did not demonstrate any verifiable symptom magnification. The claimant did not demonstrate any positive Waddell signs (Malingering, deception) during the examination."

Several months after the doctor's examination, I received a certified letter from my prison stating I had to report back to work a few weeks later. I called the prison and spoke to the Return to Work Coordinator to see if I could get my reporting date moved back because my wife was due any day with my third daughter. She mentioned the FMLA (Family Leave Act), but I didn't qualify because I hadn't worked the required amount the previous year. I asked her some more questions, which she did not know the answers to, and she said she would look into it.

I called the prison again and talked to the same woman. She was still investigating my questions and stated she needed to speak to the warden to get the answers. During the conversation, she told me my salary would be $5300 a month and that I would have to attend the four-month academy (8 weeks when I went through) again. The warden of Centinela prison gave me a 30-day extension to my reporting date, which I thought was nice of them.

During this time, I seriously contemplated if I would leave my family and go to the correctional academy again in Galt, California. After a few days, I decided it wasn't worth it, and I mentally moved on and helped my wife prepare for the birth of my third daughter. I moved three states away since my medical retirement and was established here with a home and family. There was no way that I could leave my pregnant wife and two young children while I attended the four-month correctional officer academy over 2,000 miles away.

A few weeks later, I received a letter from the California Department of Corrections and Rehabilitation saying I was terminated. The reason given was that I was Absent Without Leave (AWOL) since I never personally reported to Centinela prison on the specified date. I could have called and resigned, but I was busy with the birth of my daughter, so I never got around to it.

My fourth daughter was conceived precisely a month after my third daughter was born. She would never have been born if I had returned to the correctional academy. God had a plan for my life, and it didn't include working in a maximum-security prison and risking my life for no good reason when I have kids at home who need me there.

I am reminded of something very touching that happened to me on Centinela prison's Level IV Charlie yard. After my tour of six months in building Charlie 5, I returned to that yard as the Observation Officer for one day. The Observation Officer stays in a little office overlooking the prison yard about fifty feet above the ground. It was during the evening meal, so inmates slowly returned to their buildings after eating in the chow hall.

Two Crips who knew me from my time there glanced up, and one of them said, "Hey, it's Superman. What are you doing back here?" We laughed and talked a little as they looked up at me. Then the other Crip said, "What are you doing working here, man? You are too good for this type of place."

That statement by that man has stayed with me since then, and it means a lot to me. Even in prison, men on opposite sides of the aisle can respect and have compassion for each other. I did my best to treat each convict with the respect they had coming as a fellow man. One frequently used line to convicts who I butted heads with was, "I give you respect you have coming as a man. I expect the same in return."

At the end of the day, we were all just men doing our time here on earth and trying to live as comfortably as possible. Our interactions back then have stayed with me and made me a better man and father. I thank you all for motivating me to always be in the best shape mentally, physically, and spiritually. God bless you!

Special thanks to the following convicts who challenged me to be a better man: Downer, Dantana, Tio, T-Dog, Catman, Cornfed, Trouble, Dumps, T-Baby (RIP), Pancho, Termite, Tiny, T-Bone, Flaco, Rascal, Jahvo, Silk, Lucky, Diablo, and Sharky. There are many more of you, but I can't recall your street names.

About the Author

Eric has emerged as a highly accomplished investor and Day Trader, engaging in trading activities with a substantial value of stocks annually. He enjoys the status of a dedicated husband and father, being blessed with four wonderful daughters who hold a special place in his heart. Eric's existence revolves around upholding the virtues of a devout Christian, a devoted husband, and a caring father guided by the grace of God. His journey has been transformative, considering his challenging upbringing, and he now stands as an illustrious testament to the boundless possibilities achievable through faith in God.

Eric joined a criminal street gang as a teenager, and he was eventually arrested and put in a cage at the Long Beach City Jail. He dropped out of Jordan High School in Long Beach, California, in the 10th grade. Eric eventually got on the right path by the Grace of God and obtained his GED the same month that he would have graduated. He joined the United States Coast Guard at 18, and after four years of faithful service, he was honorably discharged.

The following is an excerpt from his autobiography: "California Prison Confessions."

"It was a typical beautiful summer night in Long Beach, California, and the three young teens fighting in the musty garage starkly contrasted the night's serenity. A teen called Bones was thrown against a wall, and a muscular teenager nicknamed E Double (me) rushed towards him and violently punched him in his lower back. Another youth named Tim Loc held Bones against the wall during this attack. E Double's knuckles landed with a thick-sounding thud as Bones grimaced and moaned in pain from each successive blow.

There's a look of pain and fear in Bone's eyes as E Double mercilessly lands blow after blow to his kidneys. E Double has spent years hitting the heavy bag in his garage, so his punches are devastating for his age. The beating lasted a minute, and the two teens stopped attacking the unfortunate victim. Amazingly, they all shook hands and embraced each other. We were all friends, and this was our modest gang initiation into our small clique called Six Feet Under."

Our tiny neighborhood gang in North Long Beach, California, had several members of various races: White, Black, and Hispanic. The definition of a criminal street gang according to the California Penal Code is as follows:

"As used in this chapter, 'criminal street gang' means any ongoing organization, association, or group of three or more persons, whether formal or informal, having as one of its primary activities the commission of one or more of the criminal acts… having a common name or common identifying sign or symbol, and whose members individually or collectively engage in or have engaged in a pattern of criminal gang activity," California Penal Code 186.22(f).

Some of our associates committed serious crimes such as burglaries, drug sales, stealing cars, carrying guns, vandalism, and assaulting people. Although we were nothing but young punks, we were a criminal street gang according to the California Penal Code.

The FBI did a study entitled "Street-Gang Mentality: A Mosaic of Remorseless Violence and Relentless Loyalty." I want to quote a relevant part concerning young males who do not have a father or other positive male role models in their lives while growing up:

"All gang members lacked male role models in their households, and when they lived with their mothers, they were rarely home because of work schedules. Gang members often lived temporarily with various people. All but one gang member reported that one or more immediate family members had a criminal history or abused drugs. Gangs attracted them because of their loyalty, stability, and sense of group identity."

There is an epidemic in this country of boys masquerading as men who don't take their responsibilities as fathers seriously. Many fathers aren't involved in their children's lives; if they are, they are a horrible example of what a real man should be. One of the main factors in young men ending up in the penal system is the lack of a father or, at the very least, a positive male role model when they were growing up. Absentee fathers are causing society to pay a high price for their selfish and callous actions.

Every day, I strive to be the best dad to the four beautiful daughters God has blessed me with. I live by the motto, "Be the man you needed as a child." I will not allow the actions of emotionally abusive people to define who I am or hinder my advancement in life. You can choose to be bitter or better. I strive for excellence because living well is the best response to abusive people.

Eric Sturgess

God bless you and yours. Romans 10:9-13

For those seeking to connect with Eric or gather additional insights about the California Prison Book Series, please visit his official website: www.PrisonPanos.com.

Made in the USA
Monee, IL
04 November 2026

67387603R00252